LYNDA GRATTON
THE SHIFT

THE FUTURE OF WORK IS ALREADY HERE

WILLIAM
COLLINS

William Collins
An imprint of HarperCollins*Publishers*
77–85 Fulham Palace Road
Hammersmith, London W6 8JB
www.harpercollins.co.uk

This William Collins paperback edition published 2014

1

First published in Great Britain by Collins in 2011

A catalogue record for this book is
available from the British Library

ISBN 978-0-00-752585-0

Printed and bound in Great Britain by Clays Ltd, St Ives plc

For my mother Barbara's grandchildren
– the 'regenerative generation' –

Carla, Max, Christian, Frankie, Dominic, Hunter,
Freddie, Tilly, Jasmine, Eve and Summer

CONTENTS

ABOUT THE AUTHOR

Lynda Gratton is Professor of Management Practice at London Business School, where she teaches an elective to MBA students on the future of work. In 2009 she was ranked by *The Times* as one of the top 20 business thinkers in the world, described by the *Financial Times* as the management guru most likely to impact on the future, ranked second in the HR world by *Human Resources* magazine, received India's Tata Award for services to HR and named as one of the 2010 Fellows of the American Human Resource Institute. Her courses at London Business School attract participants from all over the world, while her programme on the transformation of organisations is considered the best in the world. She has written six books and many articles including articles for the FT, the *Wall Street Journal, Harvard Business Review* and the *MIT Sloan Business Review*. She has won a number of prizes for her writing and research, and her books have been translated into more than 20 languages. Lynda advises companies in Europe, the USA and Asia, and currently sits on the Human Capital advisory board of Singapore Government. Lynda is the founder of the Hot Spots Movement (www. hotspotsmovement.com), dedicated to bringing energy and innovation to companies. The movement has offices in London, Singapore and California, more than 5,000 members, and advises over 40 companies and governments around the world.

Preface
TOMORROW'S WORK BEGINS TODAY

It all began with one of those simple questions that teenagers have a habit of asking. Seated at the morning breakfast table, I found my train of thought interrupted by my eldest son Christian who, 17 years old and fresh out of school, was clearly pondering his future.

'I'm really keen to be a journalist,' he remarked to his brother and me.

His brother Dominic, two years his junior, perhaps inspired by his lead, followed on with 'And I'm thinking about medicine.'

Both sentences were spoken with sufficient query that I took them as questions rather than statements of fact.

Having been a professor in a business school, and an advisor to companies for nigh on three decades, I consider myself something of an expert in the why and how of work. Of course, I am also the first to acknowledge that my sons, being teenagers, are unlikely to have much interest in my opinion. But it struck me on that busy morning that I did need at least a point of view about the future of work. The challenge was this: what was my point of view? I began to realise that, despite my years of advising companies and researching work, all I could muster that morning was a rather half-baked, old-fashioned set of assumptions, combined with 'tidbits' of data that seemed both hopelessly out of date and extraordinarily incomplete.

Over the following few months, as I pondered on their question, I found that more and more people asked me about their working future. I recall how one of my smartest MBA students wanted to know how he could create a future working life that allowed him to be more of a father to his own family. He explained to me that he believed it was crucial that he spent more time with his yet-to-be-born child than his own father had spent with him as a child. Others wanted to know where to live to gain the most value, the competencies they should focus on and the career paths they should develop. At the same time, the executives I taught wanted to know when to retire, what to do when they reached 65, how to take a gap year, what to say to their companies. Then my research team ran, with colleagues at Unilever, a session with kids under the age of 10. We asked them to talk about their ideas about work. They talked robots and transhumans, computers and global warming. Even at 10, they had begun to play out these future scenarios. And to cap it all, the human resource executives I teach at London Business School seemed to be deeply concerned that their companies were too hierarchical and bureaucratic, and too slow moving to catch up with the trends they saw emerging.

I put these anxieties and questions down in part to the 2009/10 global recessions that rattled everyone. I was feeling the impact myself in my own teaching. Back in 2000 my colleague Sumantra Ghoshal and I had chosen four companies to write extensive case studies on, which would then be taught both at London Business School and also around the world. We chose companies that at that time were in the top five in their sectors and generally admired. From banking we chose the Royal Bank of Scotland; from industry, BP; from investment banking, Goldman Sachs; and Nokia from the technology sector. By mid-2010 RBS had made one of the largest losses in banking history; BP was haemorrhaging oil into the Gulf of Mexico and being castigated by the US Senate for its leadership competence; and Goldman Sachs was in the process of a significant fine from the trading commission. Only Nokia was unscathed, although its share price and value seemed paltry against the mighty Apple. And of course, until 2009, I had directed the Lehman Centre at London Business School. Even ivory tower academics began to feel the winds of change.

When I talked to executives in Nokia and Reuters about the technological developments that are around the corner, and to colleagues at Shell about the coming energy challenges, and indeed to other academics about the growing employee distrust and anxiety they were observing, I began to realise that what I was witnessing was more than simply the backlash from the recession. Added to that, in my twice-yearly visits to India and Africa it was clear these continents were transforming in a way I had never previously witnessed. It began to dawn on me that this was not going to be business as usual. Instead I began to realise that we were entering a time of real flux and possible transformation, and that I was ill equipped to answer the questions I was being faced with.

What I needed was a point of view about the future of work that was more thoughtful and expert than the rather vague and ill-formed views I held. I knew that these questions I was being asked about the future of work were crucial. Work is, and always has been, one of the most defining aspects of our lives. It is where we meet our friends, excite ourselves and feel at our most creative and innovative. It can also be where we can feel our most frustrated, exasperated and taken for granted. Work matters – to us as individuals, to our family and friends and also to the communities and societies in which we live.

I also knew that many of the ways of working we have taken for granted in the last 20 years – working from nine to five, aligning with one company, spending time with family, taking the weekends off, working with people we know well – are all beginning to disappear. And what's coming in its place is much less knowable and less understandable – almost too fragile to grasp.

However, despite this fragility and the difficulty of grasping the future, I needed answers – and so do the people who asked all these questions. So, of course, do you. Perhaps you don't need absolute answers. But what you do need, like me, is a point of view, a basic idea of what the hard facts of the future are, and a way of thinking about the future which has some kind of internal cohesion, which resonates with who you are and what you believe. You and I, and my children, and others who are important to us, need to grasp the future of work because we have to prepare ourselves, and we have to prepare others.

To understand better these profound changes, I began my journey with the goal of discovering, with as much fine-grained detail as possible, how the future of work was likely to evolve. I was interested in day-to-day details like: What will friends, my children and I be doing in 2025? How will I be living my working life at 10.00 in the morning? Who will I be meeting for lunch? What tasks will I be performing? Which skills will be in the ascendant and most valued? Where will I be living? How will my family and friends fit with my work? Who will be paying me? When am I going to retire?

I also wanted to discover more about whether in the future our thoughts and aspirations could change. Questions like: What will be going on in my working conscious in 2025? What sort of work will I be aspiring to? What will be my hopes? What will keep me awake at night? What do I want for myself, and those who come after me?

These are the day-to-day events and fleeting moments of thoughts and aspirations that will influence the working lives of you and your colleagues, and those of your children and friends. These are important questions since it is from this fine-grained detail that our daily working lives are constructed.

I soon discovered that while, on the face of it, these are relatively simple questions, in reality the answers are not straightforward. At an early stage of this journey it began to dawn on me that you couldn't describe your working future simply as a straight line from the past into the present, and then on to the future. Instead, I began to see the future as a set of possibilities, a number of ways forward, and the opportunity to travel on different paths. But the question remained of how best to draw these possibilities and different paths.

My mother is a great maker of patchwork quilts. As a child, I remember her assembling fragments of material over many years – material she had used earlier, or which had been donated by friends, or which she had bought. Over the years the height of the material scraps in the patchwork box increased, and every couple of months my mother would take them out and look at them closely.

What she was looking for was a pattern that she could discern from the pieces. She was looking for the pieces that would naturally fit together to create a pattern that made sense. Once she had decided which to keep and which to discard, she set about arranging those pieces she kept. She moved the pieces this way and that, until she decided how best to assemble them into the quilt. At this stage she made a rough layout on the floor of the bedroom, and then began the long task of making the first rough stitches to hold the pieces together. Once this had been done, and she had made any final changes to the location of the pieces, she set about the laborious task of hand-stitching them together.

I am reminded of my mother, and her construction of the quilt from the many pieces of material, as I craft this book about the future of work. It is a book that I hope will be uplifting without being ridiculously positive and Pollyanna-ish, and illustrative without being constraining. In the crafting of this book I have followed the same path my mother took as she fashioned the patchwork quilt. I have, over the years, kept many scraps of ideas and borrowed some from friends. More recently, I have assembled a wise crowd of people from across the globe to bring their insights and ideas. Then, having gone about the process of looking for patterns, I decided what to discard and what merited keeping. I have, like my mother before me, embarked on the long period of hand-stitching the pieces together to form a patchwork of the future of work. This book is the result of that long process.

I believe passionately that the scale of change we are going through in this decade puts into stark relief many of the assumptions we have held dear about what it takes for us to be successful. It is perilous and foolhardy to ignore these changes. It is also naive to imagine that what worked for the past will work for the future. To do so puts in jeopardy our own future and the future of those we care about. Predicting the future of work, and crafting a working life that brings happiness and value, are two of the most precious gifts you can give yourself and those you care about. Don't leave it too late to make the decision to think and to act.

Introduction
PREDICTING THE FUTURE OF WORK

Why now?

What we are witnessing now is a break with the past as significant as that in the late eighteenth and early nineteenth centuries
when parts of the world began the long process of industrialisation. What we know as work – what we do, where we do it, how
we work and when we work – has already changed fundamentally in the past when the Industrial Revolution transformed
work, beginning in Britain between the late eighteenth (around
1760) and early nineteenth centuries (around 1830).[1] It seems
likely that the period we are moving into will see as fundamental
a transformation – although of course the outcome is much less
clear.

To get an idea of the velocity of the changes that can sweep
away so many assumptions, consider the period between 1760
and 1830. Within a period of less than 100 years – that's only
four generations – there occurred a fundamental and irreversible
shift which changed the experiences of every worker in the UK,
and was to be felt across the world as industrialisation spread
first to Europe and then to North America. Before that time
work – whether it be ploughing the fields, weaving of wool,
blowing of glass or throwing of pottery – was an artisanal activity engaged with largely in the home, using long-held and metic-
ulously developed craft skills. From the late eighteenth century
onwards these craft skills began to be transformed as the

manufacturing sector was developed and began to transcend the limits of artisanal production.

Looking back with hindsight and a gap of over 200 years, we can learn much from the trajectory and speed of revolutions in working lives. The Industrial Revolution began gradually and relatively slowly to change working lives. The economic growth throughout this period was little more than 0.5% per person per year, and while we now think of the 'dark satanic mills' as being the key motif of this time, in fact textile production often constituted less than 6% of total economic output within Britain. In reality, the growth in total productivity during this apparent revolution was in fact slow by modern standards.[2] This was an evolution rather than a revolution; gradual rather than progressing through breakthrough changes; and based on continual and small changes rather than a series of massive innovations. For those living through this period it would not have been seen as a time of immense change, and it is only when the broad sweep of history is viewed that the extent of change can be put into perspective.

The core of any revolution in the way that work gets done is inevitably changes in energy. When true innovations occur in the production of goods or services, they are the result of a capacity to unearth new sources of energy or to apply existing sources in a radically more efficient way. The first Industrial Revolution, although it had an impact on working lives, was not an energy revolution. The movement that took place at this time, from farming to fabrication, was not inherently innovative; the artisan remained the primary source of productive activity. That's reflected in the modest growth rates throughout the late eighteenth and early nineteenth centuries.

The real revolution in the working lives of people began to occur in the mid to late nineteenth century, when British scientists, unlike their European contemporaries, began to be experimental. It was this culture of innovation, with the ideas of organisational and technological restructuring rapidly picked up by entrepreneurs and industrialists, that transformed working lives. It enabled a new class of practical scientists to emerge and to excel.

This was the emergence of the engineering class and of a culture of innovation.[3] The real shift in work came with a change in energy – the power of steam that was rapidly integrated into the embryonic factory system. This transformation came as the consequence of a new energy source in the shape of steam, with a new spirit of enterprise and innovation. It was only when engine science combined with an emerging engineering culture that a new source of energy – steam – integrated into the productive process.

In the fifty years that followed the closing decades of the nineteenth century, a true revolution in work had occurred. The emergence of an engineering class signalled the professionalisation of practical science and the institutional pursuit of innovation. This also saw the transformation of the working lives of people across Britain and later the developed world. Work became more regimented, more specialised. The workplace and the work schedule became more compartmentalised and hierarchical.

This was the embryonic stage of Fordism – the rise of the engineer as the organiser of economic activity, and the decline of the artisan. The layout of a factory was as important as the technology within it, embodying as it did the power structure of the organisation. In this second Industrial Revolution, engineers redesigned factories to make employees fit into the production line. By doing so workers lost their autonomy, becoming simply as interchangeable as the parts they created.

As we look to the world of work we now inhabit, and the decades to come, what we are seeing is the potential reverse of this trend, from hierarchy and interchangeable, general skills to the reinstatement of horizontal collaboration and more specialised mastery.

What is clear is that the current scale of transformation is as great as any witnessed in the past. Again it is powered by an energy transformation (in this case computing power); again going through periods of slower and then more rapid change; and again depending on a new set of skills and an emerging class of skilled people.[4]

However, as we shall see, this time the impact of the Industrial Revolution is global rather than local, the speed ever more accelerated and the disconnect with the past likely to be as great. It is clear that our world is at the apex of an enormously creative and innovative shift that will result in profound changes to the everyday lives of people across the world.

Patching together the future

Faced with the magnitude of these changes, how do we both make sense of them, and indeed ensure that we and those we care about are able to do the very best they can over the coming decades? I've used the story of my mother's quilt-making as a metaphor for the task that we are all faced with as we prepare for the future. As I attempt to make sense of the future for myself – in a sense to stitch together the pieces that are important to me – I cannot help but be occasionally overwhelmed with the sheer complexity of this endeavour, very much as I suspect my mother must have felt at the beginning of her craft. I wonder if indeed it is worthwhile to try and make any predictions about our working life in 2020, 2025 or beyond, as far out as 2050? However, what has spurred me on is that, the more I have learnt, the more I have come to believe that while this endeavour is indeed complex it is also incredibly worthwhile. It is worthwhile because you and I, and those whom we care about, need some sort of realistic picture of what the future might bring in order to make choices and sound decisions.

Think about it this way: I am now 55 and could expect to live to my mid-eighties – perhaps even into my mid-nineties. My two sons are currently aged 16 and 19 and they could well live more than a century. If I work into my seventies, then that's 2025, and if my sons do the same they will be working into 2060. Take a moment now to make the same time period calculations for yourself and others who are important to you.

Of course, all the decisions about your working life don't need to be made now. In the case of my children, for example, I expect they will adapt and change and morph over the next 50 years – just as I have done through my own working career. However, wouldn't it be useful to have some picture of the future, storylines of future lives, scenarios of choice to guide and give inspiration? We need these, not only for our personal or local near-term futures, but also for remoter global futures.

Just because my children, you and I 'need' realistic pictures of the future, it does not mean of course that we can have them. Predictions about future technical and social developments are notoriously unreliable – to an extent that has led some to propose that we do away altogether with prediction in our planning and preparation for the future. Yet, while the methodological problems of such forecasting are certainly very significant, I believe that doing away with prediction altogether is misguided.[5]

The reason it is so important now at least to attempt to paint a realistic picture of the future is that we can no longer imagine the future simply by extrapolating from the past. I cannot imagine my future working life by drawing a direct line with the working life of my father – any more than I could expect my sons to predict their working lives from mine. I am not suggesting that everything will shift. Of course some aspects of work will remain the same; one of the challenges, in fact, is actually knowing what will remain stable. As the science fiction writer William Gibson famously remarked, 'the future is here – just unevenly distributed'.[6]

It has not always been so difficult to simply extrapolate from the past. For much of the ages of mankind, perceptions of daily lives were envisaged – with very few exceptions – as changeless in their material, technological, and economic conditions. This transformed fundamentally from the eighteenth century with the advent of the Industrial Revolution, when what was seen as hitherto untamable forces of nature could be controlled through the appliance of science and rationality.[7]

The past six generations have amounted to the most rapid and profound change mankind has experienced in its 5,000 years of recorded history.[8] If the world economy continues to grow at the same pace as in the last half-century, then by the time my children are the same age as me – in 2050 – the world will be seven times richer than it is today, world population could be over 9 billion, and average wealth would also increase dramatically.[9]

What is important about my sons' questions about their future work is that they are living in an age in which they face a schism with the past of the same magnitude as that previously seen in the late nineteenth century. The drivers of that change were the development of coal and steam power. This time round the change is not the result of a single force, but rather the subtle combination of five forces – the needs of a low-carbon economy, rapid advances in technology, increasing globalisation, profound changes in longevity and demography, and important societal changes that together will fundamentally transform much of what we take for granted about work.

It is not just our day-to-day working conditions and habits that will change so dramatically. What will also change is our working consciousness, just as the industrial age changed the working consciousness of our predecessors. The Industrial Revolution brought a mass market for goods, and with it a rewiring of the human brain towards an increasing desire for consumption, and the acquisition of wealth and property. The question we face now is how the working consciousness of current and future workers will be further transformed in the age of technology and globalisation we are entering.

What is inevitable is that, for younger people, their work will change perhaps unrecognisably – and those of us already in the workforce will be employed in ways we can hardly imagine. This new wave of change will, like those that have gone before them, build on what has been accomplished in the past, made up of a gradual process with some possibly unpredictable major waves. It is about increasing globalisation, industry and technology. But, as in the past, these changes will also bring something that is qualitatively different – new industries based around renewable energy sources, new developments of the internet, and indeed new ways to think about work.[10]

The reality is that predicting the future is a matter of degree, and different aspects of the future of work can be predicted with varying degrees of reliability and precision. For example, I can predict with some accuracy that computers will become faster, materials will become stronger and medicine will cure more diseases so that we will live longer. Other aspects of the future, such as migration flows, global temperatures and government policy, are much less predictable. It's more difficult to predict, for example, how the way we will relate to each other will change, or how our aspirations will evolve.

If I think about my own future and that of my children, and factor in the uncertainty we face, then of course it's a good idea to develop plans that are flexible, and to pursue ideas that are robust under a wide range of contingencies. In other words, it is wise to develop coping strategies in the face of uncertainty. However, what is also important is to strive to improve the accuracy of our beliefs about the future. This is crucial because, as I will show, there might well be traps that we are walking towards that could by avoided with foresight, or opportunities we could reach much sooner if we could see them further in advance.

Knowing something about the future helps us to prepare for our future, it influences the advice we give others, and could have a fundamental impact on the choices that we, our family and friends, our community and our company decide to make; about the competencies we decide to develop, the communities and networks on which we focus our attention, or the companies and organisations with which we choose to be associated.

The Future of Work Research Consortium

The challenge is that even with my own three decades of knowledge about work I find the future of work still fiendishly difficult to predict. That's why, by way of preparation, I created a research consortium designed to tap into ideas and knowledge from across the world. The research takes place every year – beginning in 2009 and progressing to more global and diverse groups every subsequent year.

Each year, my research team and I begin by identifying the *five forces* that will most impact on the future of work (these are technology; globalisation; demography and longevity; society; and natural resources); we then go about amassing the *hard facts* for each of these five forces. These hard facts for each of the five forces are then presented to members of the research consortium. This consortium is perhaps one of the most fascinating experiments ever conducted between management, academics and executives. In a sense it creates a 'wise crowd' of people. In 2009, for example, more than 200 people participated. They were members of more than 21 companies from around the world including Absa (the South African bank), Nokia, Nomura, Tata Consulting Group (in India), Thomson Reuters and the Singapore Government's Ministry of Manpower, together with two not-for-profit organisations, Save the Children and World Vision. In 2010 the number of participating companies had risen to 45, with over 15 from Asia including SingTel in Singapore and Wipro, Infosys and Mahindra & Mahindra from India, and Cisco and Manpower from the USA.

The research began in earnest in November 2009, at the London Business School. At this point we presented the hard facts of the five forces and asked executives to construct *storylines* of a day-in-the-life of people working in 2025 on the basis of what they had heard. We then went on to repeat this exercise with many more people in Singapore and India. The storylines that began to emerge became the blueprints for the stories I will tell later in the book. These are important because, while they are works of fiction, it is through these descriptions of possible everyday life that we are able to imagine the interplay between different ideas and knowledge. These storylines of a day-in-the-life in 2025 are not, of course, forecasts. What they portray are ways of seeing the future, and of assembling different versions of the future. They are crucial because in them we can begin to see just how much the future is full of possibilities.

Once the research team and consortium members had developed the storylines, they took the initial conversations about the hard facts and storylines back to their own companies. Over the following months they brought back the thoughts from their wider community, and from more than 30 countries. At this point we were able to work together virtually in an elaborate shared portal, and also to discuss the emerging ideas in monthly virtual web-based seminars. We followed this up later with a series of workshops in Europe and Asia. At the same time I tested out some of my initial thoughts through a weekly blog, http://www.lyndagrattonfutureofwork. It is these ideas, insights and anxieties that became stitched into the storyline narratives and brought depth to the conversation. They are also the basis of the personal reflections that you will come across in the debate that follows.

The paths to the future

As we looked more closely at the future, what became increasingly clear was that in fact there is not one but many possible paths to the future. It is certainly possible for each one of us to construct a path into the future that simply accentuates the negatives of the five forces. This becomes a future of isolation, fragmentation, exclusion and narcissism. This is the *Default Future* in which the five forces have outpaced the possibilities of taking any action. In these storylines we see people who may have been very successful in one aspect of their life, but who have failed to take positive action around an important issue or have only . taken actions that are straightforward and seemed easy to take. In the Default Future no one is prepared to work together to take cohesive action or to change the status quo. In this future, dealing with the current problems takes place without consistency or cohesion, and events outpace actions.

There is also a future where the positive aspects of the five forces are harnessed to create a more crafted outcome. These are career and life stories in which collaboration plays a key role, where choice and wisdom are exercised, and actions create a more balanced way of working. In these stories of a *Crafted Future* people are experimenting with ways of working, learning fast from each other, and rapidly adopting good ideas. These are storylines where the forces that transform work could result in the possibility – the promise, even – of a better future. It is the future that can emerge when people actively make decisions and wise choices, and are able to face up to the consequences of these choices. It is a future in which people can work more harmoniously with others, where they can become more valued and masterful, and where the different parts of a working life can be integrated in a more authentic way.

The storylines within the two paths capture possibilities; they are a way for us to explore the future, and indeed construct our own future. A word of warning: these stories are not in any sense mechanical forecasts of what will be. Instead they are based on the recognition that each one of us holds beliefs and makes choices that can lead down different paths; they reveal different possible futures that are both plausible and challenging.

Taking the right path: the shifts

Each one of us would want to choose the Crafted Future rather than succumb to the Default Future. But how do we ensure we are on the right path? The journey that I went through, and the journey I am inviting you to take, will make you question your mental map of the future, just as it has for me. You and I already have a mental map of the future – that's what has been driving the decisions we have already taken, and the choices we have already made. The question is: is this the right mental map, and are you on the right path?

In understanding what is the right path, it is crucial to have as much information and knowledge as possible about how the future will emerge. My research team and I have understood this deeply and will present it to you as the stories unfold. It seems to me that the storylines, hard facts and scenarios demand that we re-examine our assumptions, and ask three key questions:

* What are the potential milestones or events that could particularly affect me and those around me?
* What are the most significant factors that will influence my working life, and how could these play out?
* Therefore, what should I be doing over the coming five years to ensure I am on the right path to creating a future-proofed career, particularly in view of the turbulent times ahead?

My aim in this book is clear. It is written to support you as you develop your own point of view about the future – and your own path to creating a future-proofed working life. To do this you will have to understand the hard facts with as much depth as possible; to play through the possible scenarios and storylines to understand what they mean to you; while at the same time really being aware of the aspects of your specific context that will shape the choices you have. Only then can you look hard at your mental models and assumptions of the future and construct a path that will ensure your working life is robust, purposeful and valuable.

So, in creating a future-proofed working life, what are the assumptions that will need to be questioned, and what are the implications for how we live our future working lives? I am predicting that there are three shifts in assumptions which each one of us will have to make in order to craft a meaningful and valuable working life over the coming two decades.

First, our assumptions that general skills will be valuable has to be questioned. It seems clear to me that in a joined-up world where potentially 5 billion people have access to the worldwide Cloud, the age of the generalist is over. Instead, my prediction for the future is that you will need what I call 'serial mastery' to add real value. That has got crucial implications for under-standing what will be valuable skills and competencies in the future, for developing deep mastery in these areas, and yet being able to move into other areas of mastery through sliding and morphing. It also has implications for an increasingly invisible world, where self-marketing and creating credentials will be key.

Second, our assumptions about the role of individualism and competitiveness as a foundation for creating great working lives and careers have to be questioned. In a world that could become increasingly fragmented and isolated, I believe that connectivity, collaboration and networks will be central. These networks could be the group that support you in complex tasks; it could be the crowd of diverse people who are able to be the basis of ideas and inspiration; it could even be the intimate, warm and loving relationships that will be at the heart of your capacity to regenerate and remain balanced. What is crucial here is that – in a world that becomes more and more virtual – strong, diverse, emotional relationships cannot be taken for granted, they have to be shaped and crafted.

Finally, as I consider the five forces that will shape our work-ing lives over the coming two decades, and see how the storylines could play out, I am struck by the need to think hard about the type of working life to which we aspire. Do we follow the old assumptions of continuously going head first for consumption and quantity? Or is it now time to think hard about trade-offs and to focus more on the production and quality of our experiences and the balance of our lives, rather than simply the voraciousness of our consumption?

It is possible for each one of us to construct a very clear view of the challenges we face, and many of the trade-offs we will have to consider. Of course, our own future, and indeed the future of those we care about, is essentially unknowable. But that does not mean that we leave it to chance. I am convinced that we can prepare for the future in a way that increases the possibilities of success. We can do this by really understanding the five forces that will change our world. We can prepare by constructing storylines of possible futures that we can use as a basis for making choices and understanding consequences. Finally, we can prepare for the future by acknowledging that some of our most dearly held assumptions are misplaced and that we will be required to make some fundamental shifts in how we think and act our way into our future working lives. By doing this we are ensuring we are better equipped to construct a working life that excites us, brings us pleasure and creates worth for others and ourselves.

PART I

THE FORCES
THAT WILL SHAPE
YOUR FUTURE

1

THE FIVE FORCES

If you want to understand the future, you need to start with the five forces that will shape your world over the coming decades. What's more, you need to understand these five forces in some detail, since it is often in the details that the really interesting stuff can be found. For me it has been an incredibly exciting journey to collect from around the world the 32 pieces about the forces. I cannot remember being so excited about getting up in the morning and researching and writing. I have been fascinated, surprised and intrigued by what I have found. I had no idea that in 2010 China was building 45 airports; or that the centre of innovation of handheld money devices is Kenya; or that by 2025 more than 5 billion people will be connected with each other through handheld devices. These are the hard facts that I will share with you in order to create a deeper and more accurate view of the way your working life will change. They are also the hard facts that will aid you as you begin to decide how you will construct your future working life, and indeed the advice you will give to others. In finding and putting these 32 pieces together, I have been influenced by the need to be global rather than local; historical rather than simply of the moment; and broad rather than narrow.

Taking a global focus

One of the challenges about understanding the future is that much of the contemporary research and books about technology, oil or globalisation tends to take a single-region focus – typically either the USA or Europe. This makes sense as the boundaries are well understood and so the context is agreed up front.

However, this local focus does not suit my purpose for this book. In the past, I have been delighted that people across the world have read my books, and my hope is that this book will resonate with people across the world. So it's really important to me that wherever you are reading this book you have some sense of inclusion. But it is not just you as a reader that creates the need for a global viewpoint. Perhaps more than at any time in the history of mankind, the story of the future is a 'joined-up' story that can only be told from a global perspective. For example, it is impossible to imagine future carbon usage and the impact it could have on work patterns without knowing something about China's likely industrial development. It is impossible to understand potential future consumption patterns without knowing something about the savings preferences of the average US worker.

So, for both these reasons, my mission is to create a global perspective. However, I am acutely aware that as I have developed the 32 pieces that follow there are many missing regions. The challenge is that if I wrote a sentence or two for every region, then what follows would become more like an encyclopaedia and lose the flow I believe to be crucial to a story that's worth reading. So, generally I have assumed a global vantage point, and focused on specific regions when I believe something particularly interesting is happening there.

Looking back to a historical focus

It is slightly odd in a book about the future to be often casting a glimpse back to the past. Of course there are books that are resolutely future focused. However, I believe that if we want to increase our ability to understand the future of work we also have to glimpse back to the past. Taking a historical perspective can be useful in both creating a sense of momentum and velocity, and also providing a view of historical precedence. This is important for, as we have seen, there are clues to the future of work in both the first Industrial Revolution of the 1870s and indeed in the changes in production that occurred around the 1930s. It also seems to me that knowing a little about the past can serve to bring deeper insight into the future. This is particularly the case when we come to think about societal trends, including family structures and consumerism.

Understanding the broad context

Over the following 32 pieces you will see that I range far from the confined space of work itself. We will take a look at how we have lived and might live in the future, our family structures, our modes of consumption, oil prices and institutional trust. I have chosen to take this broad brush because it is clear to me that work cannot be seen without acknowledging the broader context. Work takes place in the context of families, expectations and hopes; it takes place within the context of the community and in the context of economic and political structures.

As I put these pieces together I am reminded again of my mother's quilt-making. Over the years she collected scraps of material from many sources and then one day would sit down and work out a pattern from the pieces. I have to admit that one of the reasons the earlier metaphor of my mother's fabrics and the quilts appeals to me so much is that, although I am not a maker of quilts, I am a collector of fabrics. Almost any trip I go on, I come back with tiny snippets of embroidery from Seoul or swathes of silk from Mumbai, or woven grasses from Tanzania. I even have a small woven Aboriginal basket made from pine needles. I've always patched together information in the same way. I like to travel and talk to people, and every year I make a point of visiting Asia, Africa and America.

Being a business professor is a huge advantage in this endeavour since I'm not trying to sell my ideas as I might in consulting, and I am not hiding my views as I might if I was an executive in a multinational company. I find that people tend to talk with me openly, sharing their hopes and confiding their fears. And, of course, perhaps the biggest advantage in being a professor is that I have the luxury that few have of extended periods of time to think and write. This has been crucial because, as you will discover, while this is an incredibly exciting journey, it is also very complex and it is only with time and reflection that I have been able to take a perspective and view of these pieces.

To help you find you own way through this maze of information, I have assembled the pieces of hard facts about the future under five broad headings: Technology; Globalisation; Demography and Longevity; Society; and Energy Resources. The truth is that these are rather superficial ways of categorising and the reality is that they can be re-sorted in many other ways. But it strikes me that this is a good place to start.

I have then created for each of these broad areas about five to eight smaller pieces. Each of these pieces has some kind of internal consistency and tells a story on its own: a story, for example, about how the West is ageing, or how the developing countries are becoming powerhouses of innovation, or how the population of the world is moving from the countryside to the city. I've chosen each of these pieces because I believe they could be important to your future, your children's future or the future of your community. It is up to you to decide what to do with the 32 pieces as you craft your personal point of view about the future.

So, let's take a closer look at the five broad forces that will shape the future of work, and the more detailed pieces that create a deeper understanding.

The force of technology

Technology has always played a key role in framing work and what happens in working lives. When we fast-forward to our working lives in 2025 and even out to 2050, we can only do so by knowing something about how technologies will develop in the near term – and by taking a guess at the possibilities for the long term.

Technology has been one of the main drivers of the long-term economic growth of countries; it has influenced the size of the world population, the life expectancy of the population and the education possibilities. Technological changes will continue to transform the everyday nature of our work and the way we communicate. Technology will also influence working lives in other deeper and more indirect ways – the way people engage with each other, their expectations of their colleagues, and even their views on morality and human nature. You don't have to be an out-and-out supporter of technological determinism to recognise that technological capability – through its complex interactions with people, institutions, cultures and environment – is a key determinant of the ground rules within which the games of human civilisation get played out.[1]

That's not to say, of course, that the experiences of technology of those living in 2025 will be similar across the world. There have been, and no doubt will continue to be, large variations and fluctuations in the deployment of technology. That's because technological developments do not happen in isolation but instead are dependent on context – be that cultural, economic or the values of people. What's more, the deployment of any particular aspect of technology is not inevitable and will not necessarily follow a particular growth pattern. It could be that some technological developments will create revolutions in work while others will be a slower and steadier trickle of invention. It may be that in the future, as there has been in the past, there will be important inflexion points at which technologies divide and history will take either path with quite different results.

The Cloud, the technology net that creates the means by which people across the world can access resources, is a case in point. Technologically it will be feasible within the next decade for anyone with access to the Cloud around the world to access the World Wide Web and all the enormous information held in it. However, it could be that in certain countries and regions and at certain times, issues about security and access will severely limit the deployment of the Cloud. However, in spite of these likely variations in deployment, the impact of different growth patterns across the world, and contextual variations, what is clear is that technological developments will continue on a broad front.

For those of us on a journey to understand the future, the question is what might we expect this broad front to be – and how will it impact on day-to-day working lives in 2025 and beyond? Here are the ten pieces about technology that we will see played out in the storylines that follow.

1. **Technological capability increases exponentially:** one of the key drivers of technological development has been the rapid and continuous fall in the cost of computing. We can expect this to continue and it will make increasingly complex technology available in relatively inexpensive handheld devices.
2. **Five billion become connected:** this capability will be combined with billions of people across the world becoming connected. This will take place in both the megacities of the world and rural areas. The extent of this connectivity will create the possibility of a 'global consciousness' that has never before been seen.
3. **The Cloud becomes ubiquitous:** rapidly developing technology will create a global infrastructure upon which are available

services, applications and resources. This will allow anyone with a computer or handheld device to 'rent' these on a minute-by-minute basis. This has enormous potential to bring sophisticated technology to every corner of the world.

4. **Continuous productivity gains:** technology has boosted productivity from the mid-1990s onwards, and we can expect these productivity gains to continue with the possibility of advanced communications at near-zero cost. Interestingly, in this second wave of productivity the emphasis will be less on technology and more on organisational assets such as culture, cooperation and teamwork.

5. **Social participation increases:** a crucial question for understanding the future of work is predicting what people will actually do with this unprecedented level of connectivity, content and productive possibilities. Over the next two decades we can expect the knowledge of the world to be digitalised, with an exponential rise in user-generated content, 'wise crowd' applications and open innovation applications.

6. **The world's knowledge becomes digitalised:** there is a huge push from educational institutions, public companies and governments to make available the knowledge of the world in digital form. We can expect that this will have a profound impact, particularly on those who do not have access to formal educational institutions.

7. **Mega-companies and micro-entrepreneurs emerge:** these technological advances will lead to an increasingly complex working and business environment – with the emergence of mega-companies that span the globe. At the same time, millions of smaller groups of micro-entrepreneurs and partnerships will together create value in the many industrial ecosystems that will emerge.

8. **Ever-present avatars and virtual worlds:** increasingly work will be performed virtually as workers hook up with each other across the world. Their virtual representatives – avatars – will become central to the way virtual working occurs.

9. **The rise of cognitive assistants:** at the same time, bundling and priority mechanisms, such as cognitive assistants, will act as a buffer between ever-increasing content and the needs of workers to arrange their knowledge and tasks.

10. **Technology replaces jobs:** much of the productivity in the coming decades will come as robots play a crucial part in the world of work, from manufacturing to caring for an increasingly ageing population.

These are the ten pieces of the technology force that will shape the world you will live and work in. As we shall see in the stories that follow, technological developments will not only be at the heart of the Default Future's dark side of fragmentation and isolation but will also be a part of a Crafted Future where co-creation and social participation are the norm. Before we move on, take a moment to ask yourself which are the most important pieces for you, which you can discard, and also to consider those technological aspects that have not been considered, but which you believe you need to know more about.

The force of globalisation

The workplace that dominated most of the twentieth century allowed producers and sellers a fairly relaxed existence. Thinking back to my first real job – as a psychologist for British Airways – much of the world was broken into relatively stable markets. BA had a near monopoly on the UK travelling passenger, and if the company did not make its predicted revenue the UK Government, as the owner of the airline, was there to bail it out. I recall getting into the office at 9.00, taking a one-hour break in the staff canteen on the other side of the airport, and then leaving my desk at 5.30 for a leisurely trip home. No work was expected at the weekend, the holidays were good, and of course I had the pleasure of deeply discounted travel perks – oh, and did I tell you about the BA pension scheme?

Economies of scale and stable markets (often supported by monopolies, oligopolies and regulations) protected large companies like BA from competition. If you worked for a smaller company, then you only competed with other local services and industries. The focus of these companies was on the production of goods and services at a reasonable price and in a form that consumers would not reject out of hand. Research and development departments did exist, but they tended to change around the margin, and costs could be planned for, thanks to unions negotiating wage rates for entire industries.[2]

That's not to say, of course, that national economic activity took place in complete isolation. There has always been economic integration and trade within and between nations. We may have assumed that globalisation is a recent phenomenon because we tend to take a local view of history. In fact, for thousands of years there have been complex networks of trade across regions.[3] Putting a precise date on the origin of these global linkages is difficult, since it depends on factors such as human migration, improved transport links and ever more substantial trade. Whatever the answer, the important point is that the forces that transcend the local have been operating for a very long time.

However, globalisation, as distinct from global history, emerged in the wake of the Second World War, following the agreements reached in the Bretton Woods Conference in 1944 that led to the establishment of truly international trade institutions.[4] Before 1944, trade was constrained by the sheer cost of moving goods around the world, the difficulty of sharing information across countries, and defensive governmental protectionism. After 1944, moving goods around the world became increasingly cost effective; developing technologies enabled information to be rapidly shared across much of the world, and government barriers to trade began to dissolve. As the goods and services available began to globalise, so consumers transformed the way they thought about meeting their needs. Rather than simply buying from the local supplier, people in many countries began to have a real choice. The result of this era of trade liberalisation was that the world volume of trade in the manufacturing sector rose 60-fold between 1950 and 2010.[5]

As we take a closer look at how the forces of globalisation will impact on work in the coming decades, I have selected eight pieces about globalisation that I believe to be crucial and which will become part of the future storylines.

1. **24/7 and the global world:** since the 1940s, the combination of political will and motivation and technological innovation has created the means to join up the world and, in so doing, has pushed ever greater globalisation.

2. **The emerging economies:** probably the biggest globalisation story since 1990 has been the emergence onto the world's manufacturing and trading stage of emerging markets from China and India in Asia, to Brazil in South America. With large domestic markets and increasing determination to export goods and services, these emerging markets have rewritten the rules of global trade.

3. **China and India's decades of growth:** since the Cultural Revolution in China, and the liberalisation of markets in India, both countries have experienced massive growth – fuelled by a joint domestic market of over 2 billion consumers, and the capacity to be the 'back office' and 'factory' of the world. As we shall see, as the goods and services created by workers in these countries move up the value chain, so too the global aspirations of local companies increase.

4. **Frugal innovation:** once seen primarily as the manufacturer of the West's innovations, the developing markets are increasingly leading the world in low-cost and frugal innovations that are now being exported to the developed markets of the West. This will have a profound impact on the globalisation of innovation over the coming decades.

5. **The global educational powerhouses:** it's a numbers game. With a joint population of 2.6 billion in 2010, predicted to rise to

2.8 billion in 2020 and 3 billion in 2050, India and China are rapidly becoming key to the talent pools of the world. Added to that, a propensity to study the 'hard' scientific subjects, and investment by local companies in talent development, will ensure that increasingly companies will look to India and China for their engineers and scientists.

6. **The world becomes urban:** from 2008, the proportion of the world's population living in urban centres outweighed those in rural centres, and the trend will continue. At the same time, innovative 'clusters' around the world are attracting a disproportionate number of the most talented and educated people. The mega-cities of the world, often ringed by gigantic slums, will become home to an ever-greater proportion of the population.

7. **Continued bubbles and crashes:** booms and busts have been features of economic life for centuries, and we can expect them to continue to rock the world in the coming decades. This is combined with a need for the populations of many developed countries to rein in their spending, and to substantially increase their savings.

8. **The regional underclass emerge:** we can expect that in an increasingly connected and globalising world the underclass, while still located in specific regions (such as sub-Saharan Africa), will also extend across the developed and developing worlds. This global underclass will be marked by their inability either to join the global market for skills or to have the skills and aspirations to become one of the army of service people who care for the needs of the growing ageing urban populations.

From the 1950s onwards globalisation has been one of the driving forces in the shaping of how we work. As we can see from these pieces, this is only likely to increase, bringing with it both positive aspects in terms of an ever-increasingly global marketplace for talent and work, and also a darker aspect of continuously growing competition and fragmentation.

The force of demography and longevity

This, above all other forces, was the topic that most fascinated the members of the research consortium. We quickly understood that technology is changing everything and will continue to do so, and that natural resources are depleted and carbon footprints must be reduced. However, it was demography and longevity that really captured the attention of many of those in the Future of Work Consortium. I guess the simple reason is that the force of demography and longevity, more than any other forces, is intimately about us, our friends and our children. It's about who is having babies, and how long these babies are going to live. It's about how many people are working, and for how long. It's about the four generations and how they are going to love and possibly hate each other. Demography and work are intertwined – and understanding the hard facts of demography is crucial to crafting a reasoned view of the future of work. There are three key aspects of demography that will influence work in the coming years – generational cohorts, birth rates and longevity.

Generational cohorts are people born at roughly the same time, who as a consequence tend to have rather similar attitudes and expectations. They are often brought up with the same child-rearing practices and have similar experiences as teenagers and young adults. This is a particularly sensitive period for acquiring a moral and political orientation. These shared experiences produce what has been termed 'generational markers'. These are important since they provide clues about how these generations will behave as they move into positions of decision-making at work and have increasing access to resources.

By 2010 there were four distinct generations in the workforce – the Traditionalists (born around 1928 to 1945), the Baby Boomers (born around 1945 to 1964); the Generation X (born around 1965 to 1979) and Gen Y (born around 1980 to 1995). Coming up are Gen Z (born after 1995). The Traditionalists had their main impact on organisational life between 1960 and 1980.

By 2010 they were already over 65, making up between 5% and 10% of the workforce. Between 2010 and 2025 the majority of this generation will have left the workforce. However, we can expect some part of their legacy to live on in organisational life since this generation were the initial architects of many organisational practices and processes which subsequently survived for decades.

In many ways, the coming decades will be defined by the actions of the largest demographic group the world has ever seen – the Baby Boomers. This period saw around 77 million babies born in the USA, while the birth rates of many European countries reached as high as 20 per thousand, nearly five times the rate in 2010. In 2010 they were in their 50s and 60s and by 2025 most will have left the workforce, taking with them a huge store of tactical knowledge and knowhow; and also, if some commentators are to be believed, much of the wealth of the next generations. More importantly, as this huge bulge leaves the workforce, the post-1960s reduction in birth rates across the developed and much of the developing world will see significantly fewer people taking their place. This has huge implications for the retention of knowledge in companies and the challenge of severe skill shortages.

The following generation – Generation X – is the generation that in 2010 are in their mid-40s and will be in their mid-60s by 2025 – so in 2010 they were entering the height of their earning power, beginning to see their children growing up. This is a generation that grew up in a time of economic uncertainty, the Vietnam War, the fall of the Berlin Wall, the 1973 oil crisis, the dotcom bubble, the Iran hostage crisis, all of which reduced their expectation of a long-term relationship between employee and employer.[6] They also increasingly witnessed their parents divorcing. In 1950, 26% of US marriages ended in divorce; by 1980 this had climbed to 48%.[7] They were there when computers came into the home, when video games began to be played and the nascent internet began to connect them.[8] While the Baby

Boomers believed the world to be a place of future positive growth, this was not the case for Gen X. In real terms, Gen X US men in 2004 made 12% less than their fathers at the same age in 1974.[9] This was on top of significant personal investments in education, joining a workforce behind a generation of Baby Boomers, and competing in a weak global economy.

By 2025 the Gen Y'ers (born around 1980 to 1995) will be aged between 30 and 45 and at a crucial stage of their working lives. This was the first generation to have grown up alongside the bulky embryonic forms of personal computers, the internet, social media and digital technologies. Many Gen Y'ers closely followed the rapid technological evolution of their time and now have an intimate knowledge of, and perhaps even admiration for, the devices and platforms they use. Their social habits and behaviours shifted as they increasingly used text, email, Facebook and Twitter to communicate. They talked to their friends online, and played with strangers in MMORPGs like World of Warcraft and Second Life.

Gen Z by 2005 had reached their first decade, and by 2025 will be around 35. From 2020 onwards they will be taking an increasing role in the business life of companies across the world. Called by some the Re-Generations and by others the Internet Generation, this group is often defined by their connectivity.[10] Although we cannot be sure how they will develop as a generational cohort, we know something of their early experiences. Generation Z will be the first generation to grow up surrounded by the trends we have discussed, and the challenges and opportunities that we have talked about will weigh heavily on their minds, helping to form who they are and what they do.

At the same time, with regard to birth rates, there are complex demographic patterns emerging across the world. The developed world is ageing fast and hardly reproducing itself. That's why by 2050 one in three people across the developed world will be drawing a pension. This has huge implications in many respects, particularly where a country decides to spend its money. In the

USA, for example, the Congressional Budget Office predicts that spending on entitlements will grow from 10% of GDP in 2010 to 16% in 2035.

The soon-to-be-retiring Baby Boomers are primarily a phenomena of post-World War birth rates. Since that time, birth rates in much of the developed world have been in decline, caused by a combination of increasing female education, personal choice and enhanced child medical provision. In China the 'one child per family' government regulation introduced in 1979 has drastically curtailed the growth of the population, from an average of 5.8 children per family to 1.7. However, lowering birth rates is not a worldwide phenomenon, and we can expect to see birth rates remaining high in many of the developing regions of the world such as sub-Saharan Africa and rural India. Clearly difference in birth rates will impact on the availability of labour and skills and also on the labour migration routes we can expect to see forming over the coming decades.

In Europe the working population is rapidly ageing due to low birth rates, longer life expectancies and in many countries low immigration. By 2050 it is estimated that the median age of Europeans will rise to 52.3 years from 37.7.[11] In some European countries this challenge is particularly pressing. In Italy, for example, 25% of Italian women are childless with another 25% having only one child.[12] Estimates indicate that Italy will either need to raise its retirement age to 77 or admit 2.2 million immigrants annually to maintain its current worker-to-retiree ratio.[13]

However, of all the forces, demography and longevity are the most situationally and contextually based, with contradictory aspects across the world. For example, birth rates are indeed falling in Italy – but they are soaring in Ethiopia. People are certainly living longer in Sweden – but across the border in the Soviet Union life expectancy has dropped. With regard to the demographic groups, it is clear for example that Gen Ys in Boston want meaningful work and the opportunity to develop – yet in Shanghai the most talented Gen Ys are leaving one company to join another for an extra $1,000 a year. As a consequence of these contextual differences, the overriding proviso for the demographic force is 'Well, it depends', and so as you patch together the future of your work and that of others you need to keep this uppermost in your thinking.

Having said that, there are some basic rules of thumb that can be applied when understanding and predicting demographic and longevity trends.[14] With regard to the attributes of the generation, the greater the wealth and job security of Gen Y, the more similar their views are to the stereotype of Gen Y. That's why, for example, educated and professional Gen Y'ers in Mumbai are rather similar in their aspirations and goals to educated Gen Y'ers in Silicon Valley, but very unlike Gen Y'ers who are living in Mumbai's slums.[15] Here are the four specific pieces about demography that have been patched into the future storylines.

1. **The ascendance of Gen Y:** by 2025 this group will begin to make their needs and hopes felt in the workplace. We can expect that their aspirations for a work/life balance and for interesting work could well profoundly impact on the design of work and the development of organisations and working conditions.

2. **Increasing longevity:** perhaps one of the most important aspects of the coming decades is the extraordinary increase in productive life – which will allow millions of people over the age of 60 who want to continue to make a contribution to the workplace.

3. **Some Baby Boomers grow old poor:** longevity will enable millions of people across the world to continue to make a contribution to the workplace. The challenge will be creating work for them, and we can expect a significant proportion of them to join the ranks of the global poor.

4. **Global migration increases:** over the coming decades migration will increase both to the cities and across countries as people move to gain education or better-paid work. We can also

expect to see an increase in the migration of carers and supporters from the emerging to the developed countries.

Demographic and longevity forces will influence our work in positive ways – allowing us to live longer, healthier lives and to work productively into our 80s. It could also be that the ascendance of Gen Y – brought up in a more cooperative and productive way – will have a positive impact on the collaborative context of work. We can also expect migration to allow the most talented to join others in the creative clusters of the world. However, there is also a dark side of demography: increased longevity means that many millions of people around the world do not have adequate provisions for 90 or 100 years of life and will struggle to find work. Migration may enable the most talented to move to creative clusters, but it will also break apart families and communities and lead to the isolation that could be such a crucial motif for the future.

The force of society

It would be a mistake to imagine that we humans remain the same as the forces of technology, globalisation and demography swirl around us – leaving us perhaps battered, but fundamentally unchanged. Mankind has changed in the past, and will continue to change in the future. The question is how these changes will manifest themselves. If we look back to the first Industrial Revolution, huge swathes of people moved from the countryside to the towns to work in factories. These experiences transformed the way that people saw their lives and their communities. They changed the way people thought about themselves, they changed the way they thought about others, and they changed their hopes and aspirations for work.[16]

But this process is not straightforward. The future will be elusive when it comes to predicting human behaviour and aspirations. Yes, we want to be ourselves and autonomous ... but wait, we also want to be part of a regenerative community. Yes, we are excited about technology and connectivity … but we also yearn to be comforted and crave time on our own. These are important paradoxes, which those at work will be increasingly faced with in the coming decades.

However, the fascinating aspect of the past, the present and the future is that, while the trappings may have changed, the basic human plot remains essentially the same. As Maslow described all those years back, we want safety for ourselves and those we love; we like to be cherished and find a sense of belonging in the communities we live in; we need a sense of achievement and of a job well done; and for some, we also want a sense of what he called 'self-actualisation' – the feeling that we have done the best we could and have fulfilled our potential.[17] This is the basic plot that has defined the lives of people, their families and their communities from the very beginning. What has changed are the trappings, the trappings of technology and connectivity, and the trappings of the material goods that surround us.

I remember taking my young son Dominic to Tanzania to spend time with the Masai in the Masai Mara. Dominic and I were standing on top of a hill looking over the empty plains below, talking with a young Masai warrior about his life. As we talked we were interrupted by a sound very familiar to Dominic and me – the sound of a mobile phone ringing. From his pouch the warrior extracted his phone and talked in the excited way people across the world talk on their mobile phones. When he finished the conversation I asked him who he was talking to.

'My brother,' was his reply. 'He had taken the goats out to find pasture this morning, and he has just rung me to tell me that after three hours walking into the scrub they had found fresh grass for the goats to eat.'

The trappings may have changed – but essentially the warriors are still as concerned about feeding their goats as they were many centuries ago.

Here are the seven pieces about society that will play a central role in shaping the future of work.

1. **Families become rearranged**: across the world family groups will become smaller and increasingly 'rearranged' as stepparents, stepbrothers and sisters displace the traditional family structures of the past.

2. **The rise of reflexivity**: as families become rearranged, and work groups become increasingly diverse, so people begin to think more deeply about themselves, what is important to them and the lives they want to construct. This reflexivity becomes crucial to understanding choices and creating energy and courage to make the tough decisions and trade-offs that will be necessary.

3. **The role of powerful women**: over the coming decades we can expect women to play a more prominent role in the management and leadership of companies and entrepreneurial businesses as they join the top echelons of corporate life. This will have implications for women's expectations, the norms of work, and indeed the relationships between men and women in the home.

4. **The balanced man**: there is growing evidence that men's perception of their role and the choices they make are also changing. Faced with the consequences of their fathers' choices, it seems that there will be an increasing proportion of men who will decide to make a trade-off between wealth and spending time with their family and children.

5. **Growing distrust of institutions**: trust is about the relationships between the individual and their community and work. It is based on the perception of whether others can be trusted to deliver. Across the developed world it seems that levels of trust in leaders and corporations have fallen, and may well continue to fall over the coming decades.

6. **The decline of happiness**: perhaps one of the most surprising aspects of working life is that, in the main, increases in standards of living – beyond a certain level – have been

accompanied by decreases in happiness. If the trajectory of consumption continues, there is no evidence that this decline will be reversed.

7. **Passive leisure increases:** one of the headline stories from the industrialisation of work has been the significant increase in leisure time. Up until the 2010s much of that time was spent in passive television watching. It could be that in the coming decades the growth of virtual participation will create a significant 'cognitive surplus' which can be focused on more productive activities.

At first glance these piece about the societal forces look bleak: a future of dislocated families, ebbing trust, general unhappiness, ever more voracious consumption and little in the way of work/ life balance. Certainly as we construct the storylines for the Default Future these pieces play a key role in the themes of isolation and fragmentation. However, it could also be that this force is the most positive of all in the sense that it is most dependent on personal actions and choices. So as we will see as we construct the storylines for the positive, Crafted Future, within these seemingly bleak forces are rays of hope as rearranged families create a greater openness to differences, as Gen Y exercise their choice for more collaboration in the workplace, and as women are able to have their voices heard with more vigour in the boardrooms of 2025.

The force of energy resources

The way we will work in the future is intimately wrapped up with our access to energy and the impact this access will have on our environment. Of all the five forces we considered in the Future of Work Consortium, people felt most concerned and yet powerless about this one. For many it felt that a spectre was haunting them – the spectre of ever-increasing energy costs and of a rapidly changing climate.

These are forces that began with the first Industrial Revolution and have been gathering pace ever since. It's clear to many governments, to businesses and to each one of us that the actions we are taking are having a detrimental impact on the environment. The central challenge is one of short term versus longer term – an issue we will encounter at various times in thinking through these five forces. Of course we care about the environment and the future of the planet – but these are all longer-term issues. In the short term, for many people and companies and even governments, there is no immediate stimulus to drastically reorganise their policies, companies or lifestyles to avoid some of the projections we will consider in the hard data. As many of those engaged in the conversation about the Future of Work remarked, the consequences of climate change seem like a distant fiction that currently has very little influence on their everyday decisions. Yet this is likely to change considerably by 2025, and we can expect issues of energy usage and climate change to be at the centre of the working agenda by 2030. By then, many of the outcomes of fossil fuel depletion and visible climate change will begin to impact on the daily working life of people across the world.

One of the members of the Future of Work Consortium was Shell Oil, and we found their resource scenarios for 2050 a very useful starting point from which to develop the more detailed pieces. For over 30 years the scenario team at Shell Oil have worked with experts from around the world to construct scenarios of the future use of energy, releasing these scenarios every few years. In 2008 they released the two scenarios they believe most accurately describe the paths into the next 50 years. These scenarios consider the effects of various levels of reform and progress in terms of policy, technology and commitment from governments, industry and society in order to provide a glimpse into the possible futures of energy. The interesting aspect of the Shell scenarios is that neither conclusion reached is infeasible. They display a cautious sense of optimism without forgetting the severity of the facts.

In both energy resource scenarios we are faced with an impending and necessary restructuring. We can either run the course of the present energy framework, adapting to emerging challenges as they arise, or alternatively, begin to construct a new energy framework that integrates local, regional and global networks into a new international architecture of sustainability. Whereas the first scenario (which they term Scramble) relies on the activities of national governments to secure their future energy supply, the second (termed Blueprint) emerges as a consequence of grassroots coalitions (recall those 5 billion joined-up people) that bring together individuals, companies and other institutions to construct a new foundation for energy and resource generation and control.

In the Scramble scenario, over the coming decades, governments around the world scramble to attempt to guarantee the maximum amount available to them of the dwindling resource pool. In asserting their autonomy rather than agreeing to cooperate, governments increasingly compete with each other to secure energy for their domestic consumers. This has the impact of preserving high-energy prices and putting increasing strain on the existing energy infrastructure. In this scenario, although prosperity persists throughout the 2010s and 2020s, this relentless scramble and competition for energy resources continues to increase the gap between the rich and the poor. Many of the resource gains that are made are due to the resurgence of the coal sector. In this scenario multilateral governmental institutions find themselves too weak to subsidise the creation of a global clean energy sector. To supplement the use of finite coal reserves, domestic investment is instead directed to the expansion of nuclear power and a modernised biofuel industry. In the short term they manage to sustain economic growth throughout the 2020s.

However, in the longer term (2020 and beyond) the scenario is increasingly negative. In the Scramble scenario governments increasingly have to react to the emerging constraints of the traditional energy framework, imposing solutions that often have immediate benefits but long-term negative consequences. Coal is not without its environmental problems, while nuclear fuel produces nuclear waste, and the biofuel industry competes with the food industry, pushing up prices of food to unsustainable levels. As a consequence, by 2025 the uncoordinated efforts of governments to secure resources have ensured that the existing framework is stretched to its limit, eventually necessitating draconian measures on production, consumption and mobility. For the governments of China and India, still in the process of developing a modernised industrial economy, these constraints prove hard to enforce. In Europe and America the introduction of a carbon tax and the scrutiny of the carbon footprints of individuals and companies put pressure on people to work from home and live austere lives. It is only when governments, companies and individuals reach this impasse that substantial steps to create a new energy sector are taken. Having failed to cooperate sooner, instead insisting on competing to use what remained of traditional energy reserves, nations begin to realise the extent of this undertaking. Not only do they have to restructure their energy framework completely, but they also have to confront the oncoming consequences of their lack of restraint.

The second Blueprint scenario reveals the beneficial aspect of confronting climate change and energy problems sooner (that is, before 2020) rather than later. It is also a scenario that depends both on a sense of urgency and the flow of information. It relies on the practical actions of well-coordinated coalitions who have acknowledged the implications of climate change, and are quick in their efforts to secure a safe and sustainable future. These coalitions include companies with mutual energy interests, cities and regions conscious of their future energy requirements, and a whole host of other institutions that are united in formulating low-carbon ventures. In this scenario general awareness of the damaging effects of climate change, and the initial successes of creative and efficient experiments and practices in infrastructural development, play key roles. Productive processes and lifestyle choices are quickly emulated by others on a national and regional scale. As more and more people come to accept the threats that a high-carbon economy poses to their environment and livelihood, pressure on governments, including those of developing countries, increases investment in emission-reduction projects. Emissions trading schemes offer incentives for the establishment of low-carbon ventures, while giving more traditional sectors the opportunity to adjust.

In this scenario, the Blueprints established by these multiple actors quickly create a culture of sustainability, helping to fuel a more effective international consensus. In turn, this consensus mitigates the inefficiencies and uncertainties that might otherwise continue to undermine a dis-integrated, bottom-up approach. In order to stay at the forefront of innovation, many technologically developed countries bring about an era of brave policy-making that incentivises the creation of new and efficient infrastructural foundations. This establishes the emergence of new and innovative firms that become global leaders in exportable carbon management technologies and systems. Meanwhile, China and India commit to various international frameworks that guarantee technology transfer and secure an energy-efficient future. In rural areas of Africa, cheap and efficient wind turbines and solar panels ensure cost-effective access to energy and help make electric transport increasingly viable. Energy prices, though initially reflecting the cost of infrastructural reorganisation, remain affordable in the long run and continue to fall as wind and solar technology become more efficient.

These two scenarios, Scramble and Blueprint, are not polar extremes – neither is unrealistic. Yet they do differ substantially. The first is one of denial and competition, while the second is of acknowledgement and cooperation. Both inevitably confront the hard truths of climate change without sacrificing economic growth. These are the three pieces of the energy force that will have the most profound implications on the future of work.

1. **Energy prices increase:** Over the coming decades the easily available energy resources of the world will be depleted. At the same time, countries such as China and India will increase their resource requirements significantly. One of the most immediate impacts of the rising cost of resources will be that the movement of goods and transportation of people will have to be significantly reduced.

2. **Environmental catastrophes displace people:** the correlation between carbon dioxide emissions and temperature increases was already causing concern by 2010. By this time, changes had begun to occur in the many ecosystems of the world, sea levels began rising, wind patterns had changed and heat waves and droughts had become more prevalent.

3. **A culture of sustainability begins to emerge:** one of the implications of the dwindling of easily accessed energy resources could be a renewed interest in sustainability and widespread adoption of more energy-efficient ways of living, with a brake on vicarious consumption. These cultures of sustainability could have a profound impact on the way that work gets done.

As we consider the dark and bright impact energy resources will have on the future of work, it is easy to become overwhelmed by the negative. However, as we will discover, it is possible to cast the task ahead in a positive light, one that can rejuvenate faltering economies, promote greater equality and foster innovation. It could constitute, to some extent at least, an energy revolution that echoes that of the late 1800s, with the culture of sustainability having as much impact as the engineering culture had on Victorian Britain. It is possible that the collaborative spirit will influence business ventures and government policy, creating greater transparency and integration even beyond the energy sector. There are already clues to these scenarios in the other forces. The technology force implies 5 billion people connected with each other, creating a 'cognitive surplus' that could well become the momentum and energy behind the grassroots-led initiative of the Blueprint scenario. What's more, as the demographic force shows, the generation who will be leading the world in 2025 – Gen Y – are extremely aware of the energy and environmental challenges they are faced with. Perhaps more than any other generation before, they are capable of creating the cooperative and empathic skills that will be so crucial for the emergence of the Blueprint scenario.

Crafting your own working future

You have now taken a glance at the 32 pieces that make up the five forces that will shape the coming decades of your work life. Now the task is to begin to work with these pieces to craft the story of your own future of work, and from this begin to create a deeper understanding of your options and choices.

As you look at these pieces the challenge is to make them your own and from them to craft your own story. Just as my mother worked with her fabric pieces to craft her quilts, so you need to go through a process of filtering and selection. Right from the beginning, there will be some pieces you will want to discard, others that will surprise you and you'll want to know more about, and some you will fall in love with and want to understand more to make your own. Then, once you have initially sorted the pieces, you will want to look for patterns and begin to create a deeper structure that resonates with your own context and values. These are the actions you will want to take with the pieces:

* **Discard:** one of the most important aspects of creating a beautiful quilt is to know what to leave out. The same is true with crafting your own story about the future. As you look back on each of the pieces about the future, there will be some that you can immediately discard. It may be that you don't agree with the data, or that you know it's not going to be important to you, or that it is something that you cannot imagine

resonating with your picture of the future. Feel free to discard as many of these pieces as you wish.

* **Embroider:** as you looked through the pieces, there will be some that intrigued you and created a sense of wanting to know more. As we take a closer look at the stories of the future, you will see that I provide more detail for each of the pieces and also have highlighted references and resources that you may find interesting.

* **Discover and collect:** as you begin to put these ideas together and look at them in a more holistic way, you may decide that there are bits completely missing that I have failed to find in my own quest. I've had this feeling with my own fabric collection. I can recall that for years I wanted to see the silks of Varanasi, which are legendary in their luminosity and beauty but which required a trip to the upper banks of the Ganges to find them. It took me years to actually make the trip – but as soon as I did my first priority was to take a closer look at the fabrics. I am sure that as you take a closer look at the pieces I have collected, there will be some that are missing and that you will want to devote energy to finding. That's wonderful – but do come to www.theshiftbylyndagratton.com to post what you have discovered – I'd love to take a closer look at what you have found.

* **Sort:** I have presented the pieces to you in the simplest of categories, by the impact they have on the five forces. But as you look closer you may find that for you there are other ways of categorising these pieces. For example, you may want to sort them in terms of how much you find them personally intriguing, or the extent to which they will impact on your own future, or by the way they will impact on the region of the world in which you live.

* **Look for patterns:** in a sense this is the most creative aspect of making a quilt. You have discarded the fragments that don't fit, embroidered those that you value highly, and sorted them in categories beyond the most obvious. Now is the time to

stand back and see if you can find an emerging pattern. The challenge with these pieces about the future is to find a pattern that makes sense to you, and resonates with how you believe your future will emerge. It's only at this stage that you can move into the next phase of working out the shifts you will need to take to ensure that you have future-proofed your work and career.

You may recall that this was the task I set the members of the Future of Work Consortium. I asked them specifically to take the pieces and to construct a day in the life of someone working in 2025. Many of these initial storylines were negative. They reflected the anxiety and concern people felt as they thought about the forces. As you will see, the major themes to emerge from this initial task were themes of fragmentation, isolation and exclusion. It is these themes we will next explore in more detail. After presenting these storylines, I will then describe in more detail the specific pieces that seem to play a contributing factor in the creation of the storylines.

Once the negative, default storylines had been created, we went back to the original pieces with the task of re-sorting them to create more positive storylines – what I have called the Crafted Future. These show how the pieces from the five forces can also create work for the future, a future that has co-creation, social participation, micro-entrepreneurship and creative lives at its centre.

As you begin to think through your own future of work, do download the *Future of Work Workbook* I have created for you – it's available at my website, www.theshiftbylyndagratton.com, where you will also find a series of short videos in which I describe the forces and trends in a little more detail. By the way, whilst you are there do sign up for the monthly newsletter to stay in touch with developments.

PART II

THE DARK
SIDE OF THE
DEFAULT FUTURE

It is the subtle and unique combination of the many aspects of the five forces that will create the context in which your future working life is lived. For some it could be that technology is the crucial driver, while for others it could be demography or globalisation. However, for most of us it will not be a single force but rather the combination of these forces that creates our context. To understand the many combinations these forces can take, the members of the research consortium created storylines of people working in 2025. Of course these storylines are fictitious. However, by thinking through the intersections and relationships between the forces, these possible scenarios are revealed. We can really begin to imagine how people will live their working lives in 2025.

There is the storyline of Jill, whose frantic and fragmented life reveals how the technology and globalisation forces have created a 24/7 joined-up world that leaves her with little time to concentrate, observe and think, or even to play.

There are Rohan and Amon, on the face of it both successful professionals living in Mumbai and Cairo. But scratch beneath the surface and their minute-by-minute living reveals a life devoid of easy companionship, with little by way of family ties. They are caught in the intersections of a world that is simultaneously becoming increasingly urban, where energy costs have moved relationships to the virtual, and where family ties and ebbing trust have left them isolated and lonely.

In the USA we find Briana, with little by way of skills or ambition, joining the poor who can be found in any city around the world. Hers is a working life shaped by continuous economic bubbles and crashes, and she is the victim of the relentless replacement of semi-skilled jobs by technology. She has also seen austerity grip the West, and the rise of the underclass trapped in ageing cities.

It is through the experiences of these characters that we can truly understand how the five forces will shape our future, and how they will interact, influence and create momentum. Through the eyes of our future workers we can see the paradoxes they face, the choices they make and the troubles and anxieties they experience. Like theirs, our own future working lives will have dark and light aspects depending on our context and choices.

However, these are not uniformly dark lives – working lives rarely are. Rohan, for example, is a highly competent surgeon in Mumbai and has achieved mastery at the core of his work, and Jill has a group of friends, which I will call the 'Posse', that brings her enormous pleasure. What's important about these stories from the future is that they illustrate an aspect of a working life that is missing or unbalanced. It is by considering these imbalances that we can draw a thread from the past to identify their pathway, and to the future to describe their outcomes.

As you think about each of these stories, I urge you to reflect on these questions:

* Have you noticed any of these future phenomena in your own working life – are they already resonating with you?
* Do they sound plausible for others in the future, and what are the drivers behind these phenomena?
* What would these mean to your working life and the lives of others?

The final question addresses the issue of choices and consequence, of assumptions and shifting assumptions. It ties directly with the three future-proofed shifts I believe will be crucial in creating meaningful work in the future. For example, the shift from the shallow generalist to something much more masterful and skilled – which in a sense is what sits at the heart of Briana's story. Or the shift from isolation to connectivity – which is a choice that Rohan and Amon have failed to make. Or indeed the shift from the voracious consumer that is the basis of Jill's life to a more balanced life in which meaning and experiences play a more central role.

These are four stories that illustrate what we might think of as the Default Future. That's the future which emerges when the tough decisions are ignored. If, as you read these stories, you find them chilling, then they simply serve to illustrate how crucial it is to think hard about how work life will emerge, and to be prepared to question some deeply held assumptions, and make some tough shifts.

2
FRAGMENTATION: A THREE-MINUTE WORLD

Jill's story

It is 6.00 a.m. on a cold morning in London in January 2025 and Jill is awakened to the sound of the alarm. As soon as her eyes begin to focus, her attention is grabbed by the 300 messages that flash up on her wall screen. During the night, colleagues, friends, current employers and our future employers from across the world are keen to share their ideas with her, check information and ask her opinion on pressing issues. Getting out of bed, as her eyes become accustomed to the dawn light, the first hologram call comes in. Over the next ten minutes Jill works with her avatar, as it is needed for a meeting across the globe that will begin in two hours' time and will require broad directions.

By 7.00 Jill is connected to her cognitive assistant that has created the timetable for her day and made the preparations for the teleconferencing and video-presence connections she will need. Her first conference call is to her colleagues in the Beijing office who are keen to link up with her, and so the next 30 minutes is spent in a conference call with the team. As she listens to their voices over the telephone she is able to work on another 30 messages – thank goodness for the mute button! The next 50 minutes are spent still in her bedroom taking another quick look at the nighttime messages, briefing her avatar and working on a project that is key to the group.

By 10.00, still in her pyjamas, Jill snatches a quick bite of breakfast, holds back on the demands from her colleagues for yet more feedback from them, and logs on to her worksite to see if any new work has come in overnight.

The next hour is spent on conference calls to clients, negotiating a couple of deals and agreeing delivery times. She has the final call with Mumbai before they go offline. They are using the recently developed hologram technology to project themselves, and Jill is pleased with the clarity of the representations. It is 10.30 and her team in Boston are awake and keen to ask her opinion about a particular deal they have put together: it involves linking with the Shanghai team so she agrees to brief her Chinese colleagues the following morning.

By 11.00 Jill is ready to take the train into the office hub that has been built about 10 miles away. This hub is used by any employee of the company who lives in the vicinity and provides an opportunity for people to work together in an office environment. As Jill jumps on the train she spends the next 15 minutes on her handheld computer answering more messages and taking a couple of calls to her team members. There is a particularly tricky problem in Johannesburg and her colleagues are keen to get her advice about how to proceed with the sales. By 11.30 Jill has arrived in the hub where she takes a quick look around to find a workstation that is vacant and then logs in, saying a quick hello to the others who have also decided to work in the hub that morning. Some of the people she knows, others are new faces.

Her boss Jerry is keen to talk with her about the daily sales figures, so by 3.00 p.m. she is patched through to his home office in Los Angeles. It's early morning there, so he has chosen to use his avatar to present for him – no one wants to be seen working in their pyjamas. The conversation goes pretty well – one of Jill's major clients is a telecoms company based in Rwanda in West Africa and they are negotiating a substantial order for the chips for handheld devices. Jill had caught up with the client earlier in the day, so was able to brief Jerry about how the process was going and the likely revenue stream. Jerry also wants Jill's views on how best to build the market in Patagonia and Peru. For the last two decades, Essar in Kenya and MTN in South Africa have been leaders in the field and have been particularly adept at encouraging their customers to use their mobiles to make money transfers. It's become big business, and Jerry is keen to know Jill's views on how their experiences in Kenya could be transferred to the steadily growing markets of Chile and Argentina. His plan is to link with the Chinese telecom giant that is making impressive investments in these countries.

By 4.00 the conversation with Jerry is over, so Jill takes a last look at her messages before her 4.30 team briefing. It's an opportunity to catch up with her US team members and also to hear their views on the situation in Rwanda. A couple of them have gone to the company hub in downtown Phoenix and have booked the telepresence room for the next 30 minutes. Jill waits a moment for the telepresence to be free and then is able to link through to her group. As always the sound and visual quality is first class – and she is able to really get a real sense of how the Phoenix team are feeling about the project. By 5.00 the conference is over and Jill grabs her bags before rushing to the station to get the train home. For Jill, it is a ritual that she cooks supper at home every Wednesday when she is at home, and today is Wednesday. She is in the local supermarket by 6.00 to pick up the evening food and opens the door to her home by 6.30.

A moment of peace – food on the table, conversation with her teenage daughter and a great cup of coffee.

By 10.00 p.m. that evening Jill is in her study booting up her videoconference to Beijing; she wants to catch up on one of her team members before their day begins – Jerry wants to form a stronger partnership with the Chinese telecom company and she wants to know her colleague's view on how best to do this. By 10.20 the videoconference is over and Jill has her last cup of coffee before turning on the television to catch the evening news.

Her eyes are caught by the fires that are raging across Russia, and by the floods that continue to devastate Pakistan. As her eyes close her final image is of Greenpeace protesters calling for the protection of the small part of the Amazon forest that still remains …

Welcome to the fragmented world, where it seems that no activity lasts more than three minutes, and where those in employment are continuously competing with people across the globe to strive to serve the different stakeholders they work with.

Do you think your world is already fragmented? Right now you are already likely to be interrupted at least every three minutes.[1] If you feel that technology is already out of control, fast forward to 2025 and it's only got worse. It's a global world that's so interconnected that working 24/7 is the norm, a world where 5 billion people are connected to each other through their handheld devices and as many as want to can connect to you. Imagine it – no peace, no quiet, no reflection time. Constantly plugged in, hooked up, online.

Work began to really fragment from around 2000. This was the time when internet access reached half a billion people, when desktop computers and email brought hundreds of messages into your daily inbox, and when your mobile phone began to interrupt you as often as it could.

Rewinding to the past: a pre-fragmented day in 1990

Can you remember a time when work was not fragmented? Perhaps the writer Jared Diamond is right that this has become 'creeping normalcy'.[2] The fragmentation of our working lives has unfolded so slowly that the build-up of pain occurs in small, almost unnoticeable steps. As a consequence of this slow unfolding, we accept the outcome without resistance, even if the same outcome, had it come about in one sudden leap, would have earned a vigorous response.

It reminds me of the story of the frog and the boiling water. The story goes like this. If you throw a frog into a pan of boiling water it jumps out as fast as possible to escape. However, if instead you place a frog into a pan of cold water, and then heat the water very, very slowly, the frog acclimatises to the slow increase in temperature and never tries to escape – until it is eventually boiled alive.

Have we indeed become so used to this 'creeping normalcy' that we fail to recognise what it means to our working lives now, and even more so in the future? To test this idea, let's try and recreate a pre-fragmented working day by rewinding to the past rather than fast-forwarding to the future. I'm going to rewind to 1990 because it's a time when mobile phones were very rare, and when many offices outside of the West Coast of the USA did not have internet connection, and when no homes had internet connectivity.

To get a feel for this, you will either have to recollect from your own experience (as I am able to do), or find someone who was working 20 years ago and can describe to you in detail a typical working day. It's important, by the way, that they describe the working day in detail – that's where the important stuff lurks. Here is my memory of how a working day in 1990 played out for me – as far as I can remember.

At that time I worked as a senior consultant in one of the large UK-based consulting practices. I wake in the morning, have breakfast with my husband while listening to the news on the radio, and then leave for work at 8.00. By 9.00 I am in the office and my assistant joins me to go through the letters that have arrived that morning. On average, 20 letters arrive every morning, so we go through these letters and I dictate to her my responses. By 10.00 I spend two hours working on a proposal for a client; this I write by hand and it is then taken through to the typing pool to be typed. By 12.30 it's lunchtime and I join my colleagues in my office for a quick lunch in the local pub.

By 1.30 I'm back at my desk and ready for two meetings with my team. It's 3.00, and I'm in a cab to the headquarters of a multinational to present to a group of potential clients. I'm back in the office by 4.30 to sign the letters I dictated that morning to my assistant, to take two more telephone calls, and to check the proposal that's now back from the typing pool. I make a number of changes to the proposal and send it back to the typing pool. By 5.30 the office is beginning to empty. I round up a few friends in the office and we wander across the road to the local pub for a quick drink before getting back home by 6.30 and dinner with my husband at 7.30.

By the time I reached home, my working day was over. Perhaps I brought home a document or two to read, but not often. I certainly did not write anything at home because I did not have a typewriter at home – and of course there was no computer. So my means of production was pretty much limited to the office hours. I certainly never, ever spoke with clients after 6.00 p.m. They did not have my home number, and mobile phones were not in use.

I don't mean to be Pollyanna about the past. I could tell the tale again, adding in the fact that this was a deeply sexist workplace (I was the first female senior consultant and considered something of a freak), and that it was very unhealthy (we smoked constantly in the office and drank at lunchtime and every evening). This is no exercise in nostalgia. But as we look forward 10, possibly 20 years from now, it's useful to also look back. By looking back we can get a good idea about velocity and direction, and about the rhythms and trajectories of working life.

However, before we leave this day in 1990 let me ask you to take another look at this story and consider what's missing. Did I talk with my friends about where to meet that evening? No – I did not have a mobile phone and they did not ring me at work – so we made the arrangement well in advance with few last-minute changes. Did I have a close working relationship with my clients? Yes – we did not use the internet and so instead we met, spoke on the telephone or exchanged letters. Finally, did I link into clients all over the world? Well, yes and no. I did indeed have a client in South Africa and we exchanged letters and faxes, and talked on the phone. I went over to Pretoria three times a year and stayed for two weeks. At that time, two weeks was considered a decent length of time for what was called an 'overseas trip'.

What I want to draw your attention to is that, unlike Jill's, mine was not a fragmented day. If you watched me with a stopwatch you would have found that on average I spent about half an hour on each activity. When I wrote the client proposals I was uninterrupted for two hours. Only 20 letters arrived, they were read and replied to by the next day, no one expected instant responses – and if the timing was too long we could always say, 'The letter must have been lost in the post!' There was no internet, in fact I did not have a typewriter in my room, typing was the job of my secretary and the women (they were all women) in the typing pool.

I've chosen 1990 as the date for our memory experiment because in many ways this year marked the beginning of the extreme fragmentation of work. Over the following 10 years the forces of technology and globalisation began to snip work into ever-smaller pieces. By 2000, and the following decade, this fragmentation began to become really noticeable. In 2006, for example, the popular author Stefan Klein wrote *Time: A User's Guide – Making Sense of Life's Scarcest Commodity*.[3] At the same time, the academic community began to study this fragmentation. By 2008 a group of scholars from Australia and Finland had co-authored *Discretionary Time: A New Measure of Freedom*, documenting the time pressure felt by people across the world.[4] Work had begun a process of fragmentation that has accelerated over the last decade, and there is every sign that this acceleration will continue over the coming decades.

You could say that because the increase in fragmentation has been 'creeping' rather than instant we have all become boiled frogs. I bet if I was to be transported from my life in 1990 to 2010, I would be amazed, probably horrified, by the fragmentation of my life. But like everyone else, it has happened so slowly that I have made very little resistance.

As I reflect on Jill's storyline, I think about the impact of fragmentation around me, in the programmes I teach, the executives who reach for their mobile phones the moment I stop teaching – even though we have shown how important reflection and concentration are to the learning process. Or the way my children manage to watch television, update their Facebook entry and watch a movie on their computers – all at the same time.

Our world have become ever more fragmented over the last 20 years, and, as we can see in Jill's story, for many people this fragmentation will only increase in the coming 20 years. Is yours a world of fragmentation? If it is, or will increasingly be so, then it is important to understand the consequences of fragmentation.

When your working life fragments

Does it matter that our lives are so fragmented and will increasingly be so? Does it matter that globalisation and technology will increasingly bring fragmentation to those in developed countries, and also spread it to those in developing countries? What's the real downside of fragmentation – who really misses out? As we reflect on our current working lives, we can assume that overload and time compression will only increase over the coming decades. So what effect will this have? I believe that fragmentation, overload and compression will decrease concentration, reduce our capacity to really observe and learn, and could make the future working lives of our children more frenzied, more focused ... and less whimsical and playful.

The concentration of mastery is lost

When our working time fragments, then one of the first victims is real concentration. Breaking up her life into such small pieces has meant for Jill that she never really has the time, the opportunity or the focus to become very good at anything. She has never concentrated enough to achieve the mastery that would put her in a different league and which, as I will argue later, is going to be so crucial for future success. There is no doubt that Jill is good at what she does, but the challenge is that she has never learnt to be really, really good. The reason for her lack of mastery is wrapped up in her three-minute life. It takes time and concentration to become masterful, and Jill has neither time nor concentration.

The importance of time and concentration is shown clearly in psychologist Daniel Levitin's study of people who have achieved mastery. He looked at the lives of 'composers, basketball players, fiction writers, ice skaters … and master criminals'.[5] He found that, despite their very different areas of skill, they all had one thing in common. What they all shared was a capacity to concentrate on developing their skill for long periods of time. In fact, he found that 10,000 hours is the common touchstone for how long it takes to achieve mastery. That would translate to Jill concentrating and practising three hours a day, for ten years. Of course, Jill does not aspire to becoming a concert pianist or a world-class novelist, so this level of concentration would be excessive. However, to gain real value in the world she inhabits, Jill does need some form of mastery – and at the moment she rarely achieves concentration of more than three minutes, let alone three hours.

The capacity to observe and learn is reduced

It is not just concentrated practice that suffers. When a working life is as fragmented as Jill's – broken up into three-minute time frames – what also gets lost is the opportunity to simply sit back and watch others more skilled.[6] This is important since it is through watching others more masterful than ourselves that we begin to absorb the subtle changes in what they do that can be transformed into our own working practice.[7]

I notice this in the development of teaching skills. When rookie assistant professors join London Business School they are expected to teach an MBA class in their first year. The experience can be gruesome. They get their timing wrong, the class overruns and the students are up in arms. They fudge their exam rating and marking protocol, and the class loses confidence in them. They fill their slides with hundreds of words and the students cannot read them. The list of what can go wrong is endless. At first, in order to try and make the whole experience less tough we decide to write a list of 'dos and don'ts' to help. But, though useful, the list never covers all the challenges. For example, we might have told them to manage the timing of the class – but then found that they concentrated so much on their timing that they forgot to speak sufficiently loud for those at the back to hear.

What we learnt was that mastering the teaching of a good MBA class is a skill that takes many hours to hone. It's also a skill that has much 'tacit' knowledge embedded in it – that's the type of knowledge that is difficult to describe in the ten points, and is often held deep within the unconscious of how tasks are performed. What we began to realise is that the best way for these rookies to learn was by simply observing others teach – not once, but many, many times, and to watch very, very carefully. That's not to say this was observation with the planned outcome of mimicry. We certainly don't want everyone to teach the same. However, by careful observation, these new professors began to learn deeply and to forge their own point of view about how to teach. To do this they had to concentrate, to observe for hours at a time, without recourse to checking their emails, or indeed to marking past papers!

The notion of mastery sits at the heart of the first shift I believe will be crucial for successful lives in the future. The challenge is that often the development of mastery is subtle and takes time. When our working lives become fragmented, as they inevitably will in the future, then we lose the opportunity to concentrate on watching others more skilled than ourselves. When Jill yields to a fragmented working life, she is sub-optimising the possibilities of honing deep and valuable skills and capabilities. Fragmentation means she never devotes sufficient time to move from the basics to mastery, and she rarely watches others with sufficient concentration to understand the often-subtle nuances that accompany mastery.

It is in the intersection between the forces of increasing globalisation and ever more sophisticated technological developments that work will fragment and observation and concentration are lost. The choices we make about how we spend our time, and how we focus our energy and resources, will prove to be crucial to our future success. It is through the shift to mastery that the trade-offs can be made. If not, then we, like the frogs in the warming water, will simply boil. But before we leave a future world of intense fragmentation, I'd like to consider one final aspect of working life that could also be lost – whimsy and play.

The creativity of whimsy and play is denuded
One of the most exciting aspects of the future is that it will provide extraordinary opportunities for creativity and impassioned productivity. That is in a sense what the third shift is about, and that is what drives the lives of many of the people we will meet when we take a brighter view of the future. However, here is the rub. When time becomes fragmented, and when every moment counts, then what is lost is the very chance to be creative, to play ... to be whimsical. Instead we demand instant gratification and compressed learning. If you only have three minutes, then the rewards have to be instant and the lessons delivered clearly, fast and compressed.

When time fragments, what suffers is whimsy and play. I remember as a child being enchanted by the cookery writer

Elizabeth David's descriptions of how to make Mediterranean food.[8] She introduced me to the ingredients, to their sight and smell and provenance. She took four pages to describe the making of a tomato soup, starting with a trip to the market to choose the tomatoes, then a page on how to skin and de-pip them, and only then preparing them into soup. Reading her descriptions I was transported from the cold of northern England where I was brought up to the fragrant markets of the south of France. At that time I had never stepped outside of the UK – but that did not stop me dreaming.

American readers may have had the same experience when they first read Julia Child's whimsical cookery books.[9] You may recall her description of creating French classics such as *Poularde à la d'Albufera* – from the moment the chicken is bought at the market, to the moment it enters the mouths of grateful guests. What Julia Child and Elizabeth David did was to illustrate, with good humour, time and sympathy, their own cookery journey, and by doing so empathised with the novice cook on her journey. This stuff takes time. Julia's instructions for *Poularde à la d'Albufera* take over six pages – way more than a precise description of the recipe. What this more elaborate, human and emotional description actually does, however, is to connect with you the reader in a way that a ten-step recipe could never do.[10]

The challenge is that this sort of elongation of time has no place in the three-minute episodes that punctuate Jill's world. In her world, precise and short directions will always win over the more whimsical, sympathetic illustrations – after all, who has time to fuss about *Poularde à la d'Albufera*?

Well, you might say, who indeed has time to make *Poularde à la d'Albufera*, and anyway, what's it got to do with the future of work? In a sense this classic dish is a metaphor for mastery. It's similar to a rookie professor sitting patiently as they watch hour after hour while others more masterful than they teach; it's similar to the hours and hours of patient crafting that goes into learning how to write a report, prepare a presentation or lead a team.

By 2025 the attention spans of Jill and those around her have become so much shorter, so much more parcelled up, so much more prone to disruption, so much more fragmented, that it's almost impossible for her to develop and learn to the depth of mastery which will be so crucial to her success.

It's not just concentration, observation and whimsy that are lost in this fragmented world. It's also play. With fragmentation comes less time to share a joke; less time to work on an idea we love but are not sure how we will develop; less time to play, to have fun times, to celebrate the joys of working. As the working world becomes more mechanised, so the boundaries between what's work and what's play become increasingly solid. When time becomes tighter and work fragments, what can get lost is the freedom to play. Ask Jill about playing at work and she will throw her head back and laugh out loud. With every moment accounted for, with 100 emails to be answered and another on its way – playing is way down her list of priorities.

Yet we have known for some time just how important play is to building creativity and fostering new ideas and models. The challenge for the future of work is that the compression of time pushes play out. As my colleagues Babis Mainemelis and Sarah Ronson have shown, we play when we believe we have the time and space, when we feel flexible about what we are doing and free from constraints.[11] This is the stuff that play is made of. Play is important because we are more likely to love our work when we see it as play. If you are in advertising or design, you know your play through fantasy and imagination is at the core of innovation; if you are a consultant or researcher like me, your play through exploration and questioning is at the heart of how you create value. If you are a mathematician or a theorist, the play of solving problems is what really excites you. Isn't the absolutely best work to have, both now and in the future, work of which you can say, 'I cannot believe that people pay me to do my hobby'? It's those times you are simply 'building castles in the sky' – exploring new ideas, and putting old ideas together in new ways, or in other words, playing. But to play you need time and a feeling of control over constant interruptions.

The challenge with the fragmentation of the future is that both are lost. When you are 'on' all the time, what gets lost is the opportunity to blur work and non-work – to get to the opera, theatre or a sports game, events that though playful can give you new insights and ways of thinking about problems. Absolutely the best way to work creatively in the future will be to blur the distinctions between work and play. The most rewarding jobs will be those in which your work is also your passion and hobby, and vice versa.

Our world is already fragmented, but, as we shall see, the combination of technology that connects most people on the planet with globalisation that will see more work following the sun 24/7 can only make this fragmentation more profound.

The forces that created fragmentation

It matters that work becomes ever more fragmented. It matters because with this fragmentation comes the incapacity to create the focus, concentration and creativity that will be so important to the shift from shallow generalist to serial mastery. So we have to understand why work will become increasingly fragmented, and what can be done to reconnect the parts.

In describing working lives in 2025, we began to glimpse the impact that technology had on Jill's working day in 2025 compared with my own working day in 1990. The exponential growth in technological capacity and developments in Cloud technology enable Jill to download advanced programmes from the web. At the same time, her day's work is shaped by the avatars and cognitive assistants that support her. But the fragmentation of Jill's work is not just about technology – it is also about globalisation. We see it as she struggles to join up across timezones that range from Beijing to Los Angeles. She lives in a 24/7 joined-up global world, with colleagues and customers in every part of what has become a more and more industrialised world.

The force of technology: technological capability increases exponentially

Working lives like Jill's in 2025 are fragmented by the sheer breadth and depth of communication and information that weighs on everyday working life.

What underlies this is the extraordinary processing power that has grown at an exponential rate over the previous decades.[12] In fact, this annual doubling has continued every year and has been accompanied by an equally dramatic year-on-year fall in the cost of microchips. For example, in 1975 the price of a single transistor was $0.028 dollars – by 1980 it had fallen to $0.0013 and within the next decade to $0.00002. By 2010, Moore's law was showing no sign of slowing, and we can anticipate that more transistors will be packed onto smaller microchips for less money and that processing power will continue to grow at an exponential rate.

Jill's working life has also fragmented as a result of the advanced handheld device she carries around with her. The performance of these mobile devices has grown exponentially with a short doubling time (typically a couple of years). In 2010 a phone contained the same amount of computing power as a Mac from 2000. The device that Jill carries has the same processing power and capabilities as the high-end desktop computer I used in 2010. What this means for Jill is that in those evenings when she is not online with others she is using her computer to crunch the terabytes of data that have poured out that day from the Large Hadron Collider at CERN. And when she is not doing that, she is linked into the data beaming from the Mars station to join with millions of other people who are scouring the universe for alien life.

This increasing power and the falling cost have enabled these machines to be capable of ever-increasing feats of power, from simultaneous translation, to the lifelike graphics of Jill's personal avatar and the way that she has been able to build complex performance models for her clients. It could be that by 2025 miniature computers are baked into every brick, every piece of clothing and every item of food. What this means is that data is streamed into the office and homes at an extraordinary rate. But it's not just computing power that has fragmented these lives – it's also the location and speed of downloading.

The force of technology: the Cloud becomes ubiquitous

Jill is able to download highly complex data and programs anywhere, anytime. Already by 2010 most of the regions of the world had a level of connectivity that enabled fishermen in India or the weavers in Tanzania to talk with others and access some information. Over the coming decades this was augmented by an ever faster and easier connectivity to the web and access to bandwidth that enabled the telepresence and holograms which are part of Jill's everyday working life. Behind this connectivity have been rapid developments in the Cloud. This was first conceived in the early 2000s as an expertise, control and technological infrastructure that would be all-enveloping – hence the name the 'cloud'. By 2010 services, applications and resources were already available as a service over the internet, although corporate adoption of the Cloud was relatively low, only in the beta phase, and there were many concerns about security.

These concerns were resolved over the next two decades and by 2025 the global range of the Cloud had increased, with the services available becoming ever more complex. This had allowed hundreds of thousands of independent programming teams to develop their ideas, in much the same way that applications for the iPhone were developed in 2010. What Jill loves about the Cloud is that it is convenient, on-demand and allows her to work with her colleagues to pool their resources. Jill does not actually own the physical infrastructure she uses or the applications she downloads. Instead she rents usage as and when she needs it – paying only for the resources she uses.

The Cloud has also created endless possibilities for people across the world to access pooled resources. That's one of the reasons why avatars and holographs are the norm. To use her avatar or work in a holographic representation of her office, Jill simply has to hook up to the immense computational power available on demand from Cloud computing.

Notice that the fragmentation of Jill's working life is created by technology in which she has personally invested, and which she uses from her home and the hub she works in. By 2010 the gulf between personal use of technology and corporate use had already begun to narrow as more people decided to invest in home-based technology rather than rely on the technology companies provide for them. By 2010 people had already begun to see their workplace technology lagging behind their personal investment in technology.[13] Like most of her colleagues, Jill has made a personal investment in the technology in her home and the technology she carries with her.

The force of technology: ever-present avatars and virtual worlds

In the pre-fragmented day at least you had the opportunity to relax when you where 'offline'. By 2025 you are 'online' 24/7 and your presence is augmented by avatars and virtual worlds. This development had begun in 2008 when Xbox Live launched its Xbox 360 avatars, which acted as the player's emotive representative when communicating with other players. Gamers began to customise their avatars' physical appearance, dress them in clothes bought from an online marketplace, and use them to virtually interact with other gamers' avatars from around the world. Though initially limited to online gaming, the use of avatars continued to expand into all aspects of life, to such an extent that for Jill her avatar is her primary interface between the virtually connected people she works with. Jill has designed her avatar to be as near a two-dimensional representation of herself as possible. In the online games she plays, she has other more fantastic avatars – but when she is working she keeps to a form that is close to her own.[14]

One of the ways that Jill works with her colleagues is through her virtual workplace, which is a graphic representation of a workplace where all her colleagues can virtually congregate. So as soon as she logs on in the morning, she can walk through her work community to see who else is around. Her virtual timetable tells her when group sessions have been planned, and so she can link up using both her avatar and virtual 3D telepresence to talk in real time with her colleagues.

For Jill, working and learning in a virtual environment has been a way of life since she attended a virtual university in 2015. She registered and met her instructors and colleagues online and then the instructors used the virtual platform to deliver to the worldwide audience at minimum cost.

The force of technology: the rise of the cognitive assistants

The first interruption Jill has on that cold morning in 2025 is her cognitive assistant – or Alfie as she calls it. Alfie has been with her for a couple of years now. It understands how she likes to work, keeps a record of who she knows, monitors her inward communication for interesting strangers and logs the amount of time she works every day – automatically billing her employers for the hours works. Over the years Alfie has learnt how she works and how her working life can be best organised, and this has become more and more accurate to the extent that Jill now relies on Alfie for much of the everyday running of her life. Alfie checks her carbon use, reminds her when her personal carbon budget is beginning to run out, and makes sure that the travel she needs to do works within her personal carbon budget. With so much information coming through every moment of the day, Alfie helps her manage her daily tasks, prioritise what's important and manage her weekly goals. Alfie is unique – it's a machine that uses artificial intelligence to build a logic which best fits Jill's context and working patterns, and evolves as Jill's preferences become clearer.[15]

Is Alfie like a human? Ask Jill and she will tell you she could not do without Alfie to the extent that it (he?) simplifies her already highly fragmented life. Alfie is not alone. Across the globe billions of cognitive assistants are collecting information, monitoring the behaviour of people like Jill and taking actions from their preferences. This massive crowd of computers is becoming increasingly capable of learning and creating new knowledge entirely on their own and with no human help. For decades now they have been scanning the enormous content of the internet and 'know' literally every single piece of public information (every scientific discovery, every book and movie, every public statement) generated by human beings.

The force of globalisation: 24/7 and the global world

Jill lives in a world that never sleeps, with colleagues from many timezones expecting to connect to her – it's a 24/7 world. The most obvious driver of the fragmentation of her world has been computing capability and connectivity. However, behind that is an ever-globalised and competitive world that puts immense pressure on her and her colleagues to deliver with speed and accuracy.

The joining up of the working timezones across the world began seriously from 1990 onwards, when the markets of the world become truly global. It was from this time that there was extraordinary growth in emerging markets such as China and India, Brazil and South Korea, among others. In fact, by 2009 the emerging markets accounted for half of the global economy, and by 2010 were generating the bulk of the growth in the world economy. During that year the six largest emerging economies (the 'B6' – Brazil, China, India, Mexico, Russia and South Korea) grew by 5.1%. In the next two decades they were joined by a second wave of economic activity in locations such as Egypt, Nigeria, Turkey, Indonesia and Malaysia.

To get the scale of globalisation – consider that in 1995 only 20 companies from the emerging markets were listed on the Global Fortune 500. By 2010 that number stood at 91.[16] In 1990 the company that Jill often works for, Arcelor Mittal, was an unknown producer of steel in Indonesia; by 2010 Arcelor Mittal was the world's largest steel company, and by 2025 one of the world's largest conglomerates with diverse interests ranging from steel to telecoms to chip manufacturing.[17] The combination of the technological forces we have described – Cloud computing, mobile communications and collaborative computing – have the potential, in concert with the momentum of emerging-market growth, to form a tipping point for globalisation and 24/7 working. Every year, millions of new consumers and small-business operators join the global economy, even from the most rural of villages. Over the coming decades we can anticipate that the economic power of the world will shift from the developed countries of the West and Japan – to be dispersed to an ever wider group of countries and regions.[18]

Like many people working in the West, much of Jill's day is spent connecting to clients, suppliers and customers in Asia. This is a booming market fuelled in part by the sheer size of the population. In 2010 there were 1.2 billion people in the more developed regions (including Europe, North America, Australia and Japan) and 5.7 billion in the less developed regions (including China, India, Africa and Latin America).[19] By 2030 it is forecast that while the developed regions of the world will have expanded by around 44 million people, the developing regions will expand by a mighty 1.3 billion – that's more than the entire population of the developed world. Jill and her colleagues know that within five years the 7 billion living in the less developed regions will increasingly overshadow the 1.3 billion in the more developed regions.[20]

How can you reconnect the fragments?

What will it take for you to reconnect the fragments of working life into something with more cohesion? What will it take to craft a working life that has greater opportunity for sustained concentration, more time for deep learning, and for a life that has woven into it occasions for whimsy and play? What can you do to create a working life that does not leave you exhausted, and does not denude your capacity to sustain your energy and talent?

Of course it is impossible to wind back the clock to the slower-paced working life of 1990, when technology was basic and globalisation in its infancy. It may indeed be that technological developments such as the cognitive assistants themselves become part of the answer to reconnecting the fragments as they make it ever easier for people to prioritise and focus.

It is also impossible for you to significantly change the context in which you are living. Beyond moving to a desert island, you will always be part of the global economy, more and more people will want to connect to you and to others, and technology will create greater demands on productivity and outcome. So there is no easy answer to reconnecting the fragments. It is fundamentally about working from the inside out – being clear about the choices you are presented with, and being mature about the consequences of these choices.

I believe there are three future-proofed shifts that will play a role in ensuring that your future working life is not simply torn apart by fragmentation.

The first shift is your conscious construction of a working life that is based on mastery. By that I mean developing a career that is built from dedication and focus – remember, it takes 10,000 hours to learn something to the point of mastery. To do so will require the willpower to resist the temptation of fragmentation, and to be prepared to set aside significant time for apprenticeship, learning and practice.

The second shift is the realisation that the opposite of fragmentation is not isolation. The challenge is to construct a working life in the future that has both self focus and also strong relationships with others. It can be that, through the relationships with others, work can be simplified and shared. Perhaps one of the lessons we all have to learn for the future is that we tend to fragment our lives by trying to do too much ourselves, rather than creating sufficiently strong networks to really take some of the burden off our shoulders. Your relationships with others will also be a crucial balance to fragmentation as a strong regenerative community of people around you, who love and support you, could well help you to create boundaries for your time.

However, it's the last shift, from voracious consumer to impassioned producer, that is most able to address the challenges of an increasingly fragmented working life. This shift is fundamentally about the way you choose to live your working life and your preparedness to make bold choices, to confront the consequences of these choices and to exercise free will. Looking back to Jill's story, did she really have to take the call at 7.00 in the morning or 10.00 that evening? Did she really have to eat lunch at her desk on her own? Did she really have to look at hundreds of emails? These are decisions that many of the forces that will shape your working future will make ever more attractive. It will also make Jill's way of working increasingly the norm. In a global, technologically enhanced and joined-up world, there is always something you can do – whatever the time, and wherever you are. And these issues of choices and priorities become ever more poignant when you consider that Jill, like many others in 2025, will be expected to be working into her 70s. Like you, what Jill faces is a long marathon – not a short sprint.

It is clear that crafting a working life through the choices you make will become increasingly important in the coming decades.

When I think about my own working life, I did not have to make any really tough choices back in 1990; emerging technology and nascent globalisation had created a world that was a lot less frantic. If you are to address the 'creeping normalcy' of fragmentation, then it will require seeing it for what it is – constant pressure with no boundaries to protect you. In this third future-proofed shift – towards a deeper, more profound way of constructing a working life – we will address these issues. It is actively making wise choices, clearly understanding the consequences, and facing up to the sorts of dilemmas that Jill faces, that will be ever more crucial. Without this there will be no boundaries to protect people like Jill, and indeed to protect you from the ever-growing demands of a joined-up world.

3

ISOLATION: THE GENESIS OF LONELINESS

Rohan's story

As we leave Jill and her increasingly fragmented life, let's move across the world to the centre of Mumbai where, later that morning, Rohan, an Indian brain surgeon, comes online. Though skilled and masterful, Rohan experiences the dark side of the future every day of his life. Here is how.

As he wakes in the morning he moves into his home office, where he is preparing for the day's work. You might expect a doctor like Rohan to spend much of his time at a hospital, working with colleagues and meeting patients. However, like many specialists in 2025, Rohan spends much of his time working from his home office. Within an hour of waking he has accessed the technology of the Cloud to download some of the most advanced visualisation technology that he needs for the day, and takes out a subscription for three hours of use.

By 11.00 a.m. he is ready to begin surgery. Today he is leading a team of surgeons in China who are performing a particularly tricky operation. That is why earlier in the week they had contacted Rohan to provide expertise for the operation. A young woman has internal bleeding from her brain and needs to be operated on to stop the bleeding. Rohan activates his telepresence unit, and within seconds can see clearly the other members of the team and the young woman patient who is already anaesthetised and ready for surgery. As his colleagues begin to open the skull, Rohan directs the holographic representation attached to the on-site camera to show him clearly the site of the bleeding. He then activates the robotic instruments and begins to gently manipulate the brain tissue. As Rohan leads the team, he speaks in his native Hindi language, which is automatically converted to the Cantonese of the rest of the team. This instantaneous translation technology, introduced in 2020, has made the learning of specialist languages redundant, save for those who speak languages as a hobby.

For the next half hour the team work skilfully to move to the site of the bleeding. It is a relatively shallow bleed so that stopping the blood flow can be done quickly. Within an hour the flow has been stemmed and the Chinese surgeons have begun to reconstruct the portion of the skull that was removed. The surgery seems to have been a success, so it is with a good heart that Rohan sits down for lunch in the bright dining room of his apartment.

By 2.00 Rohan is ready to join the second team he will be working with that afternoon. As the afternoon begins, he connects to the team from Chile which has come online to ask his advice about a particularly difficult case they are treating. They are due to operate on a young man with a brain tumour the following day. Over the next couple of hours Rohan again uses holographic representation – this time of the young man's brain – to decide the best strategy for the operation. It takes over three hours of deep conversation and visualisation of the tumour to decide the strategy, but by 6.00 p.m. the team feels prepared and agrees to the timing for tomorrow's surgery.

It is just time for Rohan to have a quick supper before he hooks up with colleagues at Great Ormond Street Hospital in London to talk about a young boy who has been brought in this week with a suspected brain tumour. Rohan specialises in the treatment of the young, so he is pleased to be able to share his advice and good wishes for the surgery. While he will not be involved with this one, he will observe the surgery in order to give feedback to one of the junior team members.

So by 11.00 p.m. Rohan is ready for bed. He has a busy day tomorrow with a follow-up to the young man from Chile and the observation of the London surgery. It has been a busy week for Rohan, and as he thinks back he realises that he has rarely left his apartment.

Amon's Story

Amon in Cairo rarely leaves his apartment either that week. He is an independent freelancer, who works on complex IT projects. As soon as he wakes, the first action he takes is to check in with his virtual agent. He knows that every minute of the day his virtual agent is scanning the world for work that may suit Amon. It uses an exact profile of Amon's current skills and knowledge base to find the project match. It also knows something about his working preferences – when he likes to work and the sort of client with whom he wants to work.

This morning the virtual agent has presented a range of possibilities for Amon. A drinks outfit in Brazil wants a program written for their customer care team, and needs it within three days. Another possibility has come through from a Malaysian entrepreneur with whom he has worked before. He wants a particularly complex piece of software written and is prepared to pay Amon 2000 Euros for it. He also spends the next hour taking a look at two open bids for work that his virtual agent has brought him. Amon knows that he will have to respond within the next two days if he wants to enter the competition for the work.

Over the following hour he works out how long the project will take him and comes to a decision about the lowest price for which he is prepared to work. By mid-morning he has decided to go with the drinks company in Brazil. By late morning he has begun the programming and over the next six hours he works in the virtual office of the project, dropping a note to others he is working with, and chatting to a fellow programmer. By 5.00 p.m. he is ready to attend a conference call with all the project team.

By now he is at full steam and so decides that if he works into the evening he can probably get this finished. Before he finishes that evening Amon updates his personal profile, adding the recent work he completed for the Brazilian client.

Amon is a neo-nomad, picking up programming work from people he has never met, working with teams whose names he does not know, for companies far, far away.

Both Rohan and Amon have interesting working lives. Both are engaged with work tasks they enjoy and which stretch their competencies. They have found work they love and which they see as hobbies to be enjoyed, focused on and relished.

But do you notice what's missing from their working lives? Neither Rohan nor Amon spends time during much of their working day with real people. Yes, they interact with people all day – Rohan with his fellow surgeons in China and Amon with the Brazilian team. However, what they are interacting with is cognitive assistants, avatars, holographs and video presence. Neither of them frequently encounters warm flesh and blood in their daily lives. Amon's closest 'friend' is his virtual agent – and that's a computer.

They are not alone. By 2025 we face the possibility that much of the fabric of our working lives is denuded of face-to-face relationships. It could well be, of course, that these virtual relationships become as rejuvenating as face-to-face relationships. But somehow I doubt this. When you strip away daily face-to-face relationships, then you strip away the joys of easy companionship and you strip away all the possibility that relationships have of nurturing work – and, indeed, of work nurturing life.

Rewinding to the past: a day of easy companionship in 1990

To let the extent of this sink in, let's replay the 1990 memory experiment again – but this time look at the day, not through the degree of fragmentation, but rather through the lens of human interaction. In my case I will go back to the consulting practice I worked for – but this time view it as a series of social conversations. As I track my day, what's interesting is that I spent most of the day in an office with my colleagues. Sure, I have my own room – but I can glance down the corridor and see others working in their offices. The place has a feeling of easy companionship. Not that we were all friends, by the way – there were certainly people I could not stand and I am sure the feeling was mutual. The place was riven with politics, power play and hierarchies – it could be infuriating, but it was also real. You may recall that in the day I described earlier I went in the afternoon to a meeting with a group of prospective clients. Again, this was a physical meeting, and we talked for an hour or two. In the early evening in the pub, the team comes together to chew over the events of the day, share more gossip and continue the marvellous power plays.

It might have been frustrating, annoying and at times downright irritating – but I never actually felt lonely during the working day. This was a world of easy companionship. Rohan and Amon have working companions whom they know well and whom they trust. However, they rarely actually physically meet these people.

What's missing in the working lives of Rohan and Amon is the possibility of simply pushing your head through an open door and saying 'Hi', or wandering down the corridor to goad people into having another cup of coffee. Or even inviting a group out on the spur of the moment to a curry down the road.

The death of easy companionship

It could be that this loss of easy companionship, which was so much a part of working lives in 1990, will be one of the dark sides of the future of work. We humans, in the past, in the present and I would imagine also in the future, are intensely affected by the state of our relationships with others. For many of us, the aspect we value, above all other aspects of work, is our relationships with our co-workers.[1] It is no surprise that when asked why people chose to stay at work, one of the top predictors is 'I have a friend at work.'[2] And we should also not be surprised that longitudinal studies carried out by researchers at the Harvard Medical School of the lifetime health and happiness of thousands of people reveal a similar effect. Those who are the happiest in their lives are not the richest, or indeed those who have achieved the most. The researchers found consistently that the single greatest link with lifetime happiness was the extent to which people have close friends in their lives, while loneliness was associated with ill health – and was, interestingly, contagious, rapidly spreading to others. That's why easy, close, relaxed friendships have been described as such a key part of human mental health and happiness.[3]

I cannot imagine this being different in 2025. After all, across the whole history of the human race we have been intensely social, clannish people. Yet the coming forces of technology and globalisation could impact on this natural sociability in a way never experienced in the history of mankind.

So where does that leave Rohan and Amon and billions of others who in 2025 could spend much of their working day interacting with others in cyberspace rather than establishing physical contact? The simple truth is that we simply don't know. Perhaps humanity will adjust to these cyber relationships to such an extent that they will bring the positive effect that face-to-face relationships do now. After all, the early experiments with Sony's PET computer AIBO suggested that, with its puppy-like appearance and mischievous way of behaving, people rapidly learnt to enjoy it as a companion and as a playmate. Even in 2010 in Hong Kong and Japan, 'virtual girlfriends' can be downloaded to your 3-G mobile. In cyberspace and in chatroom salons a gigantic world of relationships has been flourishing. In the future we can imagine that avatars won't simply be the mainstay of the sex trade, but will also be the logical development, from call centres to financial advisers.[4] Perhaps one of the outcomes of advancing technology is that we humans will be able to substitute virtual, avatar relationships for real, flesh-and-blood relationships. Or perhaps technological developments will be such that, as some have predicted, by 2025 brain implants will ensure positive relational emotions – whatever the situation.[5]

However, I'm going to assume that by 2025 neither of these 'transhuman' adjustments has taken place. Instead what we can imagine is the slow but continuous disappearance of face-to-face contact at work, bringing with it the possibility of deep loneliness and isolation.

The dark side of the future is a working world of isolation. Advances in imaging, holographs and virtual technologies, combined with developments in the Cloud, have put the most sophisticated techniques into the homes of people like Rohan and Amon. They no longer have to go into the office to access information – it's all available to them on their handheld device or through their personal home computers. Theirs is a virtual, global existence. Their clients, patients and teams are scattered around the world – their colleagues are not in the next office cubicle, and they may not even be in the same city, region or country.

It's not that their colleagues are strangers. Ask Rohan about his peers in China and he will tell you much about them – after all, he has been leading the Chinese team in these specialist operations for more than a year and has twice spent a week with them. From his encounters over the year he has learnt whom to trust at certain times, whom to keep an eye on and who will need the most counselling after the operation. As fellow professionals he has a keen eye on their strengths and weaknesses and in the case of a couple of them has even gone so far as to mentor them outside the operating theatre. He knows them pretty well and would count a couple as friends.

However, like Amon, Rohan's relationships with his working colleagues are more often virtual than face-to-face. In the past he went to conferences around the world to meet up with other specialists in his field, but increasingly the carbon tax on flights is such that these are now being held virtually, so he simply briefs his avatar about whom he wants to meet. In his own hospital there are few people with his deep expertise and so he does not spend much time there. For Amon, his work is completely virtual. He works from his home all of the time and has never met the other programmers with whom he routinely collaborates.

Taking families out of the mosaic of work

Our relationships at work are an important part of the mosaic of our whole life relationships. However, they are only one part. For many people, what compensates for the possible lack of relationships at work is their relationships with their family members.

Work and home life can spill over in terms of energy and emotion.[6] Our work and our lives outside work are rarely hermetically sealed from each other. More often, there is a spill-over between the two that can be an emotional spillover, or could be the spillover of networks and competencies.[7]

On occasions the spillover between the two is positive. Our family home can be a place where we feel relaxed, authentic and loved. These are the positive feelings and emotions with which we enter our working day and they create the emotional foundation that plays an important role in helping us deal with the stresses and strains of working life. This positive cycle between work and home life can also be reversed. Instead of positive home emotions spilling over into work, it is our positive experiences of work that spill over to the home. We leave work and enter the home feeling positive and uplifted. Work is a place where we can gain valuable networks, develop new skills and deepen our knowledge, and these are competencies and connections that can be brought back to home as we enter it in the evening.

Of course there are also occasions when the spillover between the two is negative. Our work becomes a place where we feel angry, under-appreciated and wound up. It is these negative emotions that we bring back home, and it is these caustic emotions that can have such a negative impact on our capacity to find happiness at home. Or the caustic cycle can start with our home – perhaps it becomes a place in which we feel insecure, guilty and overwhelmed by the demands of others. So it is these that become the emotions and feelings that we bring into work.[8]

There has also been a spillover in how relationships are developed. Over the last couple of decades, relationships at home have become increasingly 'negotiated' and worked out. In part this reflects the growing economic independence of women, and also profound changes in the roles of men and women. The point here is that as we develop more relational 'muscle' at home, so we use these same relational muscles at work. If future generations become increasingly skilled at negotiating their relationships with their partners, so we can expect them to become more skilled and indeed inspired to negotiate their relationships with their co-workers, managers and businesses.

Work and home are also intimately connected in other more physical ways. If you have work that takes you physically away from the family – in overnight trips or longer projects – then this impacts on the family. If you leave early in the morning and return late at night after a long commute – then this impacts on the family. And of course the decisions you make about where to work will be influenced by the impact it will have on your family and your own personal goals for them.

So, if we want to really understand the future of work, we also have to at least acknowledge, indeed understand, the ways in which home and family are likely to change over the coming decades.

This endeavour is not as difficult as it might at first seem because what constitutes a 'home' and a 'family' began to change significantly from the time of the Industrial Revolution, and this transformation in many ways set the scene for what is to come.

Rewinding to the past: changes in family structures

To get a feel for the magnitude of the transformation of family life, rewind to the past by taking a look at your own family tree for the last two generations. As you do so, you may want to ask the following questions. How many children did my parents and grandparents have? Did any of them or their parents divorce? What is the current family structure?

For myself, both my grandmothers, Annie Evans and Minnie Stanwell, came from families of seven children. Their own childhood was interrupted by the First World War, and as a consequence in both families a number of their sisters remained spinsters because their sweethearts were killed in the early battles of the war. Those that married had smaller families than their parents – Annie had two children, one of whom, Barbara, is my mother; Minnie had only one child – my father David. None of my grandparents' brothers or sisters was divorced. Sure, there was much family gossip about a couple of marriages that had obviously hit a sticky patch – but in the main these families stuck together through thick and thin. The unravelling of families began in my family in my own generation. Of the four children that my parents Barbara and David had, only one stayed with their first partner. All the other three children divorced, and two had second families.

Perhaps your family history reveals a steadier matrimonial environment. But if it has, then it will be in the minority. In much of the world divorce is becoming the norm, not the exception, and even in countries such as India, in which divorce is still very much frowned upon, some of the old ways of staying married are breaking down.

So let's take a closer look at how Rohan and Amon relate to their family members, particularly when their daily work is complete. Like the majority of people in 2025, both live in cities – far removed from their parents and from their childhood friends. By 2025, families, even those in India, have shrunk in size. Amon has one sister, and Rohan an older brother who moved some years ago to Brazil to set up an internet trading company. They get to hook up their holograms on family birthdays, but it's been years since they actually met. Neither Amon nor Rohan has parents who live in the same city. Rohan moved from his home town of Jaipur to study at the Mumbai Medical School and left his parents there. Amon also moved from his home town to be educated.

And like many other people around the world, both Amon and Rohan have parents who live far away from them – so surely they can come and stay? Here is the other reason why Amon and Rohan see so little of their parents. Both their parents have been caught in a series of demographic trends which has meant that – even though they are now in their late 60s, early 70s – to some extent or another they continue to work. It's not that their parents wouldn't love to see them, it's just that they are still working and they live hundreds, even thousands of miles away. Rohan's parents are now in their mid-60s and both work full time; his mother teaches at the local primary school and his father mans the family store. The same is true for Amon's parents. They divorced when he was a young child – his mother moving back to the home town of Luxor in southern Egypt, while his father moved to join the extended family in Canada, and while they are now almost 70 both are still engaged in work.

So when Rohan closes down his avatar station and Amon switches off his computer, both are on their own. They are far from their family, and from their working colleagues and peers. Theirs are isolated lives with very little human contact.

So one of the real potential downsides of this steady erosion of real (rather than virtual) relationships that could be the case in 2025 is that the positive energy flow from home to work ceases, and with it some of the opportunity to tolerate work-related stress. My guess is that if we took a closer look at the health and well-being of Rohan and Amon, both will be suffering from anxiety and possibly also depression.

The forces that created isolation

When you look at Rohan and Amon's working life, at first glance they look interesting and meaningful, and in many ways their working lives are. However, as we peel back and observe their working lives in the context of their whole life, the extent of the gaps becomes apparent. And it is not just Rohan and Amon. Around the world we can anticipate that many billions of people will live isolated working lives. How did this happen?

Some of the clues can be drawn from their stories. Did you notice that Rohan and Amon both live in one of the many megacities of the world in 2025? Like billions of others, in the course of the last 100 years their families moved from rural villages to urban sprawls. Isolation came in part as a result of the world becoming urban. Another clue is that both of them have family members that migrated, Amon's father to Canada, and Rohan's brother to Brazil. The migration of vast numbers of people has also served to break up the family ties that can be so important to reducing isolation. But it is not just the globalisation forces of urbanisation and migration that are impacting on the lives of Rohan and Amon. It's also the increasing cost of energy and fuel. Two decades earlier, and Rohan would have flown to spend time with his colleagues in China and Amon may have made the trip to his clients in Brazil. But with a strong focus on the cost of carbon footprints and the rise of virtual technologies, they are both more inclined to stay at home rather than to commute or indeed to fly to meet others.

There is also something deeper going on in the working society of 2025 that we can glimpse in the stories of Rohan and Amon. Perhaps the most obvious is that the traditional families that Rohan and Amon's grandparents grew up with have been replaced with rearranged families in which divorce has become much more prevalent. In the case of Amon's parents, once they had separated his father remarried in Canada and Amon now has three stepbrothers and sisters in Toronto. But it is deeper than this. Perhaps some of the loneliness and isolation of both Rohan and Amon is that they are the members of a global society that simply does not trust each other. Amon notices how cynical people are about 'big business', and that's one of the reasons he decided to work independently – he did not want to line the pockets of one of the 'fat cats'. Rohan, as a surgeon, is in the world's most trusted profession, but like Amon he distrusts the government and is worried about corruption and sleaze.

Another general emotion in the societies in which Rohan and Amon live is a feeling of unhappiness. Rohan notices this in the patients he treats, and Amon knows himself the quiet desperation he can sometimes feel. There are many pundits asking why so many people are unhappy, and one of the reasons people have pointed to is that so much leisure time is spent passively watching television.

Together these pieces form a particularly potent recipe for isolation. From the globalisation force, the pieces around urbanisation and global migration play a role; from the carbon and natural resources force, the piece around soaring energy costs puts a break on travel and encourages virtual working; from the demographic force the piece on the rearrangement of families breaks many of the natural bonds that keep isolation at bay. Finally, the societal force brings three pieces – ebbing trust, declining happiness and increases in passive TV watching. It's a toxic brew that could potentially bring isolating work to billions of people by 2025.

The force of globalisation: the world became urban

One of the key drivers of isolation has been the explosive growth of cities and urban areas across the whole globe. In 1800 just 3% of the world's population lived in urban areas, and by 1900 this had only increased to 14%. Yet by 1950 – when the Baby Boomers were born – it had moved up to 30%. The extraordinary fact is that in their lifetime that percentage had shifted to 50% – and there is no evidence that the trend will decrease. By 2010 in many Western countries more than 75% of people lived in an urban area.

Urban and rural living have different communities and rhythms. In the mid-nineteenth century in Europe or America most people lived in the countryside, on a small farm or in a small town. The typical family grew some of its own food, raised livestock and took their surplus to the market to exchange for goods they did not produce. If, like me, you love the novels of Jane Austen or Henry James, then their vivid descriptions of life in the nineteenth century resonated with the scale and domesticity of life. Jane Austen's Emma and Henry James's Isabel do occasionally go into town – but remember that in the 1860s London was home to 3,189,000 people, New York to 813,000 and Boston to 177,000. Had our heroes been explorers, when they entered Bombay or Shanghai they would have found cities of around 600,000 and 700,000.

This all changed in the West around 1870 when a host of innovations in transportation, energy creation and manufacturing created remarkable industrial growth, which sucked the population into the towns. The great chroniclers of this migration, Charles Dickens in the UK and Émile Zola in France, described both the excitement and the misery that this created. Between 1870 and 1900 New York's population tripled from 942,000 to 3.4 million and London's nearly doubled from 3,841,000 to 6,507,000. In the East, Bombay (now Mumbai) and Shanghai also grew – from 645,000 to 813,000 in Bombay and from around 600,000 to 1,000,000 in Shanghai. 2008 saw the balance tip from a majority of rural to a majority of urban world inhabitants. By 2030 it is estimated that the number of people living in urban spaces will have risen to almost 5 billion.[9] In China, by 2010, it was almost half and half between the urban and rural populations, although of course the 54% of the population living in rural China produce a much lower share of its GDP.

What this move to the cities means is that more and more people are dislocated from their roots, living in cities where they know very few people, often in neighbourhoods with very little community spirit and activity. It's from this dislocation that isolation grows. But it is not just the migration to the cities that could be a cause of isolation – there are other migration patterns that could impact on the way we relate to work and our working communities.

The demographic force: global migration increases

The isolation that many workers feel in 2025 has also emerged from the dislocation of families and communities as people migrate to get better jobs or to escape war or natural disasters. It is true, of course, that people have always migrated ever since the first *homo sapiens* ventured from Africa across Eurasia 60,000 years ago; people have continued to migrate in order to establish new communities, move their existing communities and join other communities.[10] Since that time the pace of migration has accelerated as a consequence of commercial and technological developments, and is often spiked by occasional grand economic ventures, as well as political and ecological crises. The colonisation of the Classical period, the forced migration of the transatlantic slave trade and the mass emigration from Europe to the New World were all significant in determining the present distribution of cultures across the face of the globe. We can anticipate that while the direction and strength of migration flows are unpredictable, migration will increase. The actual rate will depend on environmental factors (rising sea levels forcing people to migrate, earthquakes leaving areas uninhabitable, drought decimating areas), political factors (refugees moving away from war-torn regions) and technological developments (labour-saving inventions putting people out of work).

Some migrants move between countries; in 1965, for example, 2.5% of the world population migrated across country borders (that's about 75 million people), whereas in 2010 the figure was 3% (that's around 214 million people).[11] This is expected to increase, as a greater percentage of the world's population becomes migrants. Movement within countries, from country-side to cities, from one city to another, has been a much more significant story over the last century. In 2010 more than 740 million people migrated within their country, almost four times the extent of international migration.[12] Migration will also increase with the wealth of a nation. In some countries people are simply too poor to emigrate. For example, in 2009 only 1% of Africans lived in Europe and only 3% lived in a country differ-ent from where they were born.[13] However, once a country develops, much of its population finds that it has the capacity to leave for more lucrative markets. In 2009, for example, in the Philippines more than 95,000 domestic staff and carers emigrated.[14]

We can also expect the migration of the most talented and skilled in any region to increase as they congregate around the major talent pools of the world. Some will choose to stay in their own country to use their skills if there is a creative cluster or productive region where they can command a salary sufficient to afford a high standard of living. Others will choose to work in developing markets in order to benefit from the short-term opportunity and to gain international experience. Others still will become truly global citizens, free to relocate at any time depending on the relative global employment and investment opportunities.

The force of energy resources: energy prices increase

In a joined-up, global world you could perhaps assume that isolation will decrease as people jump into their car, or get onto an aircraft when they want to meet their friends and colleagues. However, the current projections of the availability and cost of fuel suggest that we can expect a significant rise in energy prices, possibly to the extent of making these easy trips impossible. That's one of the reasons why Jill works in the local hub rather than commuting, and why Amon and Rohan work virtually with their colleagues in other countries rather than jumping on a plane to meet with them in China or Brazil.

The world's use of energy has been increasing since the Industrial Revolution; in fact between 1750 and 1900 the amount of energy per capita increased as much as it had done in the previous 1,000 years, with the average person using more than three times the energy that they would have at the turn of the tenth century.[15] Not only has individual energy consumption risen dramatically, but the human population also increased rapidly. The combination of these two exponential progressions, growing energy consumption per person and growing population, has initiated an energy explosion, and this trend does not show any signs of slowing. In fact, it continues to accelerate.[16]

In the twentieth century huge investments were made in the construction of fossil-fuel-based economies, and it is clear that the reversal of this long process poses substantial challenges. First, the supply of fossil fuel is finite, meaning that demand will increasingly outpace easy supply. Second, the environmental impact of fossil-fuel dependence was by 2010 widely known among scientists, if not all those outside the scientific community. Third, even by 2010 the energy framework was causing substantial disruptions to economic activity, in particular putting financial and political pressure on developing countries. For those nations with insufficient institutions to stabilise fluctuating oil prices and protect against supply shortages, the costs of food, fertiliser and transport will often rise unexpectedly.[17]

So for Rohan, Jill and Amon, accessing fossil fuels has become ever more difficult. The supply of coal, gas and oil is limited. As far back as 2005 the oil major Exxon-Mobil reported that all the easy oil and gas reserves had been found, and that future supply would be significantly more challenging to guarantee.[18] While the extent of the reserves was not fully known, in 2009 a number of estimates predicted that accessible oil and gas reserves would run out by 2042, followed by coal in 2112.[19]

Given the declining rate of fossil-fuel reserve discovery, demand for oil surpassed supply by 2015.[20] This brought about between 2015 and 2020 the period of peak oil, when the maximum rate of global oil extraction was reached before giving way to a period of terminal decline. As the reserves began to dwindle, and the cost of extraction increased, the cost of energy inevitably increased. However, the actual cost is unreliable, depending on the policies of those nations with access to fossil fuels and economic growth forecasts.[21, 22]

What has also pushed up the price of oil by 2025 is that developing nations, including the growing populations of China and India, had entered their most energy-intensive phase of economic growth. This is a phase that countries such as the United Kingdom and the United States went through following the Industrial Revolution. As China and India industrialised, so they built more and more complex infrastructure and increased their transportation infrastructure.

This had a significant impact on the use of fossil fuels since transportation is a huge user of fossil fuels. In 2010, for example, nine out of every ten barrels of extracted oil were made into transport fuels such as gasoline and diesel. From 2010 to 2040 it is estimated that cars in emerging markets like China and India will account for three-quarters of the new vehicles on the road. Vehicles such as Tata Motor Group's Nano – 'the one lakh car' – which in 2010 retailed at $2,500, had brought the possibility of car ownership to hundreds of millions of people. As China and India industrialise, so their populations want to run refrigerators, watch television and use air conditioning. As aspirations have risen, and as modern technology has becomes increasingly affordable, so more and more consumers will be plugged into the global energy framework.[23]

As a consequence of this, there has been much focus on the reduction of carbon footprints to limit unnecessary energy expenditure. This has been achieved primarily through virtual working and e-commuting. Even by 2010 more than 75% of American and British households had internet access and their inhabitants could theoretically work from home. In Jill's country, the UK, for example, a working population of 29 million[24] commuters in 2010 spent more than 20 million hours travelling to and from work every day, losing at least an hour of their time and costing more than £266 million a day in lost productivity.[25]

Societal force: families become rearranged

It's not just the move to the anonymity of the cities, the uprooting of communities or the cost of travel that created isolation. What was also a factor in the isolation of these stories was changes in family structures. Across the world the nature of relationships and families changed dramatically. With a few noticeable exceptions, family size reduced. Even in areas that historically had large families, the trend was to have smaller families. In Bangladesh, for example, by 2010 the birth rate had fallen from 6.8 children per woman to 2.7, in just 50 years. These smaller families are rarely as simple as Mum and Dad and a couple of children. In its place are much more complex and convoluted arrangements of multiple marriages, multiple families and multiple extended families.

It was Gen X who experienced the break-up of families to the greatest extent. This is the generation that in 2010 are in their mid-40s and will be in their mid-60s by 2025 – so they are entering the height of their earning power. This is a generation that grew up in a time of economic uncertainty, the Vietnam War, the fall of the Berlin Wall, the 1973 oil crisis, the dotcom bubble, the Iran hostage crisis, all of which reduced their expectation of a long-term relationship between employee and employer.[26] They also increasingly witnessed their parents divorcing. In 1950, 26% of US marriages ended in divorce; by 1980 this had climbed to 48%.[27]

This of course has implications for isolation, but it also has other just as profound consequences. For the sociologist Anthony Giddens this is a 'basic transition in the ethics of personal life as a whole. Both kinship and gender were once seen as naturally given, a series of rights and obligations which biological and marriage ties created.'[28]

> In the separating and divorcing society, the nuclear family generated a diversity of new kin ties associated with the so-called recombinant families ... Kinship ties often used to be taken for granted basis of trust; now trust has to be negotiated for and bargained for. People have to work out how to treat relatives and, in doing so, construct novel ethics of day-to-day life.

So in place of the traditional family are ever more complex arrangements that have to be negotiated and agreed. The relationships between family members have transformed, but so too have the relationships between communities and institutions as trust in many institutions has ebbed and people are more and more wary of both the state and large institutions.

Societal force: growing distrust in institutions

One of the drivers of isolation is the feeling of mistrust. We are more likely to reach and connect with others if we trust the people and communities we live in, and less likely to do so if we don't trust them. Trust is not simply about whether you like another person, or institution, it's a much more active emotion and is typically based on the expectations we have of the future. We trust people, institutions or brands because we believe that they will deliver. You may have a friend you really like, they are great fun and wonderful to have at a party, loved by all. However, you don't trust your friend because you know that they are likely to come really late when you've asked them to come early, or they botch the task you are sharing with them. Trust in communities and societies is important because it serves to lubricate, to make easier, the everyday transactions of working life.

What and whom we decide to trust is a crucial decision made every day. Trust gets us out of a state of uncertainty. If you don't know what's going to happen, then you cannot make plans – the firmer your plans, the stronger the trust, and vice versa. Trust enables us to see the future; it lubricates relationships and the exchange of knowledge and is crucial to cooperation. Trust makes things predictable, it brings us together and helps us work together. It is perhaps one of the most precious commodities a community or an organisation can have.

Physical isolation, influenced by the move to the cities, increased migration and family breakdown have led to physical isolation. The isolation we witness in these storylines is also the result of an ebbing of trust in each other and in communities.

Year after year, many surveys have shown that trust in politicians, the judiciary and companies has declined. For example, a 2009 study by the Davos World Economic Forum found that trust in leaders is low, and declining. When asked if they trusted leaders, the percentage of respondents who said they had a 'lot of trust' or 'some trust' in religious leaders was 41%; leaders of Western Europe 36%; managers of the global economy 36%; executives in multinational companies 33%; and leaders in the USA 27%. Asked if they felt trust had increased, stayed the same or decreased, around 40% thought it had stayed the same and 40% believed it had gone down.[29] Yet while leaders and institutions are not trusted, professionals are – in a 2009 survey, 74% trusted doctors 'a lot' and 68% trusted teachers 'a lot'.

There is no evidence that the decline of trust in institutions is because politicians or company executives are acting in a less honourable way than in the past. There is no question that politicians from the beginning of time have on occasion acted in a sleazy way, or that companies have dishonoured and let down their employees. However, what is clear is that there are other factors around trust that in part account for the present ebbing of trust and will continue to do so in the future.

The most obvious of these factors is transparency. Reputation is created out of a filtered set of an infinite number of events and actions on the part of politicians and executives. Clearly the media play a key role in both filtering and accentuating this information. Recall how in late 2009 the UK's *Daily Telegraph* led on the sleaze and scandal of politicians' expenses week after week. This news was sent around the world, digested and redigested and, of course, resulted in the erosion of public trust in the British government. Social media also play an increasing role in the distribution of bad news. Blogs, YouTube, Twitter and Facebook all expose the deviant actions of corporations and governments within nanoseconds of the event. I remember how Domino's Pizza learnt the true cost of transparency when a video of its employees doing unsanitary things to a pizza surfaced on YouTube and was viewed by millions. A PR disaster of similar proportions was suffered by Nestlé after their Facebook fan page was quickly transformed into a message board where environmentalist critics could air their grievances, and upload defaced Nestlé logos and videos criticising the company on ethical grounds. The power of these 'twitstorms' is enough to sweep even the most agile PR agencies off their feet and can often cost millions of dollars to counteract or subdue.

At the same time, national psyches around the world have been battered by record numbers of corporate bankruptcies, many of them household names: Royal Bank of Scotland, Kmart, United Airlines, Lehman Brothers, GM and Chrysler; and the seemingly never-ending litany of corporate scandals – with Enron perhaps taking pride of place in the gallery of villains. We trust companies when they provide rather than conceal information (recall how Enron concealed crucial information); when they are clear about their interests (recall how Enron was overflowing with conflicts of interest); and when there are consequences for their actions. The trust that Rohan and Amon feel in corporations and governments has been eroded as the press and social media have become increasingly vigilant in watching the behaviour of those in power and the actions of the organisations of which they are members.

The ebbing of trust can be related to the loss of communities. The decline of community relationships, previously based on community activities such as bowling or local societies, has eroded the local trust that underpins global trust.[30]

The ebbing of trust has also occurred as a result of the increasing short-term nature of working contracts. Jill works part time for a multinational company; Rohan has a joint appointment with the Wockhardt Hospital in Mumbai and the St Michael Hospital in Shanghai; and Amon is self-employed. The diversity of their working forms reflects a growing proportion of work that is short term, less predictable and more market-driven. As work has becomes more flexible, so too the contract between employer and employee will become more and more open to violation. Jill and Amon have heard many stories of people believing they will be trained, but were not; being promised a promotion that did not materialise; expecting the job to be secure, but finding themselves out on the streets within months; who thought they would be coached and supported, but nothing happened.[31] In part this reflects the breaking of the old 'parent/ child' implicit contract that the role of the organisation was in some measure to 'care' for the employee. If that contract ever actually existed, the layoffs of the 1980s and 1990s put paid to it. Increasingly employees all over the world have realised that it is they alone who can be trusted to shepherd their career.

Yet while countless national, international and corporate studies of trust have shown that year after year people's trust in institutions has declined, the picture is not really as clear as this. While we may say we don't trust corporations, in practice we eat the food that these corporations make, drink the water they pipe to us, and drive on the roads they construct. We even give them our credit card information when we talk with them on the phone. It would seem, then, that although we may not say we trust executives, in reality our actions suggest a rather robust trust in the corporations that provide the material sustenance to our everyday living.

Societal force: the decline of happiness

When you don't trust governments or institutions, then it is easier to feel isolated. It's also easier to feel isolated when you are unhappy. There has been a steady decline of happiness in much of the developed world. Of course, the notion of happiness is as ephemeral and multifaceted as trust. Trust in a sense describes our relationships and expectation of others – whilst happiness describes our relationship with ourself. Just as trust lubricates the transactions that are crucial to day-to-day living and working, so too happiness lubricates our own day-to-day behaviour.

In the 1990s the political scientist Robert Lane[32] found that happiness had declined in many developing countries over the previous decade. With regard to simple 'happiness' scores, between 1972 and 1994 in the USA, for example, the percentage of people replying that they were 'very happy' had steadily declined from 35% in 1972 to 30% in 1994. The extent to which people reported they were 'very happy' with their marriage, 'very satisfied' with their jobs, and satisfied with the city or place they lived in had also declined in the two decades from 1973 to 1994. At the same time, depression had risen in many developed countries – for example, the number of adolescent suicides doubled in many countries in the years between 1970 and 1990.

What is interesting about happiness, both now and presumably in the future, is that the relationship between happiness and economic development is curvilinear. People are happier as GDP per capita increases. However, the law of diminishing returns steps in beyond a certain level of GDP. To be poor in many countries around the world is to be unhappy, but to be rich in developed countries is not necessarily to be happier. What appears to be happening in many advanced societies is what the psychologists Philip Brickman and Donald Campbell call the 'hedonistic treadmill'.[33] Simply put, as income increases, so too do desires and aspirations – to such an extent that no amount of increase in income, however large, will lead to greater happiness.

This perceived loss of happiness is important to the way we live and work in the future. In the third future-proofed shift, from voracious consumer to impassioned producer, we will take a much closer look at the role happiness plays at work and the ways that we can ensure that our future work is crafted to create satisfaction and happiness. For now, though, let us consider one of the main aspects of contemporary life that have been seen as one of the reasons why happiness has declined – the changing patterns of leisure.

Societal force: passive leisure increases

Over the last five decades we have changed the way we have consumed goods, and also the way we have consumed time, and we can expect this change to continue over the coming decades. Prior to the mass movement of the population to factories and cities, rural life was more likely to be delineated by the seasons and the needs of animals or farms. Sunday may have been the day of rest, but for most of the time people worked and lived. It was only with industrialisation that hours, days and weeks became more clearly delineated into working time and home time.

The other headline story about how time was spent over the last five decades – and sure to be of interest in the coming two decades – is the increasing use of leisure time. From the 1950s onwards, leisure had become part of the expectations of working life and with it the idea of the 'weekend' – to be filled with the newly emerging leisure activities of sports, dances and civic associations.[34]

Ask Jill, Rohan and Amon what they do in their leisure time and they will tell you that much of it is spent watching television. They are not alone: across the world leisure time has increasingly been filled with passively watching TV. Clay Shirky, the media expert, gives the following explanation of why this might be so.[35] In 1750, with rapid population growth and pressures of urbanisation, the gin craze swept London. Across the city, people downed the stuff in vast quantities; they bought gin-soaked rags if they could not afford a whole glass, and rented straw pallets by the hour to sleep off the effects. The reason, Shirky believes, was that being sozzled on gin provided just the right social lubricant for people suddenly tipped into unfamiliar and often unforgiving lives. It kept them from completely falling apart. In the shifts in society we have seen in the last two decades the social lubricant has not been gin, but rather the sitcoms watched by many. Watching sitcoms – and soap operas, costume dramas, and the host of other amusements offered by TV – has absorbed the lion's share of the free time available to the citizens of the developed world. On average, in 2009 over 20 hours of TV were watched per week by every member of the developed economies of the world. In a sense, watching television had become the part-time job for most citizens in the developed world.

It may have been the case that leisure time was conceived 'to be filled with the new leisure activities of sports, dances and civic associations' but in reality, as the sociologist Robert Putnam so poignantly showed, certainly in the USA, the population was 'bowling alone'.[36] By 2010 it was clear that TV watching had played a key role in crowding out social activities such as communal bowling, replacing them with solitary activities that simply served to reinforce the isolation of work. This is how researchers Marco Gui and Luca Stanca described it:

television can play a significant role in raising people's materialism and material aspirations, thus leading individuals to underestimate the relative importance of interpersonal relations in their life satisfaction and, as a consequence, to over-invest in income-producing activities, and under-invest in relational activities.[37]

The isolation that people like Rohan and Amon feel has many causes. In part it's a reflection of the mass movement of people away from the rural areas to large, often crowded and impersonal cities, and also of the family disintegration that has been such an important part of the landscape. At the same time, instead of getting out into the community, more and more time is being spent in passive television watching. The soaring cost of energy has meant that home-based working has become the norm for many people, and with it the demise of the easy companionship of offices. Perhaps it is no surprise that people feel less happy and are less likely to trust governments and institutions.

What could Rohan and Amon have done differently to build a working life that was less isolating and more communal? What can you do to avoid the trap of isolation that these characters from the future have found themselves in? In the second future-proofed shift, we address these issues of isolation head on. There is an incredible opportunity in the future – as we shall see when we rearrange the pieces into more positive storylines – to become less of an isolated, competitive employee and more of an innovative connector. To do so, there are three types of network that you should be actively building: a posse of people to whom you can turn and with whom you have created long-term reciprocal relationships; the big ideas crowd, which is a diverse and large group of networks, many of whom are virtual, from which great connections can be made; and finally, a regenerative community, who are real people with whom you can meet frequently, laugh, share a meal and relax.

4
EXCLUSION: THE NEW POOR

Briana's story

Let's stay in 2025 and move on now to watch 28-year-old Briana who lives in Ohio, right at the heart of the USA. She is living with her parents and grandfather in a rather small house, and by 9.00 she is up and on her computer. She is a devotee of the World of Warcraft and like many millions of people around the world likes to spend at least four hours a day on the game. She is a member of one of the many thousands of guilds and has spent the last couple of months perfecting archery and tailoring skills with the hope of being recruited to one of the more prestigious guilds.

By 11.30 Briana is getting ready for the short walk to the local burger bar where she has a part-time job – five afternoons a week. She enjoys the work and likes the crowd she gets to spend time with. By 6.00 the evening shift are coming in and Briana leaves for home. After a quick dinner with her family she does what she does many nights – tries to find more permanent work. She spends the next hour surfing the web to see if there are any jobs that might suit her. The challenge is that Briana left school at 16 with a head filled with reality shows and an education that left her barely reading and writing. She knows that for every online project she aspires to she is competing with smarter, more motivated and better-educated kids that China and India are churning out in the millions – and she's not coming out well.

Over the course of the evening Briana chats with her father Frank, who is also looking for work. He was once on the auto-line at General Motors in Detroit, but that factory closed more than a decade ago. Frank makes a living now working in a hardware store in Detroit, but it's long hours and doesn't really use his skills. As the evening closes Briana sits on the porch to chat with her grandfather. Now aged 68 he would love to work, but like Frank is finding it tough to get work that would interest him. He moved in with the family 10 years ago when it became clear that he was struggling to live off his meagre savings. Plus the pension he had saved up for years was woefully inadequate, eaten up by global inflation and various financial scams.

André's story

As the sun sets on the same day in 2025, lets take a look at André in the Belgium city of Liège. Like Frank, his father had been employed in the local factory and had made a good living from it – as did his grandfather. But by 2015 many of the factories across Belgium had closed, as steel production moved increasingly to China and India. One of the most significant factors was the massive pension provision that André's father's company had made. This brought the company to the brink of bankruptcy in 2015 and it had to be sold to a Chinese conglomerate later that year.

As a result of these closures, André's home town of Liège experienced unprecedented levels of youth unemployment. Like Briana, André struggled at school, never really keeping pace with some of his more gifted peers. Some of his friends from school have now left Belgium to work in the new emerging economies, but André has been left behind. No permanent employment, no pension provision and a state which is increasingly burdened by the health costs of an ageing population mean that André is struggling to make ends meet. Like Briana he picks up work when he can, flipping burgers, working in petrol stations, delivering parcels. But as the barriers to labour movement across the extended EC have reduced, so André finds himself increasingly in competition with people with more skills and experience than he, who are also prepared to work for lower wages.

Briana and André may be living in developed countries, but they are members of a global economic underclass who are excluded from joining the rapidly globalising talent pool. There have always been the excluded in the world of work. Take Rohan's grandfather, who was born in 1930 in rural India. He had little chance of ever getting out of his home village. Or Amon's grandfather, born in Egypt in the 1930s into a life of abject poverty, and little by way of education. A full-time education was simply a dream for both of them, however ambitious and clever they might have been. The same would have been true of most of the population born in sub-Saharan Africa, where being born in a country such as Tanzania would have meant a lifetime of poverty with little opportunity to flourish. For Rohan and Amon's grandfathers, and to a certain extent their fathers, the world was not a level playing field, and their grandfathers both had the misfortune to be born in parts of the world where their chances of creating substantial economic value were strictly limited.

The shifting axis of exclusion

The axis of exclusion still exists – what's fascinating is that in the lifetime of Briana and Rohan the axis of exclusion has subtly shifted. Before it was aligned primarily on where you were born – those born in rural Indian or Egypt were outside the exclusion zone, whereas those born in Europe and the USA had huge positional advantages. In the lifetimes of Briana and Rohan this alignment had begun to change. Being born in rural India did not stop Rohan from getting a college education, and those born in his village in 2025 have access to solar-powered computers with free access to the Cloud and all the treasures it contains. Many of these village children will not take much advantage of this. Their parents will not encourage them, or they simply will not have the motivation and ability to flourish in this knowledge-rich environment. But some like Rohan will – and that's what will pull them up from a village in northern India to a hospital in Mumbai.

In Briana's and Rohan's lifetime, the axis of exclusion has shifted from where you are born to your natural talents and motivation and the specifics of your personal connections. The advantage of where you are born holds much less power in 2025 than it did in 1960, when Rohan's father was trying to break through. The implication of this is that in 2025 Briana, born in the USA, and André, in Europe, have little more advantage than Amon, born in Egypt, and Rohan, in India. Simply being born into the USA and Western Europe has not brought them the advantages afforded by their fathers or grandfathers. Briana and André are not flourishing because they have neither the natural ability, the energy nor the inclination to take advantage of what's being offered in the Cloud. They are excluded with almost as much significance as Rohan's grandfather was excluded all those years ago.

In this global joined-up world, those previously excluded (because they were born in rural India or sub-Saharan Africa) are now, with brains and ambition, joining the global talent pool. Those with neither are the new poor – wherever they happen to be born.

The widening gulf of the 'winner takes all'

At the same time, the gap between those who are winners across the globe and the losers like Briana and André continues to widen. This widening gap between the losers and winners occurs both within companies and within countries.

Briana and André earn a great deal less than those running their companies. Briana, for example, is employed part time at a fast-food outlet run by a multinational company. Back in 1980 the average CEO in the USA earned 42 times the average worker's pay. By 2000 that multiple had increased to 531 times. If we simply extrapolate the increase in the multiple to 2025, then we could predict that by this time the multiple between Briana and the CEO is at least 1,000. That means for every dollar Briana earns the CEO earns $1,000.[1]

The truth is, of course, that Briana and André are pretty much unaware of the gap between them and their CEO. What they are much more aware of is the gap between them and others working in their neighbourhoods. This is particularly pertinent for Briana in the USA. In 2010 the richest 20% were on average nine times richer than the poorest 20%. André lives in Belgium where the gap is considerably less; in Belgium the richest 20% were four times richer than the poorest 20%. Again if we project these figures into 2025 we can expect a future scenario where the forces of globalisation increase these gaps in an increasingly 'winner takes all' society.[2]

What will be the impact of this widening gulf? One thing we can be sure of is that it is not absolute income that impacts on health and happiness. It is the income differentials between people in the same company or society that really count. In the rich countries that Briana and André live in, it is the symbolic importance of wealth and possessions that matters. The purchases that Briana makes say a lot about her status and identity. Because she is poor and cannot afford fancy stuff, the second-rate goods she purchases are assumed to reflect that she is a second-rate person. In a materialistic society, access to material goods is a measure of success – and Briana's possessions scream that she is a loser.

If we assume that these gaps within companies and countries increase, then we can predict with some accuracy that this will lead to increased social anxiety. It will also impact on trust – the greater the inequalities in a society, the less people are likely to trust each other. When trust wanes so does cooperation and the capacity to share and be optimistic about others.

Increasing status anxiety and shame

As the differences between working people increase, so they trust each other less. These differences in status are also likely to result in greater anxiety. The rise in anxiety in developed countries such as the USA has been reported for over three decades. For example, in studies carried out between 1952 and 1993, anxiety in US men and women has continuously increased.[3] In fact, the increase has been exponential. For example, by 1993 the average college student was more anxious than 85% of the population in 1952. It is difficult to know to what extent the trajectory of anxiety will increase, but we can assume that if we took a trajectory from 1993 to 2010, and then on to 2025, we could predict a steadily rising level of anxiety.

The most probable cause of anxiety in people such as Briana and André is linked to their feeling that they have not been successful. Anxiety increases with threats to self-esteem or social status, and the widening gap between them and the more successful members of their society has only served to accentuate this.[4] Simply put, the wider the status gap in society, the more anxiety is triggered. For many it is shame that is at the heart of their anxiety – shame that in this rapidly changing world they are stupid or inadequate, incompetent or vulnerable. Ask Briana in 2025 why she cannot get a job when kids in Shanghai are working non-stop, and her explanation will be because she believes herself to be stupid – what could be an alternative reason? What also triggers anxiety is peer evaluation and pressure, and there is likely to be a continuous increase in the extent to which people are evaluated, rated and described by their peers.

Does it matter that Briana and André, and millions of other people across the world, are experiencing increasing feelings of anxiety? I want to draw your attention to the most profoundly negative aspects of anxiety. Sadly, anxious people have shorter lifespans than those with less anxiety.[5]

Friendship can have an immensely protective effect that shields us from our anxieties because we feel more secure and at ease with our friends. However, think back to the lives of Rohan and Amon to be reminded of the extent to which this protective effect of friendship is likely to have eroded in the coming years. When they return home at night they only have their avatars to give them comfort and listen to their worries.

We also know that close communities play a shielding role for anxiety. Our sense of identity is often embedded in the community in which we live and work. It is this sense of embeddedness that transcends our individual beliefs about our own worth or position. Again, this shield could become ever more eroded in the coming years. Briana is already, like Amon and Rohan, coming increasingly adrift from her close community and finds herself in the anonymity of mass society where familiar faces have been replaced by a constant flux of strangers. When Briana's grandfather was a member of the community, singing at the local church, judging the annual flower show, a governor of the local school, it mattered less what his status was. In these close communities, people from all walks of life mixed with each other with relative ease. However, for Briana, globalisation and technology will mean that she is increasingly among strangers. The challenge is that, between strangers, social position and social evaluation are increasingly important features of a person's identity. When Briana is among strangers she is evaluated by the clothes she wears and the brands she carries.

Narcissism: the presentation of self

There is one other interesting impact of a society that increasingly judges itself on how each person looks and what they choose to consume – narcissism. By this I mean a continuous focus on the self – on describing the self, promoting the self, reassuring the self, gaining feedback about the self. One of the shadows that falls across our descriptions of 2025 is that with the status anxiety that Briana, André and many others around the world are experiencing comes a preference for self-promotion above personal modesty. In a world of strangers, and increasing transparency, people like Briana and André will be increasingly forced into propping up their egos through telling everyone how great they are and, like their peers, using a wide range of self-promoting and self-enhancing strategies to do so.

Rewind to the 1950s and a time when small communities and family ties were still the defining frames of a working life. That's not to say, of course, that it's only André and Briana in 2025 who have to think hard about how they present themselves. As far back as 1959, Erving Goffman, in his book *The Presentation of Self in Everyday Life*, described the extent to which we present ourselves to the world and play the roles we believe to be appropriate for who we are and whom we would like to become. However, what Goffman was describing was a long dance, a gradual revealing and a shared co-creation.[6]

The internet has changed all of this. We don't have to fast-forward to Briana's presentation of self in 2025 to explore what this could look like. We can simply stay in the present and observe how the young kids in 2010, that's Generation Z, are choosing to portray themselves. Here is a contemporary description from Facebook from a 17 year old – let's call her Sammy:

Interest: I love tattoos, Mini cars, the Red Sox, iPhone, UGG's, working out, drinking girly drinks, Papyrus cards, JUICY COUTURE, Sephora, being tan, Hudson jeans, and Britney Spears.
Bio: Had a bad time with a guy at school!!!! Now I am free and easy – so say HELLO to the boys.

You can also see how Sammy portrays herself by reading her blogs, catching her on Twitter or perusing her posting on Match. com. You can even see her in action in a short film she made for YouTube.

Goffman may have described the presentation of self in 1959 as a series of role-plays, but what would he have made of the current presentation of self? In a world of hyper-connectivity you spill the beans about yourself every day to anyone who is prepared to listen – and even those who don't want to. Gone are the intimate conversations over coffee about lost loves. In their place is Facebook screaming your relationship status to the world; Twitter, describing every move you make; and in case the world has not gotten enough of you, there is always YouTube to get the message across.

For the joined-up young like Sammy, it's a public confessional, instant presentation of the self. It is almost as if technology has unleashed the exhibitionist in all of us. Nothing is out of bounds, nothing is too mundane, every moment described, every feeling shared, every emotion dissected.

Fast-forward to 2025; Sammy is now in her first serious management job. What implications have this self-portrayal had on how and why she works? What's clear is that work could increasingly be a study in impression management, just as her teenage years have been. Work could also be a study in gaining feedback about impression management. A couple of years back, my colleagues and I studied a group of MBA students to gain more insight into Generation Y – the people who will be leading our companies in 2025.[7] We asked them to talk about the way they thought their work and careers would develop, and then recorded what they said. We then went about analysing their word usage and speech patterns in order to understand more fully what they cared about, and what they were expecting from work. What was fascinating was the seeming paradox they expressed about how they wanted to work. On the one hand the word they most frequently used with a negative angle was the word 'micro-management'. Over and over again we heard how these 20-somethings did not want people breathing down their necks, telling them what to do and over-supervising them.

But here is the paradox. At the same time, the word that had the most positive connotations for these young MBA students was the word 'feedback'. They craved it, they loved it, and wanted to hear more and more about 'what people think about me'. They wanted to hear it from their bosses, their peers and their work acquaintances. In a world in which they are continuously called upon to construct an image of themselves for public consumption, references from others play a crucial part.

As we shall see later, this need for feedback and self-awareness can have a bright side – the opportunity to become more truly oneself, to become an individual rather than simply one in a crowd. But what is also possible is the dark side of narcissism and status anxiety.

However, before we leave Sammy and her Facebook posting, I'd like you to take one last peek at it. Is there anything you notice about it, about how Sammy chooses to portray herself? Look at it again. Do you notice that it's all about stuff – Mini cars, iPhones, UGGs, JUICY COUTURE, Sephora, Hudson jeans. Sammy is presenting herself through her consumption of brands. She and the millions of others in the nation of Facebook are choosing to reveal and describe themselves through what they consume.

Let's step back for a moment and pause to consider this fascinating harbinger of the future. In the five-sentence Facebook entry, we can see how Sammy's way of portraying herself has been intimately affected by the world she lives in. Technology has created hyper-connectivity that challenges Sammy to present herself to millions, even potentially billions, of people. The increasing forces of globalisation she has experienced in her short life have crafted consumer brands that are instantly recognisable anywhere in the globe. If these Facebook presentations are to be believed, then these brands have also become the worldwide currency of self-presentation. To understand the impact globalisation has had on Sammy, take a final glance at her Facebook entry. As you read it, let me ask you a simple question. Where do you think Sammy lives?

> I love tattoos, Mini cars, iPhone, UGGs, working out,
> drinking girly drinks, Papyrus cards, JUICY COUTURE,
> Sephora, being tan, Hudson jeans, and Britney Spears.

Tokyo perhaps? Or in the rich enclave of Mumbai? Possibly London, maybe Moscow? I've fooled you by removing the only locational marker in the description. Sammy is a fan of the Red Sox – so the chances are she is a Boston girl. But you get my point – consumption could increasingly become the global currency of self-presentation.

How did so many people become excluded?

One of the darkest sides of the future of work is that exclusion becomes a fact of life not only in the poorest countries but increasingly in the heart of the developed countries across the world. We can see, for example, how economic turmoil and continued bubbles and crashes wiped out the savings of Briana's grandfather as they had for many other people. What is also clear is that much of the work that semi-skilled people like Briana's father Frank could have expected will increasingly be performed by robots, throwing millions out of jobs. But it is not just robots that Briana and André are competing with, it is also the billions of people who are joining the global labour market in countries right across the world. The globalisation of the labour force of the world has put increasing pressure on the West. That's one of the reasons why Briana and André's life has been punctuated by periods of recession and austerity in their home countries.

Increasingly the most talented of the world have been moving to regions in which they can meet other like-minded people and flourish. As a consequence, there are regions of the world which have become more denuded of real added-value economic development, leaving those who stay in these regions with very little by way of choice or prospects. These are regions in which the chances of getting a good job are severely limited, but it is not just location that can reduce working standards, it's also age. By 2025 there will be four generations at work. Some, like the older Baby Boomers, will have used the property booms of the 1990s to build up their pensions. But many will not have sufficient savings to retire at 65 and will find it difficult to get good-quality work to take them through the next decade. And finally, in a world where environmental catastrophes will become more frequent, the excluded of the world will come from those regions that experience catastrophic events.

The forces of globalisation: continued bubbles and crashes

One of the drivers of exclusion will be the continuation of bubbles and crashes that will create economic instability in sectors of the economy and potentially wipe out savings. As the world witnessed in early 2010, one of the many fascinating aspects of a joined-up, connected world is that contagion can spread very, very quickly. On 6 May the New York Stock Exchange reported a drop of 6% in share prices between 1.00 and 1.15 p.m. It became known as the 'six-minute recession'. Over the weeks that followed a number of possibilities emerged: perhaps it was the 'fat finger' mistake, where an operator accidentally added a couple of zeros to a sell action. The more likely suspect was the tied computer systems and programs of the world that monitor the markets constantly and sell within a nanosecond.

Contagion and the bubbles that accompany them are not, of course, recent phenomena. You only have to consider the tulip mania that gripped sixteenth-century Amsterdam to witness the extent to which exuberance can overtake sanity. What's interesting is that in the joined-up, global world of 2025 and beyond, the shockwaves caused by a local bubble or a local crash will be felt way beyond their locality. Take Enron, for example. When it filed for bankruptcy on 2 December 2001 its $62 billion of assets made it the largest bankruptcy ever at that time. Enron has been held responsible for the stock market crash of the first years of the twenty-first century; from the peak in 2001 the US and UK stock markets had fallen by about half. This was the end of the bubble that had seen shares massively overvalued. The collapse of Lehman Brothers in September 2008 saw a repeat of this, this time signalling the end of the massive boom in house prices.

There are arguments that a more joined-up, regulated world will create a potentially calmer economic environment and eradicate the boom/bust mentality of the past. However, some, like Nobel Prize winner George Akerlof and his colleague Robert Schiller, see it differently. In their view the fault lies not in the economics of the marketplace, but rather in the innermost human needs and wants, or what they term 'animal spirits', by which they mean ideas, feelings, hopes and aspirations.[8] Their argument is that the global financial crisis of 2009 made it painfully clear that powerful psychological forces are impacting on the global systems of wealth creation. They point to the blind faith and exuberant over-confidence in the boom years, when ever-rising housing prices pushed debt to extraordinary levels. These booms are typically followed by busts and the associated plummeting confidence in capital markets.

We can be exuberantly confident – and this confidence can be inflated by the stories we hear from others – and this multiplication effect of our confidence collectively leads to exuberance and speculation in the marketplace. Witness, for example, the dotcom boom of the late 1990s, the housing boom of the early 2000s or the commodity boom of the late 2000s.

We humans can also act in bad faith. The numerous Ponzi schemes, where people deliberately defraud others through investment rackets, show how a combination of bad faith and collective confidence can drive people to invest in schemes that were never going to be viable. The fall of Bernard Madoff's Ponzi scheme in 2008 – one of the biggest financial investor frauds in history – shows how the combination of greed, reckless confidence and corruption led to the loss of over $18 billion. The animal spirit of corruption has played a key role in many recessions. Akerlof and Schiller argue that each of the three economic contractions in the USA has involved corruption scandals. The recession of July 1990 to March 1991 began with the savings and loans associations and Michael Milken's junk bonds; the recession of March to November 2001 was attributed in part to the collapse of the Enron Corporation; and the recession that began in December 2007 was created in part by the housing bubble in the USA, fuelled by the sub-prime mortgages, and came to a head with the bankruptcy of Lehman Brothers.

We can be entranced by the stories we hear and the narratives of others – in many ways, of course, that's the way we learn and exchange knowledge. However, our memories of the stories we have heard tend to be short term; we remember them through more and more fog until finally we forget them.[9] The stock market boom that lasted from the mid-1990s to 2000 was in part fuelled by stories around the invention and exploitation of the internet.[10] We become confident when we hear inspirational stories, news about new business initiatives and tales of how others became rich. Of course there are also stories of people who have lost everything, who were cheated by others, of the stock market crashing – but as the years go by these are the stories that are forgotten.

Bubbles and crashes will continue and be as much a part of working life in 2025 and beyond as they have been in the past. What this means is that the worst depressions in the past – in the 1890s and again in the Big Depression of the 1930s – could well be harbingers for the future, since it was that heady combination of exuberant confidence, bad faith and corruption, and powerful narratives that was the root cause.

Many of these past events are rooted in human nature, which remains as powerful a force as ever. People are still every bit as concerned about fairness, still vulnerable to the temptations of corruption, still repulsed when others are revealed in their evil deeds, still confused by inflation, still dominated in their thinking by empty stories rather than economic reasoning. Events like the two depressions cannot be counted as things of the past. (Akerlof and Schiller, 2009, p. 73)

What is of course fascinating about the economic crisis of 2009/10 is that it is pervasive. In a joined-up, rapidly globalising world, the exuberant confidence and empty stories that created a stampede for housing in California and other communities across the developed economy created a sub-prime mortgage crisis that rippled around the world. Simply put, when we think about the future of work, we need to factor in economic instability.

Technology force: technology replaces jobs

Bubbles and crashes were part of these stories of exclusion, but added to this are the deep-rooted changes in the nature of work, and in particular the impact that technology will have on how work gets done. By 2025 and beyond we can anticipate that across the world machines are changing the shape of work. Robots in their simplest form are one of the reasons Briana's father Frank lost his job in the automobile factory in Detroit. Like his own father, he had joined the company as soon as he left school, to work in the assembly plant. That had worked fine for Frank's father, but by 2003 Japanese developments in robotic assembly had begun to be adopted in Detroit factories. Up until then semi-skilled workers like Frank and his father could be assured of a job in the assembly plant. Frank's father had been skilled at paintwork and had passed this interest down to Frank. By the time Frank had apprenticed for the paint room and had worked for a couple of years, much of the work had already been taken by an assembly of 20 high-precision robotic arms. In the following 10 years robots took up more and more of the work in the assembly rooms. At the same time, increasing volumes of car manufacturing had moved to Asia – leaving Frank and many of his colleagues without full-time work.

In 2025 Briana sees robots all around her; every autumn she sees them on the great cornfields of the Midwest, harvesting the corn used for biofuel. Rohan also sees robots in his work: while he concentrates on complex surgeries, medical robots perform low-invasive surgery. Even the care of the elderly has been outsourced to robots – Jill's elderly mother has a robot in the house that monitors her heart rate and is able to perform simple caring tasks. What this means for the future of work is that those who in the past could have been assured of unskilled manual work are now finding more of their work being replaced by robots or farmed out to the ever-emerging lower-cost regions of the world.

What is interesting is that in those economies such as the US or Germany which have been transformed by technology, computers have substituted for workers in routine and simple jobs. However, when the tasks are more complex and require innovation or problem solving, this substitution has not taken place. What has happened instead is that technology has complemented the skills and experience of the employee.[11] In a world of more and more complex technology, it is the highly skilled employees, or what I will call those with mastery, who will always find work.

The forces of globalisation: the growth of the emerging economies

The growing economies of the world offer an ever-expanding choice of great deals. Technology and globalisation have put into the hands of Rohan, Jill, André and Briana the possibility of choosing from a vast array of goods and services and to compare the costs of these at the press of a button. As the US economist Robert Reich puts it, 'Never before in human history have so many had access to so much so easily.'[12] It is what he calls 'The Age of the Terrific Deal'. It's easy to find a better deal and then to switch instantly – this finding and switching behaviour has had, and will continue to have, profound implications for the future. To survive, all companies have to dramatically and continuously improve, to relentlessly take costs out of the business, and to always keep their eyes alert for the next merger or acquisition, to continuously strive to innovate and refresh their market offerings. Without this continual push for quality, executives know that customers will simply switch to the next best deal. This works for the future of consumers, but it also has implications for the future of workers. To quote Reich again, 'The easier it is for us as buyers to switch to something better, the harder we as sellers have to scramble in order to keep every customer, hold every client, seize every opportunity, get every contact. As a result, our lives are more and more frenzied' (Reich, 2001, p. 5).

This push for choice and cost advantage has impacted on world competition as more and more work is moved to areas of low wages, putting continuous pressure on workers as they compete with thousands of others across the globe. This rapid development of the emerging economies may have only taken off since the mid-1990s, but all the trends suggest that this rise will continue faster and further. Economic commentator Adrian Woolridge puts this down to four trends.[13] First, the companies in emerging markets have increasing access to the capital markets, enabling them to move into the mega-deals previously only in the domain of developed-economy companies; next, they have huge and growing populations of both workers and consumers; third, they are skilled at volume, and will continuous seek new markets; and finally, some of the best Western companies are already looking to emerging markets as sources of innovation and growth.[14]

As we consider those who will be excluded from the world-wide economies, it is worth noting that the recession which gripped the West in 2010 may have an impact that influences work over the coming decades. In particular, the impact of the austerity measures is likely to be a major part of the economic storyline for much of the West over the coming decades. What is clear is that Western consumers and governments have been on a debt-fuelled spending spree for the last decade. American household debt rose from 65% of GDP in the mid-1990s to 95% in 2009. Contrast that for a moment with the average Chinese, who has saved at least 20% of their income. It's what Martin Woolf in a *Financial Times* article referred to as the 'grasshopper and the ant' story.[15] This is a tale told to many children in the West of the lazy, carefree grasshopper spending its summer days enjoying the sun and revelry – compared with the diligent ant who spent the summer working hard to prepare for the winter. I don't need to tell you how the story ends. For Martin, the industrious ants are the citizens of China, Germany and Japan, the spendthrift grasshoppers the citizens of much of Europe and the USA.

What is becoming clear in the West is that the age of profligacy could well give way to the age of austerity. Governments are putting in place measures to control public spending, while consumers, worried about unemployment and shrinking wealth, are cutting back on their spending. They are trading down and buying cheaper items. We can expect these spending cuts to dampen growth, creating more demand for frugality and austerity. This is already apparent in 2010, when many European countries, particularly in the south, will come under ever greater pressure to cut back on public spending.

The force of globalisation: a regional underclass emerges

In the future we can expect the underclass will be found in every part of the world, representing those people who are unable to join the global talent pool and are stuck in areas of economic stagnation. At the same time, other regions of the world will become ever-increasing magnets of talent.

In this connected world, the actual economic engines will be found in a surprisingly small number of places as the talent pools of the world begin to congregate with each other rather than be distributed evenly across the globe. It is what the University of Toronto's Richard Florida has called the 'spiky world'.[16] His observation is that the world is not flat, as Thomas Friedman contended in 2005, but rather spiky. The spiky world has creative clusters, productive powerhouses, mega-cities and rural areas. Whether or not you are in the global underclass will depend a lot on where you are born, or to where you choose to migrate.

The creative clusters will attract those who are engaged with the cluster, and those who support the primary workers. Those engaged with the cluster will be drawn to work with others like them – be that, for example, engineering, biotech or technology. They may also choose to work in an area of natural beauty, or one with a benign climate. They will themselves be supported by an army of carers – masseurs, hairdressers, chefs, travel agents, coaches, teachers and retailers – all in service to their needs (and probably also their whims). These clusters will continue to suck in both talent and those who support the lifestyle of the talented.[17]

The productive powerhouses are regions that will use established innovation or creativity – often imported from other places – to produce goods and services. Many of the manufacturing cities in Mexico such as Guadalajara and Tijuana, to Shanghai and the Philippines are already like this, while some like Singapore and Taipei are rapidly becoming the creators of innovation as well as the users. An individual's success in this region will in part depend on whether it is in the ascendant or the descendant. In much of the US, for example, these productive powerhouses have been in the descendant, with more than 1.8 million blue-collar jobs lost between December 2007 and

November 2008. By 2009 unemployment among production workers hit 16%, and it was 19% in construction.[18] Across the developed world, semi-skilled manufacturing jobs have been lost in millions as the productive powerhouses of the world moved east. Take Briana's home town of Detroit. In 2009 just 10% of adults were college graduates, and 30% were on food stamps. Like other US cities, Detroit has been hampered by its model of sprawling, car-dependent growth.[19] What's tough is that with the push to home ownership many of the population are stuck, unable to relocate because they cannot sell their homes.

The mega-cities are those cities with large population concentrations but insufficient economic activity to support all their people, so many of these mega-cities are ravaged by slums. The slums of Mumbai or Cairo and the favelas of Rio de Janeiro are places that have become increasingly disconnected from the global economy. These mega-cities and regions will, over the coming decades, face growing challenges and will become more congested and pricier. For these mega-cities to work, major new advances in transportation and environmental technology will be required. By 2010 some of these prototypes were under construction. For example, the city of Masdar in Abu Dhabi was scheduled to come on-stream in 2018 as an eco-city with very low carbon emissions.

The upside of Richard Florida's picture of the future of cities is that the most talented people will migrate to creative clusters and rising productive powerhouses. The downside is that the global mega-cities of the world are going through the same fierce competition and consolidation that reshaped global industries like steel and car manufacturing over the last couple of decades. It is likely that many of the city regions of the developed world will be particularly hard hit. Here is how Richard Florida describes the impact of this global competition on cities in the USA:

The Clevelands and Pittsburghs of this world will find themselves increasingly squeezed between twin pincers as top business functions gravitate to larger regions like Chicago, while production shifts to centers like Shanghai. The Austins and Research Triangles of the world will face competition not only from Silicon Valley but also from the up-and-comers like Bangalore, Dublin, and Tel Aviv. The world economy of the future is likely to take shape around an even smaller number of mega-regions and specialist centers, while a much larger number of places will see their fates worsen as they find themselves struggling just to stay in the game. (Richard Florida, 2008, p. 74)

This is taking a US-centric view – but pause for a minute and ask yourself how this will play out in your region of the world. In the UK, for example, what does this mean for Newcastle or Liverpool? In Germany, for Dortmund or Dresden? In France, for Marseille or the northern suburbs of Paris?

The underclass of the mega-cities will be increasingly found in the slums that surround them. By 2020 we can expect around 1.5 billion of the world's population to be living in slums, of which 400 million will be in Africa, and nearly 850 million in Asia.[20] It was once the case that cities and their suburbs or hinterlands were combined in a durable and meaningful relationship with one another. In the early twentieth century, for example, the surrounding areas of a city were an important source of labour supply and consumer demand. As goods and people moved between the two, this created a network of social relationships between the increasingly concentrated city and the increasingly extensive suburbs. With the emergence of mega-cities, instead of being connected parts these suburbs are increasingly becoming slums.[21] Far from claiming their own purpose and identity, these concentrated areas of 'surplus humanity' exhibit intense poverty and little direction.[22] This disconnection has been exacerbated by the vast urbanisation that has seen millions of people leave the land, hoping for a better life in the cities. As the slums around Mumbai or Johannesburg will attest, these hopes are rarely realised.

The final place in the world of 2025 will be the huge rural areas and far-flung places that are sparsely populated and have little concentrated economic activity and little connection to the global economy. It is here that we can expect the global underclass to be found. The fate of the underclass in the rural areas will depend in part on their access to technology. It could be that the programmes to put computers into the hands of children, such as in Uruguay and Rwanda, will eventually result in the opportunity for young people to join the global talent pool if they have the motivation, drive and intelligence to do so. That still leaves the question of what they will actually do, even if they attain some qualifications. They could possibly join the 'virtual talent pool' of the world and stay in Uruguay – linking into IT jobs through virtual markets such as those created by virtual labour centres such as ODesk. Alternatively, they will increase their skills and remuneration by migrating to one of the creative clusters, mega-cities or productive regions that has their skill as a core competence – assuming, of course, that there are no barriers to the movement of labour. However, this leaves out of the global talent pool those children who either have no access to education or do not have the economic muscle to move to a creative cluster.

The problem of inequality between urban and rural areas is not exclusive to countries such as India and China. It is a challenge for many less-developed countries. In Africa and Latin America, particularly, the scale of income inequality is a major factor in hindering national development. Though inequality in cities may be reducing, the rural regions are often being left behind. In Ghana, for example, only 2% of Accra's inhabitants faced poverty in 2005 compared to 70% in the rural savannah. It is clear that the benefits of Ghanaian growth are not being evenly distributed.[23] This poses a significant problem, for it mitigates the positive effects of economic development. An unequal society, no matter how rich its urban population, is less conducive to economic growth than an equal one. Inequality destabilises political institutions, hinders efficiency and produces high levels of child mortality, lowers levels of education and lowers life expectancy.[24]

The demographic force: some Baby Boomers grow old poor

Your location and talent will not be the only driver of your likely economic prosperity and working experience in the decades to come. Another important factor will be your age. Many of us across the world can expect in the coming decades both to live longer and indeed to extend considerably our productive lives. By 2025, 10% of the world population will be over 65 and the old/young ratio (the amount of people over 65 per 100 people under 20) will have shifted from 16/100 in 1995 to 31/100. Life expectancy will have increased from 65 in 1995 to 73 in 2025, and by this time no country will have a life expectancy of less than 50 years.[25]

Some of us can expect to live healthy lives a great deal longer than 75, and we may well choose to work, some for the sheer excitement and stimulation, others out of economic necessity as they see the inadequacy of their pensions.[26] We will want to work for the money, to gain continued mental stimulation, to keep physically active, to keep connected with others and to have something meaningful and valuable to do with our time.[27] However, of all these reasons, we can expect that working to earn money could well be a crucial issue for a great number of people over the age of 60.

By 2025, in the USA, much of Europe and Japan, most of the Baby Boomers will have retired. Their impact has extended to the entire economies of the developed world. This is because their pension fund investments and individual savings have provided much of the cash available for borrowing by industry and government.[28]

Some of those Baby Boomers and Gen X who begin retiring from 2025 will have made adequate pension provision. Many others will find that they have to work far beyond the time they expected to retire. Here is the maths. When pensions were designed in the 1950s, this is what the actuaries who developed them calculated. Work from 20 to 65 in one company – that's 45 years of solid, continual contributions. Then retire at 65, enjoy a wonderful five years – 10 at the most, and pass away at 70–75. That's 45 years of continuous contribution for ten years of retirement. And what's more the economic environment between 1950 and 2000 was sufficiently stable to deliver an annual return in the region of 4%, which meant that savings did indeed accumulate.[29]

For those born after the Baby Boomers, the maths are different. First, few can expect to work for the same employer for more than five years. As a consequence of this flux in working arrangements, the opportunity to build a continuous pot of pension contribution will be significantly eroded. Even if you have, you can expect the booms and busts that are likely to occur from 2000 to 2050 to reduce considerably the assets that some careful savers will have accumulated.

There are some observers, including the commentator David Willetts, who believe this will cause profound tensions between ageing Baby Boomers and the Generation X and Y who will have to fund their retirement.[30] He calls it 'The Pinch', the moment in 2030 by which all the Baby Boomers will have retired. His argument is tough on the Baby Boomers. He sees them as the most spoiled generation in the history of the developed world, the generation that has squandered the patrimony their prudent and parsimonious parents left them, and which seems intent on leaving little behind for their own offspring. They have used equity to release cash out of their homes – to splash out on holidays and cars. By contrast those that follow them are paying for their university education, building up high levels of debt, finding it tough to get a job, even tougher to get on the property ladder and not even thinking about building up a pension. It will be interesting to see to what extent the intergenerational tensions that Willetts predicts will come about.

The big question is whether the growing numbers of over 65s in 2025 will actually have the opportunity to work. Corporate accommodation of an ageing workforce is painfully slow, and the fact that people are living longer and healthier lives isn't reflected in retirement legislation. The first fixed retirement age of 65 was brought in by the German Chancellor Otto von Bismarck in 1881, when the average life expectancy was only 43 years. By 2010 few countries had adjusted this limit in light of the fact that most people in the developed world now live to nearly twice that age. By 2010 this political inertia had meant that a decade of potential work was being lost by employers every time they enforced mandatory retirement legislation. However, we can expect that the political stasis will eventually yield to economic pressures.[31] In Britain, for example, the fixed retirement age of 65 was axed in 2011.

What the over-65s will do in the coming decades is an interesting question. Perhaps the public sector decline in many developed countries will encourage the growth of the 'third sector', comprising voluntary and community-based service organisations. These will create new jobs with government support to rebuild decaying neighbourhoods and provide social services.[32] This is but one of a number of ideas about the working lives of the over-65s. What is clear from the demographic and longitudinal data is that this age group will be ever more present in the world of 2025, and ever more keen and eager to work in order to avoid growing old poor.

As we complete this analysis of the pieces that have created the lives of Briana, André and their families, let's finally take a look at another group who will be excluded from the opportunity for high-value work – the growing band of people who are dislocated as a result of environmental catastrophes.

The forces of energy resources: environmental catastrophes dislocate people

Across the world, unusual weather patterns are emerging, and the burning of fossil fuels and the associated carbon dioxide emissions have become a growing concern to scientists, politicians, organisations and citizens. The energy framework that had existed since the Industrial Revolution has increased the concentration of carbon dioxide in the Earth's atmosphere by about 40%. By 2010 much of the world was dependent on a fossil-fuel-based economy, and annual emissions continued to grow by roughly 80%, causing atmospheric concentrations of carbon dioxide to rise far above the natural range of the previous 650,000 years.[33] While carbon dioxide levels had fluctuated over millennia as a consequence of glaciation cycles, the relatively recent use of fossil fuels as a productive energy source has caused an unnatural acceleration in this process and started to reveal certain environmental limits. Over the previous century the global average surface temperature had increased by 0.6°C. This shift was likely to have been the largest for any century in the last 1,000 years, and had resulted in a tenfold increase in economic losses from weather-related catastrophes between the 1950s and the 1990s.[34]

In 2007 the Intergovernmental Panel on Climate Change (IPCC), representing the most authoritative assessment of current scientific opinion, concluded that over the last century there were already changes in many ecosystems around the world. Biological systems were reacting to environmental pressures, sea levels had begun to rise, wind patterns had changed, and heatwaves and droughts were becoming more prevalent.[35] The IPCC reported that temperature increases and their corresponding environmental effects were already starting to threaten human health, with regard to both heat-related mortality and the widening prevalence of infectious diseases.

Various groups, including the IPCC, have argued that if nothing is done to overcome the global dependence on oil, coal and gas, then the 0.6°C shift that occurred over the previous century is likely to be dwarfed by the developments of the next century. The most conservative estimate of the IPCC predicted a mean global warming of around 1.8°C, while more pessimistic models showed the potential for a 4.0°C increase. Given the consequences in 2010 of a 0.6°C temperature shift, the impact of global warming nearly eight times higher will be severe. Large areas of the Amazon forest could be lost to drought and fire, agricultural yields could decrease for all major cereal crops, water shortages could affect more than two-thirds of the global population and rising sea levels could force millions to migrate.[36]

The sociopolitical pressures of water stress have also already started to build in parts of the developing world. As early as 2000, protests erupted in Cochabamba, Bolivia, when the municipal water supply was privatised and prices increased to an infeasible level.[37] As the quality of life expectations increased, as populations expanded and as global warming increased drought, the demand for water, as with oil, begin to rise above supply. Over the previous century water extraction had increased in agriculture alone, from about 550 cubic km per year in 1900 to about 2,600 cubic km per year in 2000. This figure is expected to increase to at least 3,300 cubic km by 2030.[38] By 2030 it is predicted that most of India's river basins could be facing severe deficits, 300 million in China could lack safe drinking water, and South Africa could have to deal with potentially devastating rainfall shortages.[39] We can anticipate that these environmental catastrophes will throw a significant proportion of people into the global underclass.

Contemplating the dark side of the future

Through these glimpses of working lives in 2025 we can contemplate how the dark side of the future could emerge. These glimpses are important since it's only through the contemplation of the lives of others that we can begin to synthesise the different strands in our own lives. It is in the descriptions of everyday lives that we can begin to imagine how our future and the future of others can unfold.

In the details of the stories of Rohan and Amon we discovered how the future could be one of isolation, where all we take for granted – easy companionship, close family ties – are things of the past. Jill's working day is fragmented, leaving her with little time to really concentrate and learn the deep skills and mastery which will be so crucial for her success. Briana and André, both born in affluent countries, are now joined to the new global poor with little opportunity to become members of the talent pools that are collecting across the world. We have seen how status anxiety and narcissism could be the natural heirs of technology and globalisation.

These stories are not flights of fancy; rather they are the result of a dispassionate trajectory of the five forces that will continue to dominate and shape where and how we work. These are stories that have been built from what we know of the present, and crafted to reveal what we can guess about the future. For every trajectory there is a bright and a dark side. Here the lives are shown through the darkest of lenses.

What have we learnt from this initial patching together of ideas, insights, facts and figures about these storylines of the Default Future?

It could be that there are areas where we can expect further technological developments to reduce some of the darkest aspects. Perhaps, for example, the development of sophisticated cognitive assistants will bring the fragmentation and intensification of our working lives to an end. These could act as a barrier between the plethora of data we are faced with and our own ability to assimilate this and make sense of it.

However, it's also clear that there are other dark aspects of the future where we cannot look to our technological genius to find answers. There is no doubt in my mind that in the future work could be a lonely activity. There is also no doubt in my mind that if we continue to describe ourselves through the brands we consume, then the shift to quality of experience seems altogether too simplistic.

So as we move from these dark storylines let me ask you to consider these questions: Do you see any counter-movement that could change the trajectory of these particular phenomena? What would be some of the trade-offs to be made and competencies to be developed you would counsel your own children, or those around you, to make if they are to reduce this dark side of work?

I guess as we leave the dark storylines we are left with the realisation that if change is to come through the three future-proofed shifts, then it can only come with experiments and counter-movements that provide alternative scenarios. And if change is to come, that will mean that we, our children and those around us have to learn to make some hard trade-offs and to develop a whole set of competencies and abilities that are now only nascent.

Many of the changes needed to move away from the dark future may appear to be beyond the actions of any single individual. However, as we shall see in the brighter, crafted stories of the future, there are possibilities that a joined-up population could act collectively in ways they have never been able to do before. It is the collectivity, which we will explore in the second shift, that I believe will be crucial to learning how to thrive in the future. However, more is possible both in terms of being wise about choosing skills and competencies that are likely to have value in the future, and being prepared to morph through the many years of work into areas where value is beginning to emerge. This is the central theme for the first shift – from shallow generalist to developing serial mastery. But that leaves out one message that we can see throughout these stories, the message of how we can live our working lives in ways that minimise the damage to the environment and maximise our own working satisfaction and happiness. This is the final shift, from voracious consumer to creative producer.

PART III

THE BRIGHT SIDE OF THE CRAFTED FUTURE

For each of the five forces that will shape your working life over the coming decades there is a pathway into the future that is potentially negative, but there is also a pathway that can be positive and uplifting.

The negatives for our working future are clear. Technology leads to a world of ever-growing fragmentation, where the billions of people connected across the world are continuously bombarded by requests; a future where the virtual nature of nascent technology will leave many deeply isolated and craving for physical relationships; a future where the forces of globalisation have enhanced the divide between the winners and the losers; a world where a new global underclass has emerged which contains those not able to join the global labour markets through an accident of location, or through their age. Ours could be a world where Baby Boomers have taken much of the resources they created in a final orgy of consumerism, leaving the youngsters, Gen Z or the aptly named 'regenerative' generation, to clean up a badly damaged world. It could be a world where families have become increasingly fragmented. It's a world where what you are is marked by what you buy, and where trust in companies continues to ebb away, as does happiness in much of the developed countries. It's a future where the challenges of carbon have overwhelmed the world as the heritage the Baby Boomers and Gen X pass on to their children is an ever-heating world, rising sea levels and a mad scramble for the remaining resources.

In every situation there are challenges and opportunities. In the storylines of the Default Future the lives play out upon the darkest side of the five forces in a way that makes uncomfortable reading.

But look back for a moment to the five forces and you will see that they also contain within them more positive, energising and uplifting possibilities. Yes, technology will lead to fragmentation and isolation, but imagine a world where 5 billion people are connected to solve the big challenges ahead. Imagine a world where technology is not simply a force for fragmentation, but also the bearer of the world's insights and knowledge to every child on the planet.

Yes, globalisation is in danger of creating an underclass of terrifying proportions and of upending much of the manufacturing of the world to India and China. But wait – imagine if the whole world engaged in the process of innovation, and if the developing countries began to teach the West how to be frugal in their innovation. Imagine if the austerity of the West could become the beginnings of a less consumerist society, focusing on the production of experiences rather than voracious consumption.

Yes, demography can potentially pit young against old, but imagine what a working life extended to 70 could mean if work was positive and fulfilling. And while changes in society and family structures create more and more rearranged families, imagine the impact of more women taking decision-making roles in companies, and fathers being able to take a more active role with their children. There is no question that anxiety about carbon and energy casts a shadow over the growth of the industrialised world in the future, but imagine if we actively embraced a low-carbon world and decided to live closer to our work, commute less and get on planes as a last resort?

The point is this: while the future is essentially unknowable, we do know the forces that are likely to be shaping the future of work. We also know some of the consequences of how these forces will play out As the Shell scenario planners discovered many years ago, these can lead us to paint various pictures of how the future could be and the actions that are likely to lead to these possible outcomes.

So let's go back to the 32 pieces that represent the five forces, but this time create patterns from which we can derive storylines that encapsulate how the future of work could pan out in its most optimistic guise.

5

CO-CREATION: THE MULTIPLICATION OF IMPACT AND ENERGY

Miguel's story

Let's return to 6.00 on that cold morning in January 2025. This time we see Miguel in Rio de Janeiro as he goes about his day. As he wakes to the first rays of the sun he thinks about the day in front of him. It's going to be a great day, as he plans to spend it doing what he most loves – inventing ideas and tackling complex problems. His passion is urban transport, and for over a month now Miguel has been working with a group of pals trying to solve a particular thorny question. As a child born in 1996, he witnessed first hand the economic boom that Brazil had experienced as companies from across the world invested in the country. He also saw how entrepreneurs had built Brazilian companies, some like Ricardo Semler from Semco becoming known across the world for their prowess. He felt justly proud of what his country had achieved. But he was also painfully aware of the impact that rising prosperity and the emergence of a substantial middle class had on his home town. Industrialisation had put enormous strain on Rio, as it had on cities across Brazil. This had been exacerbated by many millions of people leaving the countryside to try and find work in Rio – swelling the population to over 13 million and scattering people in the favelas that sprawl across the hillsides of the city. As a teenager Miguel had witnessed how the streets of Rio became increasingly clogged with traffic. This was certainly not helped by the lack of any clear strategy for an urban transport system.

Growing up in Rio, Miguel decided to take a degree in urban planning. He was thrilled when he got a place to study at the University of Parana in Curitiba and was able to join a growing band of people dedicated to urban renewal. Once he had finished, he was determined to see the world outside of Brazil. Aided in part by a government grant, and supplemented by a series of part-time jobs, he applied to and was accepted on a summer programme at the University of Copenhagen. This was a great opportunity to learn first hand how the city had reduced its carbon footprint. During his time there he was inspired by the subtle combination of investment in electric transport, the creation of bicycle lanes across the whole town, and the pedestrianisation of city streets. His passion now is to bring these ideas to Rio. Since returning, he has been employed part-time by the city council as one of 80 advocates. These are roles part-funded by the government and a number of not-for-profit organisations all keen to change the carbon footprint of the citizens of Rio. The role he and his colleagues have is to advance the issues by coordinating with other advocates to change the public's attitude to transport.

Yesterday Miguel spent the day with a team of other advocates meeting residents in one of Rio's middle-class areas, canvassing their views on a proposed system of congestion charging. While congestion charging has been adopted by many cities across the world, the car-driving citizens of Rio have always stood against such a move, and as an advocate Miguel's role is to hear their concerns and develop strategies to influence them.

Today Miguel has decided he will devote most of his time to a submission he is preparing with a group of people from across the world to the city planners of Lucknow in northern India. This is one of India's fast-growing urban centres and has experienced the road congestion that has taken place across India. He first heard about their problems a month ago when the city planners posted a challenge on InnoCentive for problem solvers to identify strategies for increasing public transportation ridership. He had been keeping an eye open for a challenge that excited him and the fact the city was offering an award of $100,000 for the best submission was an added bonus. The challenge they set was to increase those using public transport by 20% over the coming two years.

Founded in 2001, InnoCentive is a global, online marketplace where organisations in need of innovation can post their challenges. In the past companies, academic institutions, the public sector and non-profit organisations have utilised an ever-growing global network of problem solvers. In 2010 more than 200,000 had registered as problem solvers, and by 2025 the number had surpassed 1 million.

As soon as he saw the Lucknow posting, Miguel reached out to two friends he made in Copenhagen who were as passionate as he was about urban transport. As he videoconferenced with them they decided they needed to increase the scope of the team. So last week he contacted a colleague, José, whom he had known in his university days and who now works on urban planning in Curitiba. José had jumped on the train the previous evening and was due to meet Miguel for the meeting booked for the early afternoon.

As the afternoon progresses, Miguel and José spend two hours on a scheduled hologram meeting with the rest of the team. The challenge they have is to put the final touches to the submission due in two days' time. It's a great couple of hours. The Danish colleagues live in a city that is showcased as having one of the lowest per capita carbon footprints of any in the developed world, and they are keen to share their insights. José, who has come in from Curitiba, also has much to suggest, for unlike Rio Curitiba is a Brazilian city specifically planned to reduce congestion and has a world-class urban transport system.

As the meeting proceeds it's clear that the real challenge with Lucknow is that urban Indians have embraced private car transport with as much gusto as Brazil did in the 1990s, and they have to be persuaded and incentivised to change their habits. To help them think through the question of incentivisation, the team has coopted the ideas of a Danish anthropologist. Jens has made a long-term study of how urban populations use buses and now in his 80s has agreed to mentor the team. He met Miguel when he was studying in Copenhagen and they have kept in touch ever since.

Later in the meeting they are finally joined by Apurna, a 23-year-old Indian entrepreneur who made her money in holo-gram technology. She has become as concerned as Miguel about the carbon footprint emissions of congested cities. Two years ago she formed a social enterprise foundation dedicated to reducing the carbon emissions in her home town of Lucknow. Miguel came across her through Jens, who had been on her advisory group. It's her evening now and she wants to give the team some ideas about what she sees as the real issues and challenges. As the team creates its first draft of the submission, Miguel sends it out to the 50 people in his personal innovation crowd – people he knows will have something interesting and useful to say about it. He knows that when he wakes up in the morning he can expect that his innovation crowd from across the world will have posted their ideas and insights.

What's interesting about Miguel's work is that it encapsulates what is known to be good practice in mass innovation. He has worked with a small group that has created the kernel of the idea and then invited further contributions. The project is seen as exciting, intriguing and challenging by enough people with the time, means and motivation to contribute to it. The tools he uses enable him to distribute the ideas quickly, so he can rapidly gather feedback to test and refine the ideas. By the time the proposal has been sent to Lucknow, it will already have benefited from exten-sive peer review to correct errors and support good ideas.[1]

This is not the first time Miguel has made a submission to InnoCentive. Since its foundation in 2001 it has become one of a growing number of global innovation marketplaces where creative minds like Miguel's can solve some of the world's most important problems. For Miguel, the major motivation is the opportunity to make a difference and to work with others in ideas he finds exciting and meaningful. However, the fact that successful problem-solvers can receive substantial cash awards is also good news. Over the last two years he has been involved with two submissions – one posted by a humanitarian organisation dedicated to urban renewal in south-west China, and another by the government of Tanzania. He was not successful with either of these submissions, but the feedback he got from the coaches at InnoCentive convinced him that he was on the right lines.

All over the world that January day in 2025, people like Miguel, José, Jens and Apurna are working with each other to solve problems. Solving the challenges we saw in the forces of demography, globalisation, carbon and society requires a level of innovation and creativity rarely seen in early generations. What has changed over the decades is that instead of innovation being seen simply as the domain of particular groups, companies or governments, it has become a highly collaborative, cumulative and social activity, in which people with different skills, points of view and insights share and develop ideas around them. In the 1950s the factories like those where Briana's grandfather worked in Detroit made possible the mass production of goods that became the basis of the mass consumption we saw as a key societal trend. In 2025 the technology and the web have made innovation and creativity a mass activity that engages millions of people. They have created the 'cognitive surplus' that sees billions of hours per day devoted to participation as people from across the globe combine their skills and ideas.[2]

Looking back: a day before co-creation

In the optimistic, bright side of the future, by 2025 the world has become a place where cooperation and co-creation are the order of the day and where people from across the world are both willing and able to link up to share ideas and energy. It had not always been like this. To get a feel for just how momentous some of these changes have been, let's return to our reminiscing experiment. Again, you will need to find someone who was working 20 years ago. Here is the question: 'Describe to me in detail a typical working day for you in 1990.' Last time we played the reminiscing experiment, we talked about the actual tasks of the day. This time we are going to change the focus of the reminiscence from what people did to what they thought, what was going on in their heads. Obviously this is a much more difficult task and so we might have to look wider at their context to really understand this.

In 1990 the generational cohort in the ascendant was the Baby Boomers. Born in the 1950s in a world devastated by war, they were reared to compete with the others in this gigantic population. They were also reared to be consumers – it was they, in fact, who began the whole consumer boom and the acquisition of goods that became such a crucial part of the psyche of those generations that followed them. By 1990 the Baby Boomers were in their mid-20s and 30s and the dominant force in the industrial world, with their hopes and aspirations increasingly shaping work.

Their beliefs about the world were shaped in part by the context in which they grew up, just as your beliefs will be shaped by the context in which you grew up. In the 1990s economic theories took centre stage, highlighting the importance of shareholder value and the power of the market. In this economic model people were believed to be motivated primarily by self-interest. People do what is best for themselves with little regard to the needs of others. At this time the 'carrot and the stick' was the way in which corporate behaviour was controlled.

Of course this economic model was not without its doubters. Douglas McGregor, in his 1960 book *The Human Side of Enterprise*,[3] had argued that the authoritarian management style (Theory X) was less effective than the humane style of management (Theory Y). The Theory X manager assumes that the average person dislikes work and will avoid it if they can. Therefore their role is to force performance with the threat of punishment, or the incentive of a reward – hence the carrot and stick. The Theory Y manager takes a more humanitarian approach. These ideas build from Abraham Maslow's insights about self-actualisation which assume that work is as natural as play, and people have a high degree of imagination, ingenuity and creativity in solving organisational problems.[4] However, in reality, while there was a strong theoretical alternative view of human motivation, corporations in 1990 were essentially run along the lines of Theory X. Those that worked in these corporations were predisposed to focus on the carrot and stick and on competition and winning.

This was hardly surprising in a world devastated by the Second World War with all the anxieties that brought. Plus, the booming populations of children in the USA and the UK were brought up as competitors. This was encouraged at school, nurtured in the 'tournament' career systems of companies that pitted people against each other, and made explicit in the '10% out' rule that leaders such as Jack Welsh at GE were later to make a corporate mantra. This was a world of winners and losers. A world where you got to the top through individual endeavour, working hard and making sure that you shone above all your colleagues. The most important people in your life were your boss and your boss's boss, and pleasing them was absolutely the most important way your ascent of the hierarchy could be achieved. Your status was signalled by the company car you drove, the number of windows your office had and the amount of space your secretary had domain over. Cooperating with others and reaching out to co-create was neither technologically possible nor indeed baked into the mindset of the competitive Baby Boomers.

The gift of diversity in co-creation

Much has changed since then, and indeed will continue to change in the coming decades. What we can see in Miguel's story is that cooperation is at the heart of the endeavour that he and his colleagues are engaged in.[5] What is also fascinating about this story is how different this group is to one another.[6] That's because Miguel has reached out through InnoCentive to people across the world who are as passionate about urban renewal as he is.

What's exciting about Miguel's working life is that this diversity is not simply about national differences (recall that in his problem-solving team are Brazilians, two people from Denmark and an Indian social entrepreneur). It's also about a diversity of mindset. Sure, what brought this group together was a common passion – but what they also bring is a diversity of experience and knowledge. Jens the anthropologist brings both deep ethnographic experience and a point of view about changing human behaviour which goes back over 60 years. Or consider Apurna, who brings a freshness of approach, a deep insight into the working of the Indian mind, plus a first-class education from the Indian Institute of Management in Bangalore. What is crucial about Miguel's endeavour is that he has been able to attract a diverse and differentiated pool of people keen to solve the problem. It's not simply about information diversity – after all, Miguel could simply go to Google or Wikipedia for a plethora of information. What's crucial about this diversity is that it is also based on problem-solving diversity.

We have known about the gift of diversity for years. Perhaps one of the most famous problem-solving exercises was the team that cracked the Enigma code in Bletchley Park during the

Second World War. These where not simply mathematicians, but rather a group of people from many disciplines – engineers, cryptographers, language experts, moral philosophers, classicists, ancient historians and crossword-puzzle experts. It was this combination of ideas and insights that cracked the code.

Miguel, like millions of people around the world, has understood that diversity leads to better outcomes, and in a world as complex as the one Rohan, Miguel and Jill inhabit the possibility of better outcomes is crucial.[7] Miguel understands completely that the group he has assembled from across the globe will create a better outcome than if he had simply asked his college friends their advice. What the members of the team bring is diverse perspectives on the problem of bus usage in Lucknow.

The diversity they bring is about perspectives, interpretations and the generation of solutions. Miguel sees the problem from the perspective of his experience in Curitiba and from what he has seen happening in the favelas in Rio; Jens' interpretation is as an anthropologist – bringing his deep understanding of tribal groups; while Apurna's perspective is as a young Indian determined to make a difference. This diversity within the group also enables them to bring diverse interpretations to the problem of bus usage in Lucknow. As an anthropologist Jens interprets the problem as one of tribal behaviours and how to get key influencers to change their behaviour, so he is likely to come up with ideas about how innovation can be sold to the local community. Miguel's pals from the University of Copenhagen interpret the problem as one of traffic flows on public transport systems, so they are likely to be really interested in the data on passenger movements and the frequency with which buses move around the town. The ways this collection of people from around the world think about generating solutions and predicting cause and effect will also be diverse.

What each brings is a product of their identity, experience and training. What happens when this group begins to share their very diverse ways of thinking can be simply a process of addition. The sophistication of the final solution they come up with will in part reflect the accumulation of what they each know. However, it is not just addition that is taking place as the group struggles to come up with solutions. What is also important to the sophistication of their final solution is the way in which they combine their ideas and perspectives. It's this unique combination that brings the super-additive effect that will help them come up with a solution that is exciting and workable (as Bayesian statistics would predict). Of course, it is not that all the combinations will be useful for Miguel and his colleagues as they wrestle with the problem – but some will and some will bring innovation that could be crucial to the team. For example, the combinations of Jens' ideas about anthropology and Apurna's knowledge about Indian family structure gave them the idea that if you want to get people to use buses, then persuading the teenage members of the family to travel by bus has the effect of encouraging other family members to follow.

Diversity of ideas, points of view, interpretations and solutions is a gift in 2025 because diversity trumps monocultures – collections of people with diverse perspectives and ways of seeing the world can rapidly outperform collections of people who rely on a single perspective.

The world of 2025 has the potential, as we see through the experiences of Miguel and his peers, to be a world of cooperation, where the competitive focus of the Baby Boomers has been replaced by a more cooperative spirit. Much of this has to do with the combination of technological developments and globalisation. When people have the opportunity to be connected and to share ideas that excite and interest them, then they are more likely to want to cooperate and to exchange ideas and knowledge. This has important implications for working life over the coming decades. One of the shifts we will consider is from the isolated competitive employee to the connected, innovative crowd. In Miguel and his colleagues we can see how this connectivity can play out in everyday working behaviour.

How did co-creation arise?

As we look at Miguel's story, what we can see is the way in which the five forces will shape our own working future. We can imagine how the joining together of over 5 billion people will create an incredible momentum for groups like InnoCentive to really capture the imagination and productivity of people across the world. At the same time, we can see how the digitalisation of most of the books of the world by 2025 and their free availability will create a knowledge base that has significantly boosted the prospects of even those born into the poorest of families. The way our societies emerge will also play a role in shaping this story. Imagine if, instead of watching television, people across the world decide to become actively engaged in social participation. And imagine a world where some of these surplus ideas and creativity become focused on a growing culture of sustainability. This is not just imagination – it's the reality of the positive side of globalisation, technology and society.

The globalisation force: five billion become connected

What is perhaps most striking about Miguel's story is the extent to which he is connected to so many people across the world. In fact, the decades from 2010 to 2025 witnessed an extraordinary growth in connectivity. In the year 2000, 109 million people in the USA, 73 million in the Americas, 85 million in China, 32 million in Europe, 10 million in Africa and 4 million in India already had personal mobile phones. Ten years on, and China alone had more mobile subscriptions than all of these figures combined. By 2025 we can expect the number of people connected with mobile phones across the globe to exceed 5 billion.

Even in 2010 two-thirds of the world's internet population visited a social network or blogging site, and the sector ranks higher than email in terms of internet time. As online ecosystems such as Facebook continued to expand their communicative services, they also became primary platforms of interaction. Propelled by the network effect, by which the value of a service increases in proportion to the number of its users, these social hubs grew at an unprecedented rate. What became known as Web 2.0, the social aspect of the internet, expanded fast, with even the most top-down sites allowing users to comment on stories and share them with friends and colleagues. Web 2.0 represented the first form of social media capable of capturing instantly authentic human connectivity.

The collaborative internet had become a medium to help people across the world communicate with each other. It's the combination of a computer or handheld device and the network capable of carrying data that made this possible. At the most sophisticated, this is the Cloud downloading to high-performance computers, and at its simplest a handheld device or computer and a telephone network. But even those with a simple mobile phone subscription will benefit enormously from connectivity. It only takes the simplest of connective technology for a fisherman in India to find out the price of fish in the various markets along the coast for him to decide where best to land his catch. And it only takes simple connectivity for a rural Kenyan textile maker to be sent a micro-loan that allows her to buy the threads that are crucial to her livelihood. It only takes simple connectivity to enable a Ugandan farmer to receive detailed weather forecasts so that he can plan his harvest, or for a Chinese labourer to receive his weekly schedule. Beyond the immediate benefits to work, mobile phones will also open up gateways for health and education by providing important and up-to-date information.

It is becoming clear that the bright side of technology and globalisation is unimagined global connectivity that will transform the working experiences of many millions of people and potentially propel them into the worldwide talent pool. It was this aspiration that lay behind the many initiatives designed to ensure young people have access to computers. In some cases it was governmental institutions that made the investment, whilst foundations and NGOs also played their part.[8] Take, for example, the US foundation One Laptop Per Child Association USA (OLPC), founded by MIT's Media Lab's Nicholas Negroponte with a mission to 'provide each child with a rugged, low-cost, low-power, connected laptop with content and software designed for collaborative, joyful, self-empowered learning'. In 2007 the foundation launched 'Give One Get One' in which donors received their own X0 laptop, and OLPC sent another on their behalf to a child in a developing country. OLPC had been particularly active in Afghanistan, Uruguay, Brazil, Paraguay and Haiti. Over the following decades other companies, such as Intel, Sinomanic and Inveneo, also joined the race to connect every child to the Internet. At the same time the race was on to put the world's educational material on the Web.

What was becoming ever more clear was that the ability to increase the adoption rate of connectivity was less about economic prosperity, and more about political commitment. Rwanda, for example, had invested heavily in the OLPC scheme in part because of the political commitment of President Paul Kagame, while other African nations were still hesitant about embracing the long-term benefits of connecting their rural populations.[9]

The rising levels of connectivity between 2010 and 2025 had profound implications on the regions of the world. In regions where children had access to the World Wide Web, those who are most capable and most motivated had the possibility of learning from a similar knowledge base as others. That of course did not mean that all children were in a position to take advantage of this – there could be many reasons why a child in a region did not join the worldwide talent pool. Their parents may not support them, or demand that they engage in other activities. Their peer group could mock them for wanting to learn or their teaching could be intermittent and provide little support.

However, for many children over the coming decades we can expect that access to the Web will have transformed their lives. Think back to the kids in Rohan's village and the opportunities the motivated, intelligent child will have to take advantage of the access to the internet and the knowledge held within it. As a consequence, we can anticipate that those regions which have earlier made efforts to enable their children to access educational possibilities through the Web will in the long run be those regions in which talent pools had begun to develop by 2030 and beyond.

Regional connectivity also allowed people like Amon in Cairo to work on global projects. A couple of decades ago it really would not have mattered how educated he was – the simple fact was that there were very few jobs for people with his skills in Egypt. Now with sophisticated connectivity Amon is able to compete with other workers from around the world to participate in the tasks and projects that have been advertised on the Web.

Of course, there is a downside to this. In those regions without good connectivity, workers will increasingly be at an enormous disadvantage – their children will find it more difficult to join the global talent pool and they themselves will be unable to sell their skills on the world spot market, or indeed work with others in global project teams.

Technology force:
the world's knowledge becomes digitalised

Connectivity is an important aspect of the bright side of the future, and is the engine that drives Miguel's connections with his colleagues around the world. However, it is not as simple as who is connected to whom; the other important issue is what they are doing through this connectivity.

There has been a huge push to digitalise the printed knowledge held in the world by creating the Universal Digital Library. Since 2004 various groups, including Google Books, Project

Gutenberg, the Open Content Alliance and national libraries such as the British Library and Carnegie Mellon, had been using scanning centres around the world to digitally capture books. Constant technological developments made the storage, translation and retrieval of the information in the books quicker and cheaper. Some are available free (such as public domain works and out-of-copyright material), while others have to be purchased.[10]

The digitalisation of these books became an incredibly useful source of information. For example, Rohan's brother, who stayed in the village to farm the family land, has access to the very latest ideas about seed development. He is part of a knowledge network developed across rural communities in India that provides critical agricultural information. The project was part of the million-book project developed in a partnership between the UN Food and Agriculture Organization and the US National Agricultural Library.[11] The same is true of Miguel; many of his ideas about how to solve the issues around urban transportation have come from the easy access he and his colleagues have to ideas from across the world.

Billions of people across the world have gained enormously from the many charitable foundations that put more complex learning material on the Web to be used without charge. Amon, for example, learnt his basic computing skills at the age of five from the charity 'e-Learning for Kids', a non-profit foundation that developed interactive programmes that teach languages, science, computer skills, environmental skills, maths, life skills and health.[12]

The technology force: social participation increases exponentially

It's not just e-books and e-learning programmes that helped people across the world to reach their potential – it was also the self-generated content in websites and web pages.

If we look back to 2005, in the USA alone people had access to 1,000,000,000 web pages and around 70,392,567 websites – by 2007 there were 30 billion pages on the World Wide Web. Even in 2009 there was more video content uploaded to YouTube in two months than all the new content on the US TV network since 1948, and every week 220 million new photos were being added to Facebook.[13]

By 2010 there were more than 540 million unique users on Facebook, 425 million on YouTube, 97 million on Twitter, 73 million on MySpace and 38 million on LinkedIn.[14] Increasingly an individual's personal networks had become public knowledge, their activities recorded and their interests shared. At the same time, developments in the Semantic Web allowed these massive data sets to be analysed, understood and their meaning extrapolated. By 2010 there had already been substantial steps in this direction, with sites like Wolfram Alpha able to answer questions ranging from 'How many people lived in America in 1776?' (3.47 million) to 'What is the tallest building in Brazil? (Torre de TV de Brasília). What Wolfram Alpha achieved with statistical data, future search engines – or 'knowledge engines' – will achieve with social data, making sense of the vast data aggregates now available on social networking sites.[15]

Perhaps one of the greatest achievements in self-created content is Wikipedia. Launched in 2001, it had 13,000,000 articles in 200 languages by 2009. Founder Jimmy Wales described Wikipedia as 'an effort to create and distribute a free encyclopedia of the highest possible quality to every single person on the planet in their own language'.

Over time greater and greater participation took place. In part this reflected an important work and social trend in both the creation and use of leisure time. The amount of unstructured time had grown significantly since 1945, fuelled by increases in the developed world in GDP, educational attainment and enhanced lifespan. Much of this free time had been spent watching TV – in 2009, for example, on average across the world people watched over 20 hours a week.[16] That means that a Gen X, born in 1960, has by 2010 watched something like 50,000 hours of TV.[17]

Much of the 200 billion hours of TV watched annually in the USA and indeed across the world had been passive and individual, an audience simply watching their favourite game shows or sitcoms. However, from 2015 onwards a significantly greater proportion of this time was spent actively and collectively. People chose to engage in participation as simple as downloading pictures of their pets, to more complex participation such as working in virtual crowds with others to solve a tough problem, just as Miguel has done with his colleagues from around the world.

Once freed from the passivity of the TV, even if only for one active hour a day, those connected created what Clay Shirky called a 'Cognitive Surplus' of over 9 billion hours per day.[18] It was not simply the extent of the time devoted to participation, it was also the fact that the internet, unlike TV, enabled aggregation. A million people spending one hour watching TV has no cumulative impact – a million people interacting on the internet becomes aggregate at scale.

This level of connectivity and the power of aggregation and self-creation had created wise crowds that were beginning to out-predict experts, and open source innovation that brought the very best ideas of the world together. It had also begun to mark the death of the classic hierarchy. In its place emerged a more peer-to-peer way of working and an understanding that collective intelligence could play a profound role in the world. As the physicist Philip Anderson put it, 'More is different.' When 5 billion people are connected to each other in ways that are active rather than passive, then what will emerge is ideas that behave in ways we have not experienced before, and aggregation creates and shares at unprecedented levels.[19]

Miguel is using the collaborative hub InnoCentive, a global, internet-based hub designed to help connect 'seekers' – those with challenging research problems – with 'solvers', like Miguel. These seekers are people who like him enjoy devising creative solutions to these problems. InnoCentive itself does not generate solutions; rather, it brings together individuals, companies, academic institutions and public-sector and non-profit organisations to do so. Indeed, by 2025 technology enables all kinds of unimagined connections and opportunities, whether for banking in remote parts of the world, e-learning across vast distances, or commerce among individuals or groups who will never meet face to face.[20]

The force of energy resources: a culture of sustainability emerges

One of the recurring themes in the co-creation that Miguel and his colleagues are engaging in is the creation of a sustainable way of living. That has been the central theme of Miguel's work, and the project in India is simply one of a number of sustainability projects he is working on. We can expect this theme to be played out across millions of other people. Miguel is a member of Gen Z, born after 1995. From 2020 onwards they took an increasing central role in the business life of companies across the world. Called by some the Re-Generation[21] and by others the Internet Generation, this group is defined by their connectivity. They've been weaned on reality TV and have embraced the intrusion of 24-hour global news into their bedrooms. They are acutely aware of the phrases 'housing crisis', 'double-dip recession' and 'quantitative easing' and they know that the ice caps are melting. This is a generation of realists and pragmatists. For them, the challenge is to rethink, renew and regenerate, since many of the issues they face – climate change and resource limitation, for example – require more tangible actions than ever before.

But despite this realism, they are also a generation that predominantly functions in the hyper-real construct of the internet. If Gen Y witnessed the emergence of this technology, Gen Zs like Miguel are the first to take it for granted. By linking the worlds of the real and the hyper-real, it is this generation that began so powerfully to bring the power of the Internet to bear on the pragmatic challenges they face.

Miguel is a member of a worldwide community that absolutely believes they hold the key to downsizing the influence of fossil fuels.[22] People like Miguel understand that the world of business and government is simply an aggregate of the individual desires of many billions of people. For Miguel this does not mean ostracising himself from the rest of the world, but it does mean that he understands his physical territory will contract while his virtual territory expands. For him, and the community he is a part of, the challenge is to leave a small footprint while attaining a high quality of life (rather than simply a high standard of living). To do this requires him to develop a renewed emphasis on what is important – and also a deep understanding of energy efficiency.

Even in 2010 these differences in energy efficiencies were being played out in countries across the world. For example, the average Japanese citizen used the same amount of energy as a Russian, yet enjoyed more than three times the latter's material well-being. The average American consumed more than twice as much energy as the average British citizen per year, yet enjoyed just 10% more GDP per capita.[23] What was becoming increasingly clear in these regional differences was that high energy use does not automatically convert to a high quality of life. It would seem that the Japanese and the British were managing to do more with less. Over the coming decades the emphasis was increasingly upon reducing individual, corporate and regional energy use.

Miguel and his community saw a particular challenge with the industrialisation of China and India, which in 2015[24] became the world's biggest energy consumers.[25] That's one of the reasons why he has decided to focus on the city of Lucknow in India as the site of his ideas. Miguel, like many other members in his community, is paranoid about limiting unnecessary energy expenditure, and keen on experimentation and adoption of any efficiency innovations as soon as they arise.

Ideas from Miguel's story will play an important role in the future-proofed shifts I believe will be crucial as each one of us learns to thrive in the future. The extent to which he has been prepared to hone his own skills and competencies resonates with the first shift we need to make, towards serial mastery. Like Miguel, you will have to be dedicated to developing skills in areas you love and which you believe will bring meaning to your working lives. In his relationships with others he has made the important second shift towards a cooperative and connected way of working. Over the coming decades, technological connectivity combined with unlimited access to the world's knowledge will create extraordinary opportunities to become part of a Big Ideas Crowd, where we can all buzz with energy and ideas. In Miguel's story you can also see how embracing the third shift towards becoming an impassioned producer has really paid off for him. In doing so you will be faced with making some tough choices, but, like his, your working future will increasingly be about productive experiences and meaningful work, rather than voracious consumption.

6

SOCIAL ENGAGEMENT: THE RISE OF EMPATHY AND BALANCE

John and Susan's story

As the sun sets on January 2025, John makes a final visit to the village elders of the small community in Chittagong he is working with. He wakes early in the morning to visit one of the sites of the water pumps he has been monitoring. He has heard that it is malfunctioning and is keen to see what the problem is. From 10 a.m. onwards he uses his mobile phone to talk with his colleagues in the USA about some of what he has seen over the last week. He catches a couple of them at home in the evening and they are pleased to hear his progress. By 12.00 John and his partner Susan are ready to sit down to a simple lunch of rice and vegetables with some of the local volunteers, and by 1.00 he is back out in the field. Then there are three hours of hard labour as he helps a team to install a water-purifying unit in one of the remote villages. By 4.00 he sits down to a meeting with a fellow NGO worker to talk about how to make progress with a particularly tough problem that has occurred as an upstream dam is threatening to collapse, with devastating effects on the surrounding villages. They decide to have supper together and then complete the day by walking home to the simple guesthouse that John shares with Susan and his young family.

John and Susan have spent the last year as volunteers in Bangladesh supporting a humanitarian aid organisation negotiating water rights for the villages surrounding the city. Every five years

John has taken six months off from his full-time work with a major US retailer to dedicate his time to supporting the very poorest in Chittagong. This year his whole family have decided to come with him. The story began for John when he was a young trainee in 2007. At that time he was appalled to see the terrible effects of the devastating flood that year on those living on the flood plain of the Ganges Delta. He was determined to do something about it and went about raising money for relief operations. Within two years he decided to increase his work with the community by visiting them and assisting in the ongoing battles they had over water. Since that early visit he kept in touch with the community, and heard from them the daily challenges they face as the water in the Ganges Delta continued to rise, flooding more and more of the arable land of the villages with contaminated salt water.

By 2015 he had decided to spend six months in a village and went back for another six months in 2020 to work on the relocation of the villages as the continuing flooding of the delta made their life impossible. By 2025 he had twinned the branch of his company in Oklahoma to the village he works with, and on this visit had brought with him the advanced computers and mobile devices the branch had bought for the villagers.

For John and Susan it has also been really important that their children understand the challenges faced by people in Bangladesh. In 2012 their son Jimmy was born, followed three years later by Gabriel. Now young teenagers, they have moved their home school to Bangladesh for the year in order to join their mother and father in the village. Connected to their home school base by a strong internet connection, they spend four hours a day studying with their peers and the rest of the day with John and Susan as they tour the villages and work with government officials and aid agencies. This has been a really fascinating experience for all of them. Jimmy has become very involved in a teenager global group that communicates to other teenagers across the world the devastation caused by global warming. Every weekend he uploads videos of what he sees and spends time coaching the village children about how best to hook up to the home-schooling material they receive.

For John it has become a key part of his life that he blends his life working as a retail manager with his time in the community in Chittagong. His year in 2025 is a culmination of almost 20 years of involvement in water rights in Bangladesh. He did not start as an expert, but over the years has learnt more and more about the challenges and the solutions and joined many other 'expert volunteers' around the world. What is clear is that the rapid acceleration of energy use across the developed and developing world has by 2025 created a raft of challenges that only a multiple of initiatives can solve.

Looking back: a pre-empathy world

In this brightest of possible futures, what had been the impetus for John and Susan and many others like them to become engaged with the challenges of a country on the other side of the globe? What their story illustrates is the rise of what we might call the 'global mindset'. Rewind back to 1990 and this global mindset did not yet exist. At that time the majority of people took their holidays in their own country, few American citizens owned a passport, and even in Europe travel was expensive. This local rather than global mindset was also largely true of companies, even large companies such as Philips, Nestlé, Coca Cola or Toyota. These were essentially companies with large home markets and what was termed 'overseas operations'. These companies had indeed established factories and plants outside their key markets – but these tended to operate as separate fiefdoms. What this meant was that managers went on 'overseas trips' sometimes for months on end, and high-potential managers were sent as ex-patriates to run overseas operations. But these managers with 'overseas operations' were a tiny minority of the total employee group. In 1990 the majority of people spent most of their time with others who had a similar nationality, background and point of view.

It's a world where most people spent most of their time with others of the same nationality and often similar experience, a world where very few people had personal computers, and where the connectivity of the World Wide Web was simply a dream. The downside of the hyper-connected world that emerged will be fragmentation and isolation. But the upside of a hyper-connected world is that through the very process of connectivity a global mindset begins to emerge as people travel more, understand others more deeply and through this understanding begin to empathise with their situations. This shift towards empathy was first noticed in the 2007 version of the World Values Survey, which had shown a clear trend towards growing empathy among the younger generation, at least in the more developed nations of the world.[1]

It was these feelings of empathy that had first connected John and Susan to a region on the other side of the world. They are not alone in their quest. Across the world of 2025, millions of other people are on the same path as John and Susan – people who have an awakened sense of empathy and who have decided to give their time to causes that are important to them. Some, like John, are linked into some of the poorest places in the world. Others use their time and expertise to load learning material on to the web, to coach and mentor people across the world, or to lobby corporations and governments in areas that they are passionate about. This world view has created greater feelings of empathy, not just for their immediate family but also reaching further out to others who are different from them and to whom they are strangers. What could happen over these 20 years is the shaping of a human nature that is predisposed to affection, companionship, sociability and empathy.

Balanced lives

It's not just empathy that has created the social engagement that has been so much a part of the working lives of John and Susan. Social engagement has also created for both of them the possibility of balancing the various aspects of their lives – be that work, charity, parental responsibilities or community commitments. This balance has been part of John's working life since the time he took a gap year between school and college. It was at this time that he became passionate about what was happening in Bangladesh. Once he finished university he began to work for one of the major retailing companies as a graduate trainee. Unusually for someone of his generation, John has stayed with the same company for most of his working life. The reason is primarily because, although they don't pay in the upper quartile, John enjoys the work, and more importantly, the company was one of the first retail groups to really give employees the opportunity to tailor-make their working sched-ule. For John this means the opportunity to spend time with his children, and to devote his attention to the issues that are important to him.

John is not alone here. All across the world people are think-ing hard about the choices that they make and the consequences of their choices. For John the issue of spending time with his children has always been a priority. Looking back to his own childhood, his recollection of his own father is hazy. His father worked for US multinational firms and spent very little time at home. When he was at home his Blackberry took up most of his time. John has always been grateful to his dad for what he had provided for the family – for example, his gap year between school and college was funded by his father's income. But what he also became aware of was the consequences of his father's choices. Yes, they had a big house, two big cars and were able to take a couple of holidays a year. But the consequence of this was that both John's parents worked full-time, his father saw very little of him, and, far away from grandparents, John had a rather lonely and isolated childhood.

When John married Susan one of the big conversations they had was about the sort of working lives they wanted to lead. At that time Susan was training to be a physician and wanted to specialise in cancer treatment. They came to the conclusion that a life more balanced than their parents' lives would be a priority. This meant for John that he continued to work with a company where he would never be rich, and for Susan that she took a job that was three days a week.

There were indeed consequences of the choices they made. It meant that they did not buy a house, choosing instead to rent. It also meant that they did not have a car – finding a place to live where the kids could walk to their social activities and Susan could walk to work. When they needed a car they simply used the rental cars parked in the main street of the town. The other lifestyle decision they made was to home-school their children. When John was at school this was a growing trend in the USA – with an increasing number of American children being home-schooled.[2] John remembers a couple of children in his neighbourhood being home-schooled and liked what he saw. Plus, from 2015 onwards the amount of material for learning had increased to such an extent that it was possible for his children to learn even the most specialist material with ease.

What had made it really exciting for John and Susan was the link-up with the school in Chittagong. John had come back with tales of how hard it was for the children of the village to get to the nearest school. As he and Susan began to home-school their own children, they saw an opportunity to bridge to the community in Chittagong. As a consequence, on one of the early visits John had made sure that a couple of simple computers were available to the children. For the initial years the internet access was very patchy, but over time a more reliable internet connection was up and running. From that time onwards, part of the role of the home school in John's town was to reach out to the school in Chittagong to share ideas about what they were learning, to mentor the students and to set up peer coaching so the Chittagong children could also coach the home-schooled children.

A highlight for John and Susan was the time they took a group of children to visit the Bangladesh school. The children had already been introduced over Skype, had conducted virtual classes together and had even played each other in online games. But despite these interactions, they had yet to meet face to face. The excitement at meeting their much-loved classmates for the first time was an extraordinary experience and one that John and Susan's children fondly remembered as they continued to support their friends in the village.

Like the working lives of John and Susan, the future of your work can progress along many possible paths. Deciding which path to take will play an important part in your capability to find and craft work that has meaning and productivity. What we can see from this story is that both John and Susan love what they do at work. Both have taken an active choice to balance and blend their work with the other parts of their lives that they valued. If you are to do this for yourself, then like John and Susan you will be called upon to make some tough choices, particularly about your standard of living and lifestyle. John and Susan were prepared to trade a big house and car for more time bringing up their children, and more time to support the village they had both grown to love. For you the equation will be different and unique to your particular needs – but, as we shall see in the third future-proofed shift, each one of us will have to confront head on what it is we want from our working lives and the trade-offs we are prepared to make to achieve this.

Why did social engagement take off?

The demographic force: the ascendancy of Gen Y

One of the central aspects of John and Susan's story is that they are both Gen Y and have some of the attributes we can see emerging in this generation around the world.

Like many other Gen Ys born around the world, John was raised by Baby Boomer parents who lavished care and attention on him and his sister. His was a generation that had longer periods of adolescence than any previous generation. Even as a child he began to understand that some people were different from him and could begin to understand the impact different parts of the world had on his own experiences. As a child he had seen television programmes about starvation in sub-Saharan Africa and the impact of global warming on the planet. Like hundreds of thousands of youngsters across the world, John took a year off between school and university, in his case to volunteer to go to Bangladesh, where he saw at first hand the devastation caused by over-population and rising sea levels.

John and his generation also had more notions of economic interdependence than any previous generation. They grew up knowing that the sneakers they wore could be made by a child labourer in India; or the reason their parent lost their job was because a competing factory had opened in China with a labour force on 20% that of the USA. They also had more cosmopolitan lifestyles – they ate sushi one day and taco another; went to Florence one year and Cambodia the next; had Facebook friends in the Amazon basin and in the outback of Australia. As a member of Gen Y, John is part of the first truly joined-up, global generation and this has made people like him more understanding of differences, better able to see the other's point of view – and, in a word, more empathic.

It's a generation who are members of virtual communities, with 'friends' all over the world, who are familiar with diversity and more accepting of differences. Already by 2010 their working preferences had emerged. This is a generation who are technically savvy, very comfortable using technology at work, and who prefer to communicate through email and text messaging rather than face-to-face contact. They are also at ease with webinars and online technology as a method of distributing information and learning.

As I discovered in my research on the ways that Gen Y are developing in the workforce,[3] the overwhelming focus of their work is on the opportunity to learn and to develop their competencies. So they are likely to choose work that has a high learning component, and peers whom they can learn from. When we asked them what they disliked about work, the overwhelming negative aspect for them was Baby Boomer bosses who over-managed and under-coached.

As this generation assumed managerial roles themselves in the 2020s, many of them, like John, cared a great deal about building families and crafting a work–life balance. They value the idea of being parents, want to spend time with their own children, and the young men want to play a more active role in bringing up their children. This is a generation that has been brought up in teams and puts a big emphasis on being team players. They have learnt to be more cooperative than their competitive Baby Boomer parents. Here is how one of our Gen Y members of the Future of Work Consortium described it:

It's not unusual for my peer group to choose working for a particular person because of what they can teach you, rather than the content of the job description. The managers/employers that do really well in terms of attracting 'bright young things' seem to be those who offer face-to-face time to develop their staff, share their knowledge and challenge every member of their team – right down to admin assistants.

And this is not just a Western perspective; here is an Indian executive's view on the Gen Ys in his office in Mumbai working for a multinational company:

> Gen Y wants a lot of freedom at the workplace (no questions from the manager as long as the job is getting done!), a chance to develop complete mastery in a particular area of work so that they are adding value to themselves, and a chance to be a part of something bigger that their immediate job. The most difficult part, however, is the time frame they are willing to give their employers to deliver on these. I think the big difference between Gen X & Gen Y finally boils down to patience. Gen X was willing to think long term/career/go through a bad patch etc. while Gen Y thinks short term/project or contract/ will quit at the slightest provocation.

Societal force: the rise of reflexivity

Take another look at John's story, this time from the perspective of the active choices he has decided to make. He actively chooses to take a year off between school and college and then to subsequently choose a company that allowed him to go to Bangladesh for periods of his life. He and his wife actively chose to home-school their children, and then they actively chose to bring them with them as they moved to Bangladesh for a year. They actively chose to rent a house rather than buy, and they actively chose not to buy a car. What we can see in John and Susan's working life is a life that has been actively crafted from making choices, rather than passively lived according to others' standards. By crafting their own stories they have created a life that is both unique to them and diverse from others.

We can anticipate that in the brightest future of 2025 John is not alone in this. All around the world we can imagine that billions of people are choosing to take control of their working lives and to craft them in a way that resonates with their own values and aspirations. This unique crafting has the potential to create a great deal of variety in what is considered possible. How did this come about? For the sociologist Anthony Giddens, what we see in John's highly personal choices reflects a more general shift in society. This is the shift from always taking the path trodden by others to a path that is more reflective of an individual's needs and preferences. As a sociologist, Giddens sees echoes of this in the changing nature of relationships between the employer and the employee; and in the changing nature of the relationship between partners in a marriage. Both these signal, and also themselves play a part in, the development of a more thoughtful, reflective and individual sense of oneself and work.

If we take a look at three decades of relationships and marriage, there is an interesting sub-plot that is revealed. My grandparents' marriage, for example, which took place in the 1920s, could well have signalled a transition point between a time when marriage was seen as an economic necessity to a time when it was conceived as a more romantic and emotional enterprise. That was certainly the case for my own parents, who eloped to marry at a young age, much to the annoyance of their mothers. By the time of their marriage the notion of 'romantic love' had been well established.[4]

With this came a greater variety of family life. Take a look at family sitcoms. In the 1960s and 1970s all across the Western world, families like mine watched families on the TV – families like that of Lucille Ball or the Waltons – good, homely families with a working father, a home-making mother and a brood of well-behaved children. My own children were raised on *The Simpsons* – a goofy dad but still a relatively stable family of mother, father and three children; then *Friends*, not a family as such but a close-knit group of twenty-somethings. By 2010 the most popular family TV show in my family is *Modern Family* – made up of a male gay couple and their child, connected in some way (here the plot eludes me) to an older, previously married father and his younger child. The plot is replete with stepmothers and fathers and stepchildren. The sheer variety of these families and their diversity is part of what Anthony Giddens calls 'reflexivity' – the invention of the self through debate and self-reflection. This is the debate that comes from the question 'Who am I?' It is questions like these that result in the energetic creation of a 'storyline' that illustrates and adds richness to our personal life narrative.

It's not just family structures that show the extent to which reflexivity has been at play. Take a quick look at the books you have about yourself and your personal development. A cursory glance at my own bookshelf reveals a well-thumbed copy of *Passages* written by Gail Sheehy in 1976 (which I can see from my annotations I read in 1978), followed by a whole shelf that mirror my own development and that of my children – books on bringing up babies, how to cope with teenagers, dealing with divorce – no doubt to be increased by whatever comes next.[5] This self-analysis is a recent phenomenon. Take a look at your parents' reading material. Your mother may have had one or two books about herself (I recall guiltily discovering a copy of Alex Comfort's *The Joy of Sex* at the back of my mother's cupboard. She was not alone in owning this book, of course; it sold a mighty 8 million copies[6]), but your grandmothers will not have read books about themselves. I recall my grandmothers certainly had no books about their development or their lives – although you might have found a copy of Mrs Beeton's *Household Management*. Theirs was not a generation that reflected on themselves; mine was, and it's likely that Gen Y and the generation that follows them – Gen Z – will be increasingly so; reflexivity is increasing, and as we think about ourselves and make active choices about our lives, so variety increases and the diversity of what is acceptable becomes ever wider.

What has also happened is that 'work' and 'life' have become increasingly intertwined. John and Susan have not slavishly followed institutional norms about what is acceptable. Instead, they have constructed a working life that reflects what is unique to them. Just as we are becoming more tolerant of variety in our personal lives, so too we have become more and more tolerant of what is deemed acceptable in our working lives.

Societal force: the role of powerful women

John works for one of the well-known retail American multinational companies that employs more than a million people in the USA and beyond. In the 1990s this company had a straightforward contract with employees – work full-time and we will pay you full-time. In fact, when John took his first trip to Bangladesh he took it as part of his holiday entitlement and was not paid for the days beyond that. By the 2000s the managers, like others around the world, began to experiment with a more flexible working contract. They began to see that for people like John the opportunity to have a more flexible arrangement was key to their staying in the company.

Over time, the view of a unitary, one-track career had begun to break down, leaving the opportunity for people like John to create a life that could be shaped around his interests and aspirations. In part this reflected the societal trends in reflexivity, but it also reflected the growing number of women in senior executive positions, some of whom more actively created role models of blended lives.

It's likely that the next two decades will see some extraordinary changes in the lives of working women across the world. You only have to think about your own mother and grandmother to see this for yourself. My own generation, born around 1950, was in a sense the first generation in which women could truly aspire to work side by side with men. I guess this was something of a pioneering generation – moving through unmapped territory, shifting aspirations and self-identity as we were confronted by the changes in the nature of marriage, the family and work. In the MBA classes I teach, I see how the current generation of young women feel immensely positive about the options available to them, and believe that they can make a significant contribution to work. Of course, there are doubts about how they can balance this with the needs of motherhood. But most have sufficient female role models around them to provide broad guidance of the options.

The members of the Future of Work Consortium could see some of these changes themselves. Here is how one described it:

> I see men doing more and more of what women have done traditionally. (I have recently met 3 stay-at-home dads who are doing an excellent job of raising kids while the mom is busy at work.) Likewise, I see women doing a lot more of what was traditionally a male dominated sphere. One thing is for sure – by 2020 or 2030 for sure, women are going to outnumber men in management roles!

In 2010 around 50% of graduates entering companies were women. In fact, in many developed countries such as the USA women were achieving greater educational qualifications than their male counterparts (in 2011, for example, there were 2.6 million more female than male university students in the USA). There are, of course, sectoral differences – women were less represented in engineering and manufacturing sectors, and more represented in some of the professions and sectors such as PR and marketing.

However, during this period of time, while women were entering companies in equal numbers to men, they were not getting to the top. By 2010 around 30% of managers were women, again with the expected sectoral differences. At that time, the percentage of women employed at senior executive or board level tended to be around 10% and was rarely more than 15%.[7]

Most of the studies of this fall-off along the corporate ladder put the reduction down to a combination of personal attributes (women do not negotiate as strongly or network with powerful men); structural issues (women tend to take specialist roles such as law or HR, which are not typically developmental escalators to the top); organisational culture (with 'masculine' traits over-valued in senior roles); and reasons of family structure (it is hard for women to return to a fast-track career after having children, and the majority of men are unprepared to take an equal role in bringing up children).

However, despite these factors we can expect these proportions to change over the coming decades. One accelerating force will be government legislation. In 2006, for example, the Norwegian government passed a law that forbade companies from employing less than 40% of women on executive boards. Over the following three years CEOs and chairmen across Norwegian companies engaged in a number of activities to find, develop and persuade women to join their boards. By the end of 2008 the exercise was considered by many a success – with women holding 44.2% of executive board positions.[8] At this point other governments voiced an interest in adopting similar legislation.

Another accelerating force will be the changing nature of the aspirations of Gen Y and Gen Z men who want to spend more time with their families. As more women get to the top, so too the corporate cultures become less macho and more accommodating to diverse individual needs.

As a result of these various pressures, by 2025 a significantly greater number of women are in senior executive positions – in some companies taking 50% of these roles. The impact of a greater number of women at the top has been to add considerably to the stock of possible role models available to younger female employees. This broader diversity has also increased the opportunities to live what we might call 'individualised' lives. Greater numbers of women at the top have also signalled the appropriateness of taking responsibility for families as a legitimate work priority.

Societal force: the balanced man

It is not just the position of women that has transformed working conditions for people like John and Susan. Something has also happened to men. Ideas about the role of men and women had begun to change in the 1980s. By 1992 the sociologist Anthony Giddens had asked the question, 'What do men want?' His answer was this: 'In one sense the answer has been clear and understood by both sexes from the nineteenth century onward. Men want status among other men, conferred by material rewards and conjoined to rituals of male solidarity.'[9] He goes on to reflect that until that time the nature of man was concealed by a range of social influences, all of which have now been, or are being, undermined. This range of concealed social influences includes the domination of men over the public sphere, the problematising of women as opaque or irrational in their desires or actions, and the sexual division of labour.[10]

As more women moved into senior positions in companies, they began to change the nature of work in all three areas of social influence on which Giddens reflects. As more women entered senior positions at work, so the domination of men over the public sphere began to wane. As more women entered senior positions, so the stereotypical description of them as opaque or irrational began to ebb, to become broader and more diverse. Finally, with regard to the sexual division of labour, as more working mothers attained significant roles, so the traditional division of home labour – where working women take the lion's share of work in the home – began to fade.

As a result of this, in many companies such as the one John works with, the culture has become less masculine and men are able to bring more of their home life to work – in the way that women traditionally had.

As we leave John's story you can reflect on some of the shifts that you have to make if you have aspirations to achieve a blended life like John's. What is interesting about John's story is that he has really embraced the second shift – and has become cooperative and connected to people across the world. But perhaps more importantly, in John's story we can see the power of becoming an impassioned producer – of making the most of experiences and of creating a working life that allows and enables him to create experiences, like those in Bangladesh, that have brought meaning and happiness to his everyday work. We can expect our world of work to change fundamentally over the coming decades – and in particular we can expect the traditional roles of men and women to evolve. If you are to make the very most of these changes, you will have to develop the insight and reflexivity that were so much part of the working lives which John and Susan have constructed. That means becoming aware of what is truly important to you, and being able to make the choices that will enable this working life to emerge.

7

MICRO-ENTREPRENEURSHIP: CRAFTING CREATIVE LIVES

The story of Xui Li, Bao Yu and Chenh-Gong

Xui Li rises at 6.00 this morning in 2025, stretching herself in the garden of her small house on the outskirts of Zhengzhou in the Henan province of China. Today will be a good day. She is expecting her grandson Chenh-Gong and is excited about what news he will bring her of his latest project.

By 8.00 she has had a simple breakfast before taking a video call with two of her embroiderers. Her love of fabrics came from her mother, who often told stories of her own life and how she dreamed of wearing something different from the Red Guards' ill-fitting and inelegant uniform. Xui Li's passion is clothes and the local handicrafts for which her region is renowned. She began her working life with a small tailoring business, using old *Vogue* patterns to make dresses for the weddings and anniversaries of the town. Over time her reputation spread, and she became known beyond her immediate suburb for the dresses she made – and, in particular, the hand embroidery on the dresses. Her speciality was embroidery that made use of small freshwater pearls. In these early years she had taken on a couple of seamstresses and opened a shop to sell her dresses. Her hope was that her daughter would join – but Bao Yu wanted to study as a teacher rather than follow her mother. Life has changed a great deal for Xui Li. She was born in a country still led by Mao Zedong, and can recall the stories her parents told her about their time in the Red Guard at work in the collective farms of the countryside.

This morning she is talking to her embroiderers about a particularly tricky dress they are working on. Xui Li no longer owns a shop; instead she is one of 10,000 business partners in the Li & Fung group. She had heard about the group more than ten years ago when a friend introduced her to one of the partners involved with embroidery on cocktail dresses. Xui Li began with a small order of crêpe de chine blouses with pearl embroidery and found she enjoyed being part of a bigger community. Now she oversees the making and embroidering of over 25 dresses a week – all of which have unique embroidery designs. She no longer needs the shop – instead trading directly with the partnership. Her conversation this morning with her embroiderers is tough. Standards in the partnership are very high; only last week she had a conference call with one of the silk manufacturing partners to ensure that the silk she would use this week was the exact weight and colour for the dresses. Today she has to check that the production quality is faultless and to be sure that logistics will get the dresses to the Li & Fung warehouse in the centre of the town by the afternoon.

Her working life is certainly more demanding than when she simply made a few dresses a week, which she sold in her one-roomed shop. Now she has to meet the standards required and to coordinate across the whole range of other partners who are involved in designing the dresses, buying and dying the silk, and stitching the dresses before she receives them for the final embroidery. She has learnt to her cost that when a particular colour is specific – then that's exactly the colour they want. What helps her keep up to date is the computer in her workroom, which is linked to all the other partners she is involved with, and gives her minute-by-minute analysis of the production chain.

By 11.00 her videoconference is over and Xui Li can sit down for a cup of tea with Bao Yu, who she has come to ask her advice about a particular problem she is experiencing with the straw bags she sells on AliBaba – one of the world's largest online trading places. Both mother and daughter are traders on AliBaba; Xui Li trades in freshwater pearls, while Bao Yu trades in the straw handbags that are handmade in the countryside. Bao Yu use Alibaba.com in English to reach out to the international marketplace, particularly to the Boston and Californian regions that are so crucial to her business.[1] Xui Li mostly uses www.1688.com when she buys the pearls from wholesalers across China. What's made a real difference for both of them is the investment the company made in 2015 in AliBaba Cloud Computing. This is an advanced data-centric Cloud-computing platform that allows them to use high-speed e-commerce data processing as well as data customisation. When Xui Li joined in 2010 there were 50 million registered users; now there are more than a billion.

After talking through a particularly thorny logistics problem, Bao Yu wants to show her mother the music she has been composing. Both spend the next half hour listening as the melody fills the room. For Bao Yu, one of the real opportunities of studying at Zhengzhou University was the opportunity to go on an exchange to South Korea. It was here that her passion for music and writing really took off. What also bowled her over was her experience of OhmyNews. Back in 2007 the site had a handful of employees, yet was able to orchestrate the work of tens of thousands of 'citizen reporters'. From across the country they submitted articles and opinion pieces on any aspect of current affairs. It was also at that time that she noticed that most of her hosts at Seoul's National University of Education had 'minihompys' (mini homepages for online photosharing, journals and networks). She began to create her own minihompy when she returned to China. Over the coming years this helped her to keep in touch with her Korean friends, and on two occasions to play host to their children.

Both live the lives of micro-entrepreneurs, Xui Li in garment embroidery, and Bao Yu in handbag manufacturing and selling.

What's interesting about both Xui Li's and Bao Yu's life is that neither are full-time employees. Instead, as Li & Fung partners and AliBaba sellers, they are both essentially independent store-owners, deciding for themselves what to sell, when to sell it, how to advertise it and how to price it.

Micro-entrepreneurs and ecosystems

They are not alone. Across the world in 2025 hundreds of millions of people are working as micro-entrepreneurs and partnering together in what have been called 'ecosystems'.[2] These are gatherings of like-minded people, gathered around an idea. It is these clusters of micro-entrepreneurs, rather than corporations, that are a crucial part of shaping the direction of the market. Like most micro-entrepreneurs, mother and daughter have chosen to work in clusters around something they are passionate about. For Xui Li it is her passion for clothes and fine embroidery, and for Bao Yu it is her dedication to keep the traditional skills of the area alive. Both have made their passion their work.

What Li & Fung and AliBaba have created for them is a shaping platform that serves to connect them with other suppliers and buyers and in doing so supports their cooperation and innovation. The role AliBaba takes is to create a shared trading platform, lay down some simple rules, and make it easy for participants to take part. They also constantly develop state-of-the-art technology to provide members with tools to assist them in this connectivity. These tools range from the item-for-sale form in eBay, which allows members to sell their products, to the rating system by which buyers rank sellers and sellers build up their reputation for reliable customer service.

Mother and daughter are really enjoying what they do – and it's no surprise that self-employed people are twice as likely to be passionate about their work as their peers who work in institutions.[3]

It is not just China, by the way, that has well-developed ecosystems which enable many thousands of micro-entrepreneurs to leverage their skills and competences. In the Prato textile industry in Italy for over 30 years more than 15,000 small entrepreneurial firms, most employing less than five people, have joined together. These, by the way, are not primitive, cottage-industry businesses but firms which use state-of-the-art equipment, joining together in cooperative ventures for functions like purchasing and R&D. Each of these ecosystems is made up of partners or brokers that tie them together. In the Prato industry these are the *impannatori* who help the small companies cooperate by bringing them together to do a particularly large order.[4]

What is a real source of joy for Xui Li and her daughter is that while the ecosystems they work in support and facilitate them, they are not controlled by them. Both are free to make their own decisions about whom to do business with, and on what terms. This autonomy has also worked well in the Prato textile industry of Italy, for out of these decentralised interactions has come some of the most beautiful material in the world, just as from Hunan has come some of the most beautiful embroidery in the world.

In 2025 Xui Li is in her late 60s and within her lifetime has seen some momentous changes in the world. In many senses the ecosystem of which she is a member is almost a natural outcome of the future forces. Technological advances have created the platform which has allowed her to join up at very low cost to so many thousands of other people. If we turn the clock back to 1990 it's clear that this level of connectivity would have been absolutely impossible. In 1990 workers communicated primarily through letters; even by 2000 email connected individuals, but did not connect groups. eBay, for example, was launched in 1996, and over the next decade its platforms and technology, like those at AliBaba, enabled ever-greater numbers of people to be connected, to become entrepreneurial, to produce and to trade.

Before we leave Xui Li that afternoon in 2025, let us linger a moment as she welcomes her only grandson Chenh-Gong fresh from his advanced electronics degree in Shanghai and revelling in his ideas. The afternoon is spent taking a look at their various projects. What Bao Yu learnt from her mother is her love of freedom and the fun – for her it's an energetic, creative life to which she feels very dedicated. When she is not trading the straw bags, she is an active member of the Sibelius community website where as a pro-am composer she publishes and shares her work. When she joined in 2010, Sibelius already had 45,000 member-contributed scores and 20 new scores arriving every day.[5] By 2025 the site is even more exciting, with whole teams from across the world joining together in complex co-productions. Over lunch, grandmother, daughter and grandson reflect that perhaps the most important lesson they have learnt is that how you express yourself creatively through what you make is infinitely more important than expressing yourself through what you buy.

Grandmother, daughter and grandson lead creative lives. For Xui Li this was nurtured during the Cultural Revolution. Her parents had very little and she learnt how to make the most of what they had. She learnt that what made her happy was working with her hands, and although much of the craft involved in the embroidery is now performed by her embroiderers across the city, she still takes much joy in the design. Born in 1981, Bao Yu was able to extend the reach of her creativity way beyond her immediate town. The Sibelius community website is just one example of how she has created some great friends through her passion for music. The spread of tools like Sibelius allowed millions of people across the world to have a sense of self-realisation. For her, creativity is not the preserve of a few people doing jobs designated as 'creative', but a possibility for many.

Both watch as Chenh-Gong uploads a film he has put onto YouTube. He has been incredibly inspired by the finely crafted videos of Lasse Gjertsen, a self-taught filmmaker from Larvik in Norway.[6] Chenh-Gong was only ten when he became one of over 2 million people who had been captivated by the short films Lasse had made. Chenh-Gong's current passion is to capture the rural life in Henan province before it finally succumbs to the rapid strides of urbanisation. He is a member of a growing group of people around the world who are members of campaigning organisations, and was an early member of a global group called 'Witness' with members dedicated to filming situations they wanted to change and then uploading them for the world to see.[7] This inspired him to become a storyteller and media producer, in particular a chronicler of the conditions under which some factory workers in Hunan province still work. When not supporting Witness, Chenh-Gong is a member of a worldwide community of graphic artists who together produce the cutting-edge animated comic strips that are such an important part of the lives of young Chinese. He is busy building a reputation through his blog sites, animations and commissions. As he shows his grandmother his work, they have yet another cup of delicately flavoured tea before watching the sun set over a far-off hill.

Why did micro-entrepreneurs and creative lives arise?

As in all the stories, I have crafted the working lives of Xui Li, Bao Yu and Chenh-Gong from the patches of the five forces. Behind these lives is ubiquitous technology. Just like Jill and Rohan, Amon and John, they all use advanced mobile technology and make use of the Cloud to download complex programs at very low cost. What has also been crucial to the success of their endeavour has been the way in which technological developments have made it possible to have continuous gains in productivity. It's also a story about how the forces of technology have enabled the emergence of mega-companies like Li & Fung in tandem with ecosystems and micro-entrepreneurs like Xui Li and thousands of others like her.

But theirs is not just a story of technology. It is also a story of how the forces of globalisation enabled the extraordinary growth that China experienced as it took its position as one of the leading creators of wealth. Beyond the forces of technology and globalisation are deeper forces, the globalisation of education and the emergence of China, and indeed of India, as educational powerhouses. This has been combined with an increasing emphasis on the globalisation of innovation, once the preserve of the West. Across China and India many companies are frugally innovating around a host of challenges that are making the lives of Xui Li and billions of others a lot easier.

And finally, Xui Li's story is one of enhanced longevity. Now in her late 60s, like millions of others around the world, she loves what she does and is determined to work productively for at least another decade.

Technology force: continuous productivity gains

What have enabled Xui Li and her family to work so productively are the major developments in technology and connectivity.[8] Historically, the productivity of work has been transformed primarily by innovations around technology. For example, much of the productivity increases in the southern USA in the 1930s could be accounted for by the arrival of air conditioning in that hot and humid region.[9]

However, from 1995 to 2000 this technologically led trend continued, with productivity gains in the developed countries the result of massive IT investments and improvements in IT products. From 2000 onwards the sources of productivity gains shifted from pure technology to a combination of technology and organisational assets such as a culture of innovation or teamwork. That's what has made Xui Li's partnership with the Li & Fung group so successful. This has worked because it's a combination of both the best technology and the most appropriate organisational capital that has been developed by creating the right structure, selecting the right people and then rigorously training and developing them.[10]

What the technology which Xui Li and her colleagues use has also done is to make it possible to communicate ideas and information at near-zero costs. Never before has it been so easy for Xui Li or her family to make a perfect and near-costless copy of an original information product. When her grandson sends a brochure to 1,000 people or uses Wikipedia, he is gaining productivity at very, very low cost. In part this is because while the price of most goods Xui Li and her family buy has increased every year, the computers they use are an exception: huge price declines coupled with significant quality improvements have been pervasive year after year.[11]

Technology force:
mega-companies and micro-entrepreneurs

What has also changed the way that Xui Li, Bao Yu and Chenh-Gong work has been the transformations in the structure of companies, and particularly in the boundaries of companies. Advances in technology have expanded the size of firms because people are more able to coordinate with each other at scale. However, advanced technology has also created more permeable boundaries between full-time workers and those who work on a project or joint venture basis. It has enabled tiny businesses like Xui Li's to hook up to others and by doing so to create these clusters or ecosystems that together have scale and power. The very same developments have also led to the rise of the global mega-companies. These, like Li & Fung or AliBaba, are able to speedily coordinate the many hundreds of thousands of people working on tasks for millions of customers. Around this central core of the mega-companies are the ecosystems of thousands of entrepreneurs running small companies all co-coordinating to create services or build products. Think for a moment about the applications on the iPhone – many thousands of which are created by individual small companies, or micro-entrepreneurs, each working with the market that is the ecosystem surrounding Apple.

What's so fascinating about these technological developments is that they make it increasingly easy to coordinate across the horizontal, without always resorting to vertical, hierarchical coordination. Even now we can see this emerging with the crowds of people who work on GNU/Linux using open source code to develop and improve the system. Or we can see it now in the way that Wikipedia is evolving to include hundreds of thousands of people who are actively co-creating a global source of information.

The globalisation force: China's decades of growth

However, beyond the advances in global technology it is difficult to truly understand Xui Li, Bao Yu and Chenh-Gong's working stories in 2025 without knowing something about China. Their country has developed incredibly in Xui Li's lifetime. As a young adult she was already upbeat and optimistic about her economic situation,[12] and in 2015 she saw China's economic output surpass that of the US.[13]

The modern economic history of China began in 1978, two years after the death of Chairman Mao Zedong, when in a speech to the Party Congress Vice Premier Deng Xiaoping made it clear the government would support private investment. Over the following decade Chinese villages such as Huaxi and Liutuan made spectacularly successful investments in village enterprises that became models throughout China. From 2005 to 2010 China's annual growth rate was more than 10%. Xui Li, like most of her friends, is a voracious saver.[14] Back in 2008 when Xui Li got her first credit card, China had only 5 million credit cards. This contrasted with America, which at a quarter the size had 1.3 billion credit cards.[15] In 2010 life was tough, she was working incredibly hard in one of the local factories and her annual wages were $3,500.

Although life was tough, like most Chinese workers, Xui Li had saved carefully for her future. Even in 2008, total gross saving (including personal, corporate and governmental) of the Chinese population was 54% of GDP. That compares, by the way, to around 15% in the USA and 20% in most of Europe.[16]

Since the 1980s, Xui Li and her colleagues had embraced their position as the factory for the world. Many of her colleagues worked in the factories that made the shoes that Nike sold and the components that Apple put into their phones. This huge manufacturing sector of which she was a part had grown as a result of the lower wages of Chinese workers, but also through the government's policy to drive manufacturing. This period also saw a rapid development of an infrastructure that supported the transportation and export of goods. In 2010, for example, over 40 airports were under construction in China. This not only allowed for the development of integrated domestic and international industrial chains, but also facilitated continuous urbanisation.

By 2010 Xui Li had begun to see her work and the work of others become more sophisticated. Before that time she had worked in one of the factories and as a sideline had employed a couple of people in her embroidery business. About that time she left the factory and decided to concentrate instead on building her business. Over the following years she saw it continuously rise up the value chain as she and her partners put more emphasis on innovations in cost reduction and customer value.[17] By 2015 she had joined the Li & Fung network of companies and this allowed her to access flexible networks that enabled her to work closely with a network of more than 12,000 companies in more than 40 countries. In the space of one decade her world had gone from local to global.

As Xui Li looks around the place in which she has spent most of her life, what's clear is that China's remarkable growth has been propelled by a handful of regions which attracted the majority of its most talented people and generated the bulk of its innovations. Xui Li knows very well that cities such as Shanghai,

Shenzhen and Beijing are a world apart from the vast rural populations of China, the majority of whom in 2010 were living on less than $150 a month.[18] Like much of the world in 2025, she can see that the powerhouses of Chinese talent are becoming ever more concentrated, and with this have come increasing regional disparities.

However, as fast growing as it is, by 2010 China was still an emerging economy: it ranked 30th in the Davos Competitiveness Index and 81st on the UN Human Development Index. Since that time the growing infrastructure built across China, the high literacy rates and skilled labour force have all worked to its competitive advantage. But Xui Li is painfully aware that it is a major challenge for China to ensure that its vast rural population benefits from the rapid growth in the industrial and knowledge sectors.

The globalisation force: the global educational powerhouses

The rise of the global creative class, of which Xui Li's daughter and grandson are members, reflects a wider educational push across much of Asia. Per capita, in 2010 Europe and the USA had proportionally more children in higher education than either China or India (India in 2010 still had 33% illiteracy across the total population), and compared to the European powerhouses like Finland (where 27% of the population aged 15 and over hold postgraduate qualifications) India and China look like laggards.

However, the reason why both India and China created such large numbers of educated people was due in part to their huge populations. In 2010 Asia had a population of over 4 billion, and by 2030 that will rise to 5 billion – with Europe and America's population relatively stable over the same period of time at around 1.5 billion.

What's also important to the educational story is specifically what Indian and Chinese students actually study. While the students of the West will study a range of topics including humanities and the arts, Indian and Chinese students like Xui Li's grandson and Rohan and his brother are more likely to focus resolutely on the sciences. As a consequence, in 2008 India and China each produced twice as many people with advanced degrees in engineering or computer sciences as the USA. It is also important to realise that in America, in the same year, 40% of masters degrees and 60% of doctoral degrees in engineering were awarded to foreigners, most of them members of the Indian or Chinese diaspora.

It's not simply that India and China had increased their educational prowess during Xui Li's lifetime. During that period these countries had also become centres of talent development. Take Rohan's brother Amit for example who, along with over 10,000 other people, received his initial training from the Indian IT company Infosys on its campus in Bangalore.

Yet despite this focus on education, what is clear in 2025 is that in the emerging industries of both India and China there is a chronic shortage of management talent. That's because, while the educational infrastructure of these countries grew fast, the development resource needs of their companies grew even faster. As a consequence, the available talent pool for managerial roles is very shallow compared to Europe or the USA, where multinationals like GE, Philips, Shell or Unilever had systematically developed large swathes of managers since the 1950s. At the same time, the economic and political histories of both countries had exacerbated the problem. In India the closed economy that had been in place until the early 1990s severely limited the development of managerial talent. In China a whole generation of people like Xui Li's parents had experienced the Cultural Revolution and had little by way of education or training during this period.[19]

The challenge for education in the economies of China and India was also one of quality. While some of the elite business schools in India and China had world-class teachers and students, many of the broader and more local universities did not. A glance at the *Times World University Rankings* in 2009 shows that, of the top 20 institutions, only two were outside the USA or Europe, with none in Asia. China's best, Tsinghua University, ranked 49th, while Indian universities failed to place in the top 100.[20]

So the challenge that companies like Li & Fung and AliBaba face in emerging markets such as China and India is to both recruit and retain employees as they grow fast (in 2010 the high-tech employee turnover in India and China was 25–30%), and at the same time produce a world-class workforce from a very shallow managerial talent pool.

Globalisation force: frugal innovation

Many of the technologies that make Xui Li's life comfortable – the refrigerator she uses, the water purifier and the car she drives – are all examples of frugal innovations developed in China or India. In the past it was the developed countries in the West and Japan that had created the hubs of innovation. This was most apparent in Silicon Valley, which had spawned companies such as Google, with a market capitalisation in mid-2010 that placed it as one of the most valuable companies in the world; or in the way that Germany continued to create high-end manufactured goods that the world wanted to buy; or how Japan became a hotbed for innovation from the 1950s onwards. This focus on the developed world was reflected in the locations of research and development laboratories, which multinationals kept resolutely in their own countries.

By 2010 this had begun to change, and continued to do so as research and innovation became a global rather than simply a developed-world phenomenon. A combination of investment, education and a strategic policy focused on new technologies had spurred the development of new clusters of innovation in emerging economies. Witness the rise of nanotechnologies and biotech in Beijing, digital media and genomics in Seoul, biofuels in Brazil and automotive technologies in Poland.

One of the drivers of frugal innovation in India and China was the return of the diaspora. From 1980 to 1999, 25% of the Silicon Valley start-ups were Indian or Chinese entrepreneurs, and between them they generated $17 billion in annual revenue. By 2005 that percentage had increased to 30%.[21] From 2010 onwards many of these entrepreneurs were using their skills and networks back in their home country as the shift of economic energy moved to Asia.

In India the powerhouses of value creation were in the IT sector, led initially by companies such as Wipro, Infosys, Tata Consulting Services and HCL Technologies. Many of these companies began their lives as the IT back office of the developed economies. However, just as Chinese manufacturers moved up the value chain, so too the IT sector in India moved up. In 1995, for example, Airbus and Boeing had both outsourced their basic back office tasks to Indian companies. By 2009 they were partnering on complex tasks such as the Infosys design for a section of the wing for the Airbus's A380, while HCL Technologies had partnered on two vital technology developments around averting collisions and landing in zero visibility.

What was fascinating was the extent to which the focus of innovation was on cost innovation – using resources more thoughtfully and redesigning products more frugally. Launched in 2008, the Tata Group's Nano car, for example, with the dream of the 'one lakh car', built innovation around manufacturing, procurement and value chains that saw the price drop to around 40% of a small European car. It was not just product innovation; Bharti Airtel had slashed the cost of mobile-phone services by radically innovating around its suppliers.

Sometimes these innovations had come through entrepreneurs creating entirely new businesses. Xui Li and her family all use money transfer from their mobile phones. This was not a Western development, but was rather pioneered by the Kenyan company Safaricom, which in 2007 launched a service that enabled users to conduct money transfers through their mobile phones.[22] In the wake of Safaricom's success, the technology was taken up by Africa's biggest cellular network operator, MTN, and rolled out across many African countries, to be followed by rollouts in China and India.[23]

The demography force: longevity increases

There is one more force that has helped Xui Li to create her working life – the fact that she, like millions of people around the world, is able to work productively into her 60s and 70s – and some work on considerably longer.

It is interesting that when the great management thinker Peter Drucker was asked what was the most important transformation in contemporary working life, he did not choose technology or globalisation. Instead he focused on what he thought was the miracle of the 21st century, the phenomenal increases in life expectancy.[24] Since the 1950s longevity in much of the world has developed to such an extent that many of the healthy children born in 2010 will live over 100 years. During Xui Li's working life this brought into question assumptions about retirement, about the employment of the over-65s and about the provision of pensions.[25]

As Drucker noted, this has been an extraordinary phenomenon. In Western Europe in 1800, for example, less than 25% of males would survive to age 60, while by 2010 more than 90% of them did. A 60-year-old man in Western Europe in 2010 had around the same remaining life expectancy as a 43-year-old man in 1800. In 2010 a person who was 60 was considered middle-aged; in 1800 that 60-year-old was elderly. All around, Xui Li sees people in their 60s and 70s doing activities that were the province of younger people only a few decades earlier. Her friends have had knee replacements in their 80s so they can continue hiking, and heart surgery even into their late 90s.[26]

There is much debate in Xui Li's circle about how long people will live – she is determined to live productively into her 100s. She keeps abreast of the latest medical technology, which is advancing at an enormous pace. In 2010 Xui Li remembers reading a piece by futurist Ray Kurzweil, who believed that between 2010 and 2050 medical advances would enable people to radically extend their lifespan while preserving and even improving their quality of life as they age. His view was that over this period the ageing process would first be slowed, then halted, and then reversed as newer and better medical technologies such as nanotechnology would allow microscopic machines to travel through the body to repair all types of damage at the cellular level.[27] Xui Li is keeping updated on progress and hopes to use all the technology available to her to live a productive and long life.[28]

In this final story playing on the bright side of the future we can see how a combination of technology, globalisation and longevity have created a good working life for Xui Li and her family. She has built a career as an entrepreneur and yet has all the advantages of linking into a strong platform and to many others in the ecosystems that will play such an important role in the future. As we leave Xui Li and her family you may want to ponder on the following questions.

First, do you see yourself working at the centre of a large company, or like Xui Li do you imagine that your working future will be more independent and entrepreneurial? If the answer is the latter, then the first shift – to serial mastery – and the second shift – to the innovative connector – will be crucial.

Next, how long do you expect to be productive? Do you like Xui Li expect to work productively into your 70s? If that's the case then this has profound implications for how you manage your energy and vigour. Perhaps, like John and Susan in Bangladesh, your hope is to craft a working life that has some balance embedded within it.

And finally, where do you expect to live? In a more and more global world there are wonderful opportunities to live in so many different places and yet still, like Xui Li, be connected to the global marketplace.

PART IV

THE SHIFT

It is enormously exciting to prepare for the next decades of our working lives. There are forces at work that over the coming decades will destroy forever many of the old assumptions of a traditional job and career. Around the world, outdated hierarchies will crumble; notions of nine-to-five working will come under immense pressure; and those who in the past would have been disadvantaged will have the opportunity to join the global talent pool. Over the coming decades there will be positive upsides for each one of us. But there will also be significant downsides. The traditional jobs and careers of the past may have been constraining and frustrating – but they did bring a measure of predictability. The nine-to-five rhythm may have created annoying inflexibility – but at least it was a rhythm and not a continuous 24-hour barrage. Opening up opportunities for people across most of the regions of the world has enormous benefits – but it also puts under colossal pressure those born into what had previously been privileged regions.

Our world is changing at an extraordinary pace, and what will go are many of the beliefs about what work is and how it is performed. In its place are greater opportunities and more choice. It is the opening of the aperture of choice that creates the space which will enable you to write a personal career script that can bring you fulfilment and meaning.

However, with this comes the necessity of actively making choices, and of being able to live with the consequences of these choices and the trade-offs they may require. The pleasures of the traditional working role were the certainty of a parent–child relationship. You could leave it in the hands of the corporation to make the big decisions about your working life. The adult–adult relationship we are moving towards is healthier and more capable of creating meaning. However, it also requires each one of us to take a more thoughtful, determined and energetic approach to exercising the choices that are available to us. It requires reflexivity – the capacity to both reflect on and to make decisions about what it is we want to become.

Thinking about the forces and the storylines, how are you going to go about crafting a working life that brings pleasure and meaning, and if you have children, what advice will you give to them? That is in a sense where I started my own journey into the future, thinking about the advice I would give to my own children about their future working lives.

Understanding the forces that will shape your future working life is a good place to start, for without this understanding it is impossible to create the possible scenarios. As we deepen our understanding of these shaping forces, what is overwhelming is the knowledge that the world is changing in a way we can only begin to imagine. However, while understanding these shaping forces is an important beginning to crafting a working future, you also need to focus these generalised, disparate forces on to your specific working life. Through these future working lives described earlier we can see how these big forces actually play out in miniature. The storylines we have just considered are miniature examples of the configuration of the forces. They show how the shaping forces of the future could configure in a way that could bring misery as more and more working people become isolated, buffered by global economic trends, and lead impersonal and fragmented lives. Yet while these dark storylines are indeed fictitious, nevertheless they contain sufficient truths to act as a warning. They warn us what to avoid if we are to craft future working lives of meaning and joy.

In the second group of storylines I configured the forces in a way that showed lives in miniature in the most positive of lights. Here we saw how it would be increasingly possible in the future to lead lives of deep cooperation and empathy, to craft lives which have balance and meaning at their core, and to build value as entrepreneurs and creative producers.

The challenge you face, of course, is to create opportunities and to make choices that accentuate the positives and minimise the negatives. How are you going to do this? My argument is that to create a great working future you will be called upon to make a number of fundamental shifts in your assumptions, and indeed in your knowledge, skills, working practices and habits. One way of thinking about these shifts is to consider them within the context of the three sources of capital or resources we all have available to us.

Building from capital and resources

The first resource or capital, which in many cultures is the one that is most lauded in careers, is your intellectual capital. That is a combination of what you know and your capacity to think deeply and intelligently about issues and challenges. It is to the building of intellectual capital that most schooling and education are directed, with the aim of increasing cognitive capability and the depth of learning. Intellectual capital plays a key role in the development of your career in the sense that it defines the areas of knowledge that you engage with, and your capabilities to work in these areas of knowledge. It is clear that in the future intellectual capital will become increasingly important in the creation of valuable jobs and careers.

The first shift addresses the development of intellectual capital. The argument I am making is that while in the past developing broad, general knowledge and skills may have been valuable, this will not be so in the future. In a joined-up, global and technologically enabled world, there will always be thousands, perhaps even millions of people who know the same as you yet can deliver it faster, cheaper and perhaps even better. In the future you will have to increasingly differentiate yourself from the crowd. You will do this by building depth and by putting in the time and resources to create a body of knowledge and skills, in other words – to achieve mastery. However, focusing on a single area of mastery is hazardous. What happens if that area becomes obsolete, or devalued, or you begin to loathe it? In the past, short working lives made single-focus careers the norm. In the future, long working lives mean that you can start deep and then slide or morph into other related areas, or even jump into something completely different. So the first shift, from shallow generalist to serial master, addresses the question of how you can best develop and deploy your intellectual capital over the coming decades.

The second area of resource or capital valuable to you in your working life is your social capital. That's the sum of all the relationships you have and the extent and depth of your networks. Some of these relationships will be strong and real sources of personal joy, while many others will be weaker and enable you to connect to diverse groups of people. The argument I am making with regard to the future of work is that the depth and breadth of these relationships and networks will become ever more vital, and that they will need to be crafted and nurtured in conscious ways.

In a world where isolation is just around the corner, finding and keeping regenerative relationships will be key. But in a world where innovation and creativity are at a premium, the diversity of networks will also play a crucial role. Success will come from the balance between the different types of relationships and networks that define your work. This will mean letting go of many of your preconceptions about what it takes to be a winner. Sure, you want to stand out from the crowd – but paradoxically it's the crowd, or at least the wise crowd, which will help you thrive. This is the second shift that will be so crucial to success in the future. It's the shift from being an isolated competitor to being an innovative connector.

So you need to both stand out with your mastery and skills, and yet simultaneously become part of a collection of other masters who together create value. Why? Because otherwise you are on your own, isolated and competing with thousands of others with no possibility of the leverage that the crowd brings.

The third source of capital or resource available to you is your emotional capital. That's the extent to which you are able to understand yourself and be reflexive about the choices you make. It's also about the capacity to build emotional resilience and forti- tude that will be so important for taking courageous action. Perhaps most importantly, emotional capital is the extent to which you are able to understand and then to make choices that create happiness in your life and allow you to live in harmony with your values and your work. In a sense the shift that accom- panies this source of personal capital is the most complex. It will require you and your friends – and your children if you have them – to think hard about what sort of working life you want. As you look at the forces that will shape your world over the coming decades, what is clear is that simply opting for a high standard of living will not be enough. What will be more crucial to the development of emotional capital will be the choices you make and the consequences you are prepared to trade off. It seems to me that increasingly the quality of experiences will trump quantity of consumption every time, and that words like 'happiness' and 'regeneration' will replace words like 'affluence' and 'luxury' as the touchstone of future working lives. So the third and final shift builds on sources of emotional capital through shifting from a working life dominated by voracious consumption to one that has impassioned production at its heart.

What has emerged so clearly from the stories of the future is that each one of us has an opportunity to create a working life that resonates with our values and is aligned with our beliefs to create a unique life script. What underlies the variety of these different life scripts is the choices made and trade-offs confronted. None of this will be straightforward. Much will require a level of focus and energy that frankly few of us have associated with decisions about the way we work. But glance back to the stories of the future if you don't believe the endeavour to be worthwhile. The interesting insight is that some of the aspects of the bright side are already with us – just unevenly distributed.

For you, your friends and your children, doing nothing is not an option. Faced with the reality of the dark side of the future, who would want to wander aimlessly into it? The challenge is what to do. Simply expending energy will take you on a path, but it will not necessarily get you to the co-creation, the social engagement and the creative lives that are so much part of the Crafted Future. What is required instead will be conscious, articulated and purposeful actions around the three shifts: to be prepared to expend the focus and determination to be a serial master; to use energy and goodwill to become an innovative connector with a rich network of diverse and interesting people; and finally, to redraft the traditional working deal that has money and consumption at the heart to something more in tune with your emotional needs for experiences and passion.

8

THE FIRST SHIFT: FROM SHALLOW GENERALIST TO SERIAL MASTER

The success of your future at work will depend in part on your ability to build the intellectual capital that will be the foundation of your capacity to create value. What that means in reality is to both understand the skills and competencies that will be at a premium, and also know how best to develop them.

To do this you will have to make a fundamental shift in your intellectual base from being a shallow generalist, who knows a little about lots, to being a serial master, who has in-depth knowledge and competencies in a number of domains. The advantage of shallow generalism was that it allowed you to hedge your bets. Because you knew a little about a lot, it didn't much matter if some of what you knew had very little value. However, as valuable competencies become the currency of the future, so too you will be called upon to make a bet about what will be valuable in the future and how best to develop mastery. Building from your awareness of the five forces that will shape your future, you will need to understand those competencies that will be more valuable and therefore worth investing in. You will also need to think carefully about the types of careers that will be in the ascendant, together with the knowledge areas that accompany them. Your challenge will be to become deep, and yet over time slide or morph, through personal development, or through new networks, into other areas of mastery. That's why when it comes to this shift I am suggesting two areas of competency:

* **Serial mastery:** the focus here is on depth, which describes the sort of career choices and competencies that are likely to be in the ascendant in the next two decades.
* **Self-marketing:** the focus here is on creating and crafting credentials, which consider some of the investments that will be necessary to ensure that you and those you care about become, and then stay, a member of the global talent pool.

The case against shallow knowledge and skills

You know you're a generalist with shallow skills when you know a little about lots of things, and when you say you are a jack-of-all-trades. Over the last 80 years the role of mastery and deep craft knowledge development, through the roles of apprentice and master, has eroded. It was replaced, outside of the old professions, by the rise of shallow generalism. This saw the rise of the non-specialist 'general manager', and also huge number of workers with limited specialist skills.

The general management role was one of the cornerstones of the traditional corporate life. These were managers who stayed within a single company, or an industrial sector, for the majority of their careers. They became the classic 'corporate men'.[1] They understood the company well and could speak for it in any part of the world. They also had the contacts with the head office that allowed them to understand the corporate ethos and culture, and to make decisions on the part of the owners of the company. The deal for these general managers was that, in return for developing competencies and knowledge that were non-transferable (it would be difficult, for example, to move in a senior position from Ford to Cadbury's because so much of their knowledge and networks were specific to Ford), they had the guarantee of a lifetime of employment.

From the 1920s onwards the majority of large corporations stuck to the traditional general manager deal. They created 'fast-track' development practices that whisked the most talented youngsters to the top, and built what was to be called 'bench strength' of possible internal candidates for the top jobs. For this cohort of managers it might be that their skills and networks were too specific to the company they worked with, and too general to bring real value outside the company. But that did not matter, because the company guaranteed that they could always work with them.

The challenge for generalists now is that the traditional contract of a job for life has been well and truly broken – leaving them in a job market which does not place a great deal of value on their general knowledge about one company.

But that's not the only group that got caught out by developing wide and shallow skills and knowledge. There was another group who, while they had never reached the top, had made a living supervising others, or who worked on projects finding information, writing reports and making recommendations.

The full extent of the future of this managerial group of people began to dawn on me when I watched my son Dominic writing an essay about bird flu. Aged 16, he was preparing for a biology exam later in the year, and this was a topic his teacher had asked him to work on and then to write an essay about. She wanted him to prepare a report on the history of bird flu, the way in which it developed across the world, and the means by which the UK government had prepared for the possibility of a pandemic.

Over the next two hours I watched as he wrote this bird flu essay. He began drafting the essay by first pulling out bird flu references in Wikipedia, then he dived into some of the medical journal articles which had taken the argument further, and finally he took a close look at the UK Government's paper on the subject. All the time he was snipping pieces from here and there and downloading data to create maps and charts. Within four hours he had created what looked to me like the sort of essay I would have written in my second year at university.

But does my son actually know anything about bird flu? In a sense he does – but this is generalist knowledge created from the scraps and scrapings of information from public sources. What he does not have is any original thoughts on it, any well-developed point of view or any valuable insights that others don't have. Hey, don't get me wrong – the guy's only 16 and I would not have expected more.

But what he did was what any bright 16-year-old anywhere in the world with access to broadband can do. He had assimilated information in a way that looks cohesive and thorough. The challenge with being a 'jack-of-all-trades', developing shallow knowledge across a range of topics, is that your main competitor is not the person sitting next to you; it's not even the person sitting in Mumbai; your main competitor is Wikipedia, or Google Analytics, or the myriad of technical applications that will replace shallow knowledge. And you think the networks that you have invested so much time in developing are really valuable – well, guess what, LinkedIn and Facebook applications are making every person with access to the internet a world-class networker.

In part, my argument against generalist skills and shallow knowledge is a swing of the pendulum back from mechanised work to nineteenth-century craftwork. With the rise of the factory, both skilled craftsmen and unskilled rural workers left the countryside to work in the factories that had been built across England and later in North America. The metaphor for the way of working that accompanied this shift was the 'wheel and the cog'. The wheel was the company that ran these factories, the cog the people engaged in production. The mechanisation of work witnessed the breaking down of work into its smallest component tasks, which could then be performed by people with limited, shallow skills and to all intents and purposes acting as automata. In the textile mills, for example, what was needed in these corporate hierarchies was hours of labour – not innovation, not creativity and certainly not the 'whole person'.

When Briana's great-great-grandfather worked in the Ford factory in Detroit in the 1930s he walked onto the factory floor in the morning, joined his colleagues on the assembly line and then returned home in the evenings. He was a replicable part of the labour machine. When he took his annual holiday or was off sick it was easy for any of the others on the assembly line to replace him.

Before the nineteenth century master craftsmen were often able to specialise because they worked alone. Artisans made a chair, a piece of clothing or a cart from start to finish with little assistance from others. But this was simple work. The division of labour made possible much more complex tasks – like building a car. The challenge now is to develop a deep knowledge of a particular area but also to create networks that tap into others' deep knowledge since tasks and jobs are a great deal more complicated than they were in the nineteenth century. We need the knowledge and depth of the eighteenth-century artisan, and at the same time the networks that enabled the division of labour to be formed in the late nineteenth century.[2]

That's not to say, of course, that all jobs in the nineteenth century simply needed shallow generalist skills. During that period of time the professionals – such as lawyers, physicians, engineers and architects – made enormous efforts to build their expertise and to ring-fence their professions against others. It was during this century that professional bodies were created that regulated entry into the professions, kept a tight hold on who could be selected, and regulated fee structures while upholding what became known as 'professional standards'. Over the coming decades these ancient professions were joined by other job groups that attempted to do the same.

However, with the mechanisation of labour it was often left to the professionals to develop deep skills that were difficult for others outside the profession to imitate.

To summarise the case against shallow knowledge and skills, broad general management skills, while valuable at a point in time, are in fact too specific to one company to be easily transfer-able, and in a world of limited contract life can lead to a cul-de-sac. At the same time, shallow skills are rapidly being replaced by knowledge repositories such as Wikipedia and amalgamation devices such as Google Analytics.

So, in order to flourish in the future, you will need to develop deep knowledge and skills. However, to do so you will also have to decide which skills and knowledge are likely to be valuable in the future, and to ensure that you develop depth in more than one area – in other words, to develop serial mastery.

Serial mastery: the importance of depth

So, if generalist, shallow skills could lead to a cul-de-sac, on what basis can valuable serial mastery be created? This is the thought exercise you can go through in order to decide how best to create a future working life of value and meaning:

* First, you will need to build a deep understanding of why some competencies are more valuable than others. This insight will become an important pathfinder in the coming years.
* Then, be as smart as possible about predicting what will be valued in the future. Of course you cannot know exactly what will be crucial – but knowing what you do about the five trends you should be able to make an educated guess.
* However, keeping these skills and competencies in mind, go with what you love.
* Then go really, really deep to gain mastery of the area.
* Finally, be prepared to move into other areas of mastery through sliding and morphing.

Understand why some competencies are valued

At any point in time some competencies are more valuable than others. Generally this is because they are easily seen to create value and others can judge them on this criterion; because they are rare and demand for the competency or skill exceeds supply; and finally, because it is difficult for others or a machine to imitate them.

Because they create value

For a skill or competency to be valuable, it needs to be easily observed to create high value. Ideas about what is valuable have changed over the years. In the eighteenth century, for example, the skill of blowing glass was valuable because glassware was increasingly important to elegant living, and much valued in the domestic lives of the wealthy. In the nineteenth century the skills of the engineer were considered highly valuable because from 1830 onwards the wealth of a town was dependent on whether it had a railway connection. No surprise that in 1830 Isambard Kingdom Brunel – the engineer behind the Great Western Railway – was the pin-up of his time and engineering was seen as an important competence to develop. From the twentieth century onwards the value of engineering waned in the UK, although it continues to be highly prized in Germany, where the designers and the engineers at BMW and Mercedes Benz are revered and engineering is considered a highly valuable skill to develop.

Over time, skills, competencies and abilities have risen to ascendancy and then descended or languished as they are seen to be less valuable, or as the basis of their value is questioned. Take investment banking for example. Richard Fuld, then the CEO and Chairman of the investment bank Lehman Brothers, earned $40 million in 2006 and $34 million in 2007. Some of the bankers in other investment banks were paid similar amounts. The justification was that what they did created such value that they were worth it. So, for example, if an investment banker brought in $100 million of revenue (or value), then to receive, let's say, $10 million for themselves was considered part of the value proposition. However, since the bankruptcy of Lehman's in September 2008 and the global recession that followed, the basis of the value of investment banking has been questioned. As a consequence the skills and competencies of investment banking are considered less valuable, and the numbers of the most talented people aspiring to join investment banking will drop.[3]

So the challenge you face is to try to predict what skills and competencies will create (or be seen to create) the greatest value in 2025.

Because they are rare

Skills and competencies become valuable because they are rare, and are seen to be rare. Clearly if everyone has the same competencies and skills, and there is a large pool of these talents, then they will not command a premium. That's the logic, for example, behind the valuation of world-class footballers. Hundreds of millions of boys in the world play soccer, and many of them dream of World Cup glory. Talent scouts from the leading football clubs scour the earth for raw talent, and even poverty is no barrier – some stars come from the favelas of South America or the slums of South Africa. Once chosen for a club, the rarity of the skills of the player is tested every time he walks onto the pitch. Tens of millions of people watch him play and draw their own conclusions about whether he is indeed unique or rare.[4]

World-class footballing talents are rare and therefore considered valuable. But it is not just footballing talents that are rare. At any point in history resources become rare because demand outstrips supply, either because those already in the occupation are leaving (mostly because they are retiring) or because the demand for the skill is rising.

These supply trends are intimately linked to demographic variables. All over the world there are industries in which the number of skilled workers who will retire over the coming two decades is significantly greater than the number capable of joining. We see this played out in the aerospace industry. At Boeing, for example, the predicted future skills gap is marked. It is one of the US's biggest manufacturers and exporters, but by 2015, 40% of the aircraft maker's skilled workers will reach retirement age. That's 60,000 skilled, knowledgeable workers who will potentially walk out of the door.[5] It is not just Boeing in the USA that will experience these skill gaps. In the US manufacturing sector generally, in 2009 about 19% of manufacturing workers were 54 and older, and only 7% under 25 years old. This is not just a US phenomenon. Across the developed world, as we saw in the hard facts of demography, the retirement of the largest cohort in the history of mankind – the Baby Boomers – will create huge skill and talent deficits.

Take the UK, for example; between 2007 and 2017 retiring Baby Boomers will create 11.5 million job vacancies. By 2010 companies had begun to face difficulties in securing specialist skills, including science, technology, engineering, maths and project management. The UK Government predicts that demand for these skills will continue to grow over the next decade. It is estimated that in the UK alone an additional 1.3 million people with professional and technical skills and 900,000 managers and senior professionals will be required by 2017.[6]

Skills also become rare when a sudden explosion of demand exceeds a readily available supply, typically when a new technology opens up a whole new portfolio of skills and competencies. For example, the competencies and capacity to program in Fortran or Java were both highly sought-after skills at the time these programs were released.

So the challenge you face is to predict what skills and competencies will be in short supply in 2025.

Because they are difficult to imitate

Finally, to be valuable, a competency or skill has to be difficult to imitate – and that can be by a technology, or by a person. When a skill can be imitated, then it moves to the lowest-paid imitators. That was the reason why between 1985 and 2010 over 768,000 back-office jobs moved to the low-wage economy of India,[7] and why in 2009 China's outsourcing industry recruited nearly 700,000 new employees.[8]

Of course, the source of imitation need not be another person; it can also be a machine. This began in the mid-nineteenth century with the weaving machines in Lancashire towns which put thousands of skilled weavers out of business and continued with the car assembly plants of Detroit. Today, the source of imitation can be an application rather than a machine. For example, publishing software has meant that one designer can do what many once could; administrative departments can be slashed with the introduction of advanced spreadsheet software; and the development of robotics is increasingly likely to encroach on employment positions in the service and care industry.[9]

The challenge you face is to find and develop competencies, skills and abilities that are difficult for others and indeed for machines to imitate. So, in the light of the five forces that will shape your work over the coming decades, what are the likely skills and competency areas that will be seen to create value, which will be rare, and which cannot be easily imitated?[10]

Future-proofed careers and skills

I am going to differentiate between careers that I believe will be in the ascendant over the coming decades and the specific skills that will be valuable. I use the word 'valuable' broadly to signify those roles that will bring value to those that perform them, and to the societies in which they exist. Some, such as those working in the life sciences, can expect to be well remunerated. Others, such as the advocates, will not receive above-average pay for their labour. There are three broad career paths that the five forces suggest will be of value (beyond those that are always of value) over the coming decade: grassroots advocacy, social entrepreneurship and micro-entrepreneurs.

Career: grassroots advocacy

In 2009 the strategists at Shell Oil developed two scenarios about the future of energy resources. What is interesting about the Shell 2050 scenario, in the 'Blueprint' version, is the role that local, regional and global advocates play. They believe that, rather than a top-down, centralised approach, in an increasingly transparent world high-profile local actors will influence the national stage. Change will come through the success of many individual initiatives which become linked and amplified around the world and progressively change the character of international debate. I believe these grassroots advocates will become the early developers of experiments and innovative solutions and adopters of proven practice. These are careers like Miguel's, who joined up with people from across the world to make the case for reducing the carbon footprints of commuting. Or careers like John's, who connected a community in Bangladesh with his home town in Oklahoma and along the way became an advocate for water policies. Or Chenh-Gong in Hunan province, who has used his filming and editing expertise to make short films about the degradation of the rural environment around his home town. I guess to call these 'career choices' is wrong. In each case, Miguel, John and Chenh-Gong does not make a living out of advocacy, but for each of these people it is a crucial part of their working life.

We can expect to see advocacy rising in any area that people care about – from the education of children in developing countries, to the eradication of endemic diseases, to the support of small businesses. Expect to see a proliferation of enterprises built around developing and supporting advocacy skills and capabilities. These could be NGOs like one of our Future of Work Consortium members, Save the Children. Already in 2010 this had a sophisticated programme of support for people who want to volunteer to work with them, and also for those who work as advocates on their behalf. Or they could be companies like Projects Abroad,which by 2010 had sent over 18,500 people to volunteer as interns in areas as diverse as teaching, conservation, medicine and journalism.[11]

Career: social entrepreneurship

For some, advocacy will be about becoming high-profile local actors who galvanise energy and create ideas about how to move forward. For others, advocacy will entail using their leadership skills and management know-how to create organisations that serve social needs. At the heart of social entrepreneurship is the will to organise, create and manage a venture to make social change. So while a business enterprise measures performance in terms of profit and return, a social entrepreneur focuses on measuring outcomes in broader ways.

For many young people, the hero of social entrepreneurship is Professor Muhammad Yunus, who back in 1976 launched an action research project to design a credit delivery system that would provide banking services targeted at the rural poor. From this initial project the Grameen Bank (Grameen means 'rural' or 'village' in Bengali) came into operation. Based on the idea of microfinance, the bank provides tiny loans to very poor people – most of them women – which they often use to start the small businesses that will lift them out of poverty. As of November 2009 Grameen had provided \$8.6bn in small loans to almost 8 million people, and microfinance had become a \$30bn global industry.

Or take Blake Mycoskie, founder of TOMS Shoes. I first came across Blake when we were speaking at the Inntown Conference in Norway in the spring of 2010. Just in from Los Angeles, Blake spellbound the audience with the story that took him from seeing bare-footed children in Argentina to building a business with a mission that, for every pair of shoes sold, TOMS would donate a new pair of shoes to a child in need. As of April 2010 they had given away more than 600,000 shoes in 'shoe drops' in more than 20 countries, supported by a large group of volunteer shoe-fitters.

All over the world social entrepreneurial businesses were springing up – NIKA Water Company, for example, which sells bottled water in the USA and uses 100% of its profits to bring clean water to those in the developing world. Or Newman's Own, which donates 100% of its total profits to support various educational charities.

But it is not just individuals who are making the running here. Across Asia and Europe in particular social entrepreneurs are gathering together in teams, networks and movements for change. Gen Y is beginning to play a role and we can expect this to gather greater momentum over the coming decades. For example, the Young Social Pioneers group in Australia actively invest in young social entrepreneurs, while Istanbul's Bilgi University does the same in Turkey.

Social entrepreneurs are becoming more and more important. By 2010 programmes on how to become a social entrepreneur were being run at the leading business schools, and their outcomes were annually ranked by both Fast Company and Business Week. What is clear, is that the internet and the social networking websites are becoming a pivotal resource for the success and collaboration of many social entrepreneurs, ensuring that their ideas are heard by a global audience, allowing networks and investors to develop globally, and creating the opportunity to make a real change with little or no start-up capital.[12]

Career: micro-entrepreneurs

What we saw in Xui Li and her daughter and grandson were three generations of micro-entrepreneurs. None of them employs more than five people, and all of them work for themselves.

Small businesses have always played a key role in the economy of developed and emerging markets. For example, in 2004, 40% of the working population in the USA worked in small business,[13] while 47% of the UK working population did the same.[14]

But what it means to be a micro-entrepreneur in 2025 will be very different from now. Although we can still expect large companies to exist in 2025 – and in fact there is an argument that these companies will become even larger – proportionally we can expect more people to work for themselves, or with a small group of other people. Many will be employed in ecosystems that become the hinterland of companies. Like the many thousands of independent people who build the applications for the iPhone, these people will be working on small parts of the value chain. Alternatively, they, like Xui Li, will be part of a much larger collaboration of many thousands of people brought together to experience economies of scale.

Whatever the mechanism of coordination, we can expect a greater proportion of the valuable work in companies to be carried out by people working independently. The main driver, of course, will be the continually falling price of IT, combined with the ubiquitous Cloud, which will allow even the smallest businesses to use highly sophisticated analytics to track orders, work with third parties and collect money. What has also become more prevalent and will continue to grow is the ability of the internet to coordinate funding for entrepreneurs – it's a method for people to donate or invest in ideas they think are exciting or profitable.[15]

Beyond the three emerging careers, we can also expect clusters of skills to become ever more valuable, rare and difficult to imitate. In particular, clusters in the life sciences and health, energy conservation, creativity and innovation, and coaching and caring will become increasingly important as the impact of the five forces is felt.

Skill area: life sciences and health

It's an absolute certainty that over the next two decades life science will become a key sector in the growth of skilled work. It's the simple truth that regardless of how good we feel, and how long we live, we always want to look better and live longer. We can expect two important life science and health clusters to emerge. The first will be the creation of what we might call 'health hubs' across the world, designed in part to cater for the needs of the ageing population of the developed world. For example, in Europe by 2010 a number of these health resorts were under construction around the Mediterranean, just as North Americans have flocked to Florida and the southern states. Turkey had begun to market itself as a health and spa specialist because of its proximity to a major geothermal belt,[16] while Eastern Europe in general was preparing itself to accommodate the growing number of Baby Boomers in search of 'Hippocratic holidays'.[17]

At the same time, clusters around the life sciences will become ever more important as universities, health and pharmaceutical companies, joint ventures and service companies work more closely together. The Bay Area around San Francisco, and 'Gene Town' in Boston and Cambridge, Massachusetts, have emerged as the first biotechnology clusters containing critical masses of academic and industrial institutions in relatively small areas.[18] In Europe, by 2010 there were three biomedical clusters, in the Oxford–Cambridge–London triangle in the United Kingdom, the French capital of Paris, and in the Medicon cluster corridor between Sweden and Denmark. In Asia the largest biomedical cluster was in Singapore, where more than 13,000 people were employed. Over the next decade we can predict bioclusters to strengthen in Kobe and Osaka in Japan. In China in 2010 biomedical research was taking place in key universities, but at that time there was not a mature biomedical cluster to fill the gap between basic research and the commercial application of these ideas. However, over the coming decades we can expect the Chinese Government to pour resources into the rapid development of these clusters.

What will these biomedics be doing? Certainly they will be in demand. In 2010, for example, despite the US recession, biomedical engineering (with a 72% growth rate) was the fastest-growing skill in the country. These are the people who over the next decade will be developing MRI machines, asthma inhalers and artificial hearts. By 2025 we can expect even more creative developments. Take the Nanomedics, for example, who will be devising subatomic 'nanoscale' healthcare devices, procedures and body inserts, including 'cargo ships' that seek out cancerous cells in the bloodstream. Or the memory-augmentation surgeon tasked with adding extra memory capacity to people who want to increase their recall ability and helping those suffering sensory shutdown. Stem cell research was already showing signs of success by 2010 and will become a massive industry in the future. These cells can be used for repairing damaged spinal cords, growing replacement organs and even perhaps constructing replacement limbs. However, stem cell research is not without its moral conflicts – it has huge potential, but also high barriers to overcome. By 2010 the green light had been given for human embryonic stem cells to be used in humans, and this was considered to be the beginning of what could be a crucial industry.[19]

Skill area: energy conservation

There will be enormous potential work in the field of energy conservation as new industries continue to be built around the capture of energy. By 2010 wind power, solar power and wave power had already emerged as nascent industries. In India substantial investments were being made in wind power, while in China energy conservation scientists were pioneering new developments in solar energy. We can anticipate a rapid acceleration of skills in energy conservation, driven in part by government mandates for zero-emission cars, and also by fiscal incentives to support the build-up of mass production. These developments in wind and solar power will stimulate a surge in electric transport – powered by battery, fuel cell or hybrid technologies. Engineers will certainly be in high demand in the sustainable energy sector, but the sector will also need PR specialists, planning specialists and indeed everything the traditional energy sector needs. In fact, there should be more jobs available in the renewable energy sector than the traditional energy sector because renewables create more jobs per unit of power, per unit of installed capacity and per pound invested than conventional power generation.[20]

These jobs in life sciences, health and energy conservation will become truly global labour markets. These are jobs that require deep and extensive knowledge, and are being developed in different places across the world. Want engineering skills? Better look at India, which graduated over 400,000 engineers in 2009.[21] Or if you are looking for IT skills, then 6.1 million graduates in China joined the labour market in 2009.[22]

The implication of this is that competition for these jobs will become increasingly worldwide, and that the predicted labour shortages in much of the developed world could potentially be filled by graduates in these 'hot' subjects from anywhere in the world. It's also important to bear in mind that location will not always be crucial to the delivery of these skills. Take Miguel, who is working with other enthusiasts from across the world to support the city of Lucknow in its attempts to reduce its carbon footprint. He is actively joining up clusters of energy conservationists from Copenhagen and Brazil in order to solve the challenges of a city on the other side of the world. Or Rohan, who is using the latest visualisation robotics to work with colleagues and patients across the world.

Skill area: creativity and innovation

Creativity and innovation are in the ascendant as the mechanisation and automation of the past are replaced by a way of working that is more organic, emergent and creative. These creative industries will flourish, and increasingly permeate everyday life, in part because, as experiences become as important as consumption, so those that invent, design and execute experiences will have valuable skills. We are beginning to learn more about the creative class through the research of people like Richard Florida and his work on their aspirations and needs.[23]

Richard Florida has calculated that, even in 2008, between 25% and 30% of all workers in developed economies were engaged in the creative sector (he includes here science and technology, research and development, the technology branches of the arts, as well as the knowledge-based professions of medicine, financial management and law).

It seems that all around the world people are waking up from the tedium of bureaucratic sameness to the colour and richness of creativity. I saw this first hand with our first Future of Work research consortium. As we neared the end of the consortium I suggested that we create (as I always do) an executive bound report. You know the sort of thing – you probably have a couple of them on your shelf. My highly creative team, Julia Goga-Cooke and Marzia Arico, were having none of this. Instead they crafted for each participant a box in which 60 cards illustrated through language, stories, pictures and cartoons the key aspects of the future. They called it 'gambling with the future' and invited groups of executives to make up games from the cards – which they did with great gusto. My guess is that for many of these executives this might have been their first real experience of high-quality design and creativity. I can imagine that as a consequence their expectations have changed subtly. I've no doubt that the next time they see a 'normal' presentation or receive a report a small part of them will think – 'Hmm … I wonder if there is another way of doing this?'

Julia and Marzia are members of a growing and influential band of people dedicated to creativity and design at work. They don't accept the default position and are always looking for an alternative way of displaying data and interacting with clients. Though there are many aborted attempts at creative reimagining, this process is important because it stirs pools that would otherwise become stagnant. We know that this 'creative class' will continue to grow in size and impact in the years to come, and the dividing line between these 'creatives' and those engaged in managing and working in organisations will become more and more permeable. As I saw with the cards and presentations, what can be called 'art' has morphed and flowed into what could be called the 'aesthetic-intellectual' sector. Take a look at the highly successful Californian company IDEO to see how a group that began as product designers have morphed over the years into designers and creators of experiences and organisational practices. Or how innovation and creativity have become increasingly important to the way in which brands are created and reputations made. How many more Tom Fords will there be in 2025 as arbiters of good taste and self-presentation?

What will the creative classes do? The German futurist Mathias Horx lists over 100 creative vocations including animators, architects, authors, ceramicists, creative managers, DJs, documentary film-makers, event agents, fashion consultants, fitness trainers, graphic designers, interior designers, media trainers, musicians, muses, painters, photographers, philosophers, preachers, publisher's readers, rappers, researchers, star cooks, storytellers, stylists, theatre directors, trainers and website developers.[24] Of course, some of these creative roles will fade and morph into allied roles, while others are at the beginning of their trajectory and we can expect them to grow over the coming decades.

What will be the day-to-day working life of these creative people? Perhaps you imagine they will live a solitary existence somewhere on a rocky island in the middle of a warm sea. Here they contemplate, consider and of course ... create. In fact, nothing is further from the truth, and in all likelihood this will continue to be a fallacy. The creative class likes to be near, and I mean really near, to others with the same skills. What's more, they congregate and cluster in large numbers in particular regions across the world, and in all likelihood this clustering mechanism will only increase between now and 2025. Creative clusters are emerging around the world, populated by people who want to learn from each other and do business with each other.[25] These clusters are being energised and fuelled from the 'inside out' through the ideas and creativity that emerge when people with related but diverse skills and abilities come together. They are becoming what I have called 'hot spots' of innovation and creativity.[26] Chenh-Gong, whose daily life we explored in the storylines of the Crafted Future, is exactly one of the creative people working in an innovative cluster in Shanghai. Like many around him he is flourishing in the mix of skills and ideas and building value from the deep diversity he is experiencing.

A final thought about joining the creative classes. Mathias Horx makes an interesting (though not entirely substantiated) point about the earning potential of the creative class. His argument is that the distribution of income in the creative class will become as polarised as it is currently among tennis players, models, designers, theatre directors, advertising creatives and opera singers. He predicts that for the creative class the distribution of wealth will go something like this: 80% will get by on a relatively low income – but they will not necessarily be unhappy; for 18% there will be enough to live well; while 2% will hit the jackpot. These are the super-talented, who are able to create great wealth through the management of their personal brand. His argument is that the professional classes (lawyers, physicians, architects, professors) create 'guilds' which in part ensure the distribution of resources across the whole profession (through minimum fees, for example). There may be superstars in these professions, but they will have to work hard to emerge. In contrast, in the emerging creative industries there is no such guild mechanism for the even distribution of resources – so they are more likely to imitate the 'winner takes all' distribution of resources currently seen in tennis players or models. An interesting thought for those contemplating joining the creative classes.[27]

Skill area: coaching and caring

In a world that will become increasingly virtual, creating supportive relationships to help navigate through life, keep overworked employees feeling great and address the challenges of growing time fragmentation will be key. That's why the skills around coaching and caring will become ever more important over the next two decades.

The American economic commentator Robert Reich calls these jobs 'purchased care' and describes them under five Cs – Computing, Caring, Catering, Consulting, Coaching.[28] Mathias Horx uses this wonderful description: 'They are the people who offer scent design, who sing our praises, who arrange our papers on our desk for a fee, who read aloud for us, and who bury or plastinate us with new rituals ...'[29]

Some of the services will be delivered virtually. So we can expect a plethora of micro-entrepreneurs developing virtual personal coaches capable of building and managing personal and professional avatars, ensuring personal 'brands' are working, and monitoring and providing advice on the development of high-value networks. Expect also to see virtual and physical service jobs addressing the challenge of time fragmentation; virtual-clutter organisers who will help to organise complex electronic lives, handling e-mail, storing data and managing identities; 'narrowcasters' – specialists working with content providers and advertisers to create personalised content.[30]

Like the new creatives, these new caring roles are an absolutely essential outcome from the way work and life will develop over the coming decades. They are aligned with the principle that by 2025 many people will choose to focus on productive experiences rather than voracious consumption – for it is they who are often the purveyors of such experiences. At the highest end these will be individually developed, tailor-made, unique experiences, crafted just for you. These are also the people who will help tread the fine line between out-and-out narcissism and a more nuanced presentation and branding of self. They will work on the development of personal blogs, ensure photographs and avatars are realistic – but more, they will craft CVs and support people like Amon and Rohan to navigate the worldwide job market. They will recommend great theatre, craft wonderful gap years and sabbatical experiences, and support personal brands through hairdressing, massage and fitness.

We can also anticipate that a particular focus of these caring roles will be on family well-being. Even as families become smaller, 'reassembled' and fragmented, we can anticipate that Gen Y and Gen Z as parents will have a strong desire to do the best for their children and cherish their families. So there will be a priority on services that care for them, educate and inspire them, and generally increase their well-being and happiness.

Where will these caring and coaching jobs be located? They will locate wherever the clients are. If the creative classes cluster together, then the coaching and caring roles will be there to support them and to ensure the delivery of a personal service. We can also expect them to be working in the emerging healthy-living regions of the world. As we shall see in the third shift, it could well be that the caring and coaching classes form the backbone of the regenerative communities that will be so crucial to the wellbeing of workers by 2025.

One final point about labour migration. In the past, many of these coaching and caring roles were filled through immigration. In 2009, for example, the Philippines exported 95,000 housekeepers and nannies to the developed countries of the world, and the hospitals of the UK had a high proportion of nursing staff from Africa. We can expect that with the potential opening up of more and more labour markets this migration of coaching and caring class will increase. For example, when Poland joined the Economic Union in 2006, over a period of two years 265,000 people came to live and work in London.[31] Typically they came into support and caring roles – cleaning, painting and plumbing London's deteriorating housing stock, and caring for the children of busy London families and older relatives.

Then … go with what you love

Here is my dilemma. You may recall that what got me started on this journey looking into the future of work was a breakfast conversation with my two sons. Christian, aged 19 at the time, wanted to be a journalist, and Dominic, at 16, wanted to study medicine. Taking a look at what you've just read, you could not be blamed for saying, 'Medicine good. Well done, Dominic!' – 'Journalism bad. Bad choice, Christian.' Did you notice that pure journalism did not figure among the top sectors for 2025? The reason is straightforward. The numbers of print newspapers read across the world has collapsed, the vast majority of online content is currently free (though unlikely to remain so), and writers who blog are competing with a million other people who can also – sort of – string a sentence together.

So what do I tell Christian, my son, who has his heart set on journalism? Of course I don't tell him anything. He is so determined to be a journalist that my opinion is of very little use. What is also clear is that going with something you love trumps going with something your parents want you to do every time. Think of all the unhappy lawyers, accountants and finance people you know who got talked into their career choice and lived to regret it. However, here is the caveat. In the future it is wise to go with what you love – but do it with your eyes wide open. For Christian this means, for example, that he must realise that he is unlikely to ever be wealthy. It also means that he will have to work incredibly hard to have his voice heard above the cacophony of the web. And finally, it means that he will almost certainly have to slide into something else or completely morph into other areas as his working life progresses.

Making the shift into the future is all about understanding choices, trade-offs and consequences. You can certainly analyse the five forces and predict which careers and competencies are most likely to be future-proofed. However, while it is both sensible and possible to make these well-grounded guesses about the future (as I have just done), the truth is that these can only ever be guesses. So, in a world where the specifics of the future are difficult to predict with great accuracy, a smart option is to go with what you love and feel passionate about. Perhaps even more than this, if you are going to be working until you are 70, then you had better find something you really enjoy doing. However, as we shall see, once you have made the choice, what you cannot do is dabble, or skate around being a generalist – you have to develop mastery.

How do you know what you love? I believe that at the heart of loving work is meaning and expertise. It's hard to love something that you feel is meaningless, and it's also hard to fall in love with something you don't think you are going to be any good at. Meaning is an intensely personal perspective. My son Christian, for example, loves the idea of being a journalist because it resonates with his own sense of what is important. Others may believe journalism is a meaningful occupation but not love it because they believe they cannot develop an expertise in it. Christian loves journalism because it's meaningful to him, and because he has had sufficient feedback about his writing and research skills to believe that he can give it a go. He is fully aware that this may not work for him – but that's where sliding and morphing come in!

Going with what you love will be crucial to the future of work. If you find what you love, you are more likely to stick with it, and to experience it as meaningful. This will be increasingly important if, as I am predicting in the third shift, we will see a move from consumption to productive experiences. In this future shift the experience of fun, of spending time with others, of being challenged and of creating meaning move centre stage. If productive experiences and meaning are to replace remuneration and consumption as the major drivers for work, then you will need to be very thoughtful about the jobs you take and the competencies you develop.

It seems to me that knowledge, creativity and innovation will be the basis by which many of us choose to make our living in the future – and all of these outcomes depend on our feelings and attitudes to our work. We cannot be creative if we hate what we do, or find it insubstantial or meaningless. We cannot coach and care for others if we find our work boring or repetitive. Sure, we can do a decent day's work, but we will not put in that extra energy that comes with the territory of loving what we do.

Being masterful

Your future will be about becoming and being masterful. It's a combination of knowing something deeply and becoming skilled in a variety of competencies. Remember my observation of my 16-year-old son's creation of a passable university-degree-level essay on bird flu. He created it during a couple of hours on Wikipedia and diving into an assortment of medical journal articles. The argument I am making in this shift is that these shallow skills will simply not be as valuable as deeper, specialist skills since so many people across the world will have access to the same information and opportunities to develop shallow skills.

In a sense this will require a return to the notion of craft development that was lost in the Industrial Revolution. Becoming masterful will also provide an opportunity to blur the lines between what you do at work and how you like to play. In the future, thinking like a craftsman will become more and more important, and if you want to be innovative and creative, then that will also require playing like a child.

Thinking like a craftsman

When I think about the future of work and the level of specialisation that's required, I am drawn to a parallel with the medieval craftsmen who created some of the marvellous objects we now treasure. The mechanisation of work during the Industrial Revolution saw the destruction of many of the old craft skills as people moved to the factories in the towns and cities, and work became more fragmented and people more interchangeable.

These medieval craftsmen honed their skills over many years. The way they learnt, taught and arranged their guilds both demonstrates a way of working and raises some interesting questions for your own working future.

To learn a craft such as glassblowing, throwing a pot or gilding a chair, the young apprentice first went through a training period that required them to repeat an action again and again. With each repetition the content changed as the craftsman became more skilled – what the sociologist Richard Sennet[32] calls circularity, 'the virtue of repeated practice'. It is in this repetition that skill and the knowledge we have from something that is outside of us move to something that is embodied within us. He has observed that craftsmen who achieve this depth of knowledge and skill do so by watching others, and by practising over and over again until the tacit knowledge, that which is unspoken and uncodified, is absorbed within them. Of course this raises some important questions about the future, when, as we have seen in Jill's story, so much of our time could be fragmented, leaving very little time for the concentration and observation that is key to deep learning and skill development.

The medieval craftsmen repeated an action to learn, and they were also careful about where they worked. Typically they lived in workshops close to each other, and near to their work. In fact they would often sleep, eat and raise their children in the place in which they worked, so that in these workplaces labour and life mixed face to face. In a sense this is a precursor to the increase in home-based working which is a natural extension of technological advances, and of the reduction of carbon footprints.

The workshops of these craftsmen were more than simply places of joint work. They were also organised into systems of guilds, which served as the hands-on transmission of the craft or the intellectual capital that was the economic power of the guild.[33] The role of the guild was to establish the requirements for selection into the apprenticeships, and the basis of promotion to master craftsman. This parallels the emergence in a number of skill areas such as law and medicine of guilds and credentials.

Once an apprentice was accepted into the guild, they typically worked for seven years, the costs often borne by the young person's parents. If successful, the craftsman, now a journeyman, would work for another five to ten years before demonstrating mastery. I do not imagine that in the future these long apprenticeships will be required since there will be machines and technology to speed the process of learning. However, it is interesting to reflect on what it takes to go from shallow to deep skills, and the extent of the tacit and embedded knowledge required to do so.

Once up and working, these craftsmen were not working as sole traders; instead the guilds controlled entry and promotion, and also the quality of the work. In these loose partnerships personal reputation, trust and personal distinction were considered the most important obligations of a craftsman. It was part of the role of the guild to provide a frame to establish their probity. This was crucial, for every craftsman knew that their prosperity depended on their making a name for their goods – with an ever more personal sign of distinction. When an apprentice initially began their craftwork they tried to imitate the work of their masters; it was only over time in a slow and long process that they began to make their own signs of distinction so others could identify the product with them.

These systems of medieval craftsmen began to break down from the eighteenth century as machines replaced the blowing of glass or the throwing of a pot. However, it is worth reflecting on what these ancient mechanisms designed to build mastery can tell us about the future. It seems to me that there are three ways we can learn from these medieval craftsmen as we think about the future of work.

First, it is likely that location, as Richard Florida has argued, will become increasingly important to the development of deep skills. Just like the medieval craftsmen, we want to be near those whom we can learn from. As the development of deep skills becomes ever more important, so will be the choices that we make about where to be located and the communities we want to live in.

Next, while technology has speeded up our process of learning and knowledge acquisition, there is a strong case that deep skills will always require significant time invested in practising, training and developing. It is possible that as much as 50% of the time spent actually performing will be spent on training and development. With regard to actual hours, as mentioned earlier, there is an argument that it takes over 10,000 hours of practice to truly achieve mastery.[34]

Finally, the craft system reminds us that personal distinction will be key to crafting deep skills – as we shall see in the next piece, walking the line between personal branding and making a mark, and out-and-out narcissism, will be increasingly important. We can see parallels about developing deep mastery in the way in which the World of Warcraft has developed. In this virtual world people travel and live in guilds, with each member developing a competency in a certain skill or craft. Individual players become highly focused and specialised in a specific area and eventually achieve mastery of their field. Like the medieval craftsman, they join guilds and begin to work with other members who are versed in entirely different skill sets. What this encourages is the development of serial mastery as those who become experts are able to reach out to others in both related and unrelated skill areas. As in the real world, those who have reached the highest levels of skills do so through thousands of hours of work. To do this often requires playing for one full 24-hour day, at least once a week. It seems that it takes as much to build skills in the virtual world of gaming as it does to develop a tangible skill in the real world. What these gamers have done is to use play to become masterful, and as we shall see, in many areas of expertise, being prepared to play can be crucial to achieving mastery.

Playing like a child

Medieval craftsmen were trained to imitate their master and, perhaps after 20 years of working, to then develop their own signature. Theirs was not a world of innovation – it was a world of imitation. While we may learn from the rigour and depth of training of these ancient craftsmen, what we also need to acknowledge is the importance of innovation and creativity. To understand this we can look from the craftsman to the child. As innovation and creativity become the stamp of high-value work, so our working circumstances will have to provide an opportunity for childlike play and creativity to flourish.

Traditionally, companies have emphasised administration as a means of creating rationality and consistency. It was not that play and joy had been entirely extinguished, but rather they did not stand at the centre of work. Yet if mastery is to be achieved that goes beyond mere imitation, then play and creativity will become increasingly important. Work becomes play when we do something we normally don't; when we stop doing something we normally do; when we carry to the extreme the behaviours we normally regulate; and when we invert the patterns of our daily social life. My colleagues Charalampos (Babis) Mainemelis and Sarah Ronson call this reversal, intensification, trespassing and abstinence – the four cardinal points of play and festive behaviour.[35] We play when we move out of our day-to-day life; when we are not constrained by the normal boundaries of time and space; when we feel free and unconstrained; when we are flexible and lose our normal association between means (what we do) and ends (the result of our actions). These are not antecedents, consequences of something else that is play; rather, they are the very stuff play is made of.

The creative classes, such as advertising agents, creative writers, designers, planners and social theorists, have typically used fantasy and imagination to fire their creativity. Athletes compete; consultants and researchers explore; mathematicians solve puzzles; therapists may use therapeutic play. These people cannot achieve mastery without playing.[36] For mastery to work, you have to be prepared to play. You will only really achieve the mastery you need if you are excited about what you are doing and love the stretch of achieving mastery, and when you feel challenged.[37]

Play is central to achieving mastery because it can result in the combination of pieces of behaviour that are not normally brought to work. It involves making connections beyond the usual working relationships, and playing with others to experiment with diverse ideas and processes. As we shall see, in developing the Big Ideas Crowd, playful interactions, social gatherings and hobbies are a great way of keeping these crowds energised.

The future of work will increasingly be about breaking down the barrier that separates work from life, and work from play. The social scientist who on a Saturday evening visits the opera, a theatre or a sports game, may observe a wealth of information and inspiration for their research on the role of emotions in work group interactions; a dinner party at a restaurant can inspire an interior designer with ideas and insights about designing restaurants. The creative mind does not stop working at the end of the work day but, rather, transcends and blurs the boundaries between 'work' and 'non-work'.[38]

This, by the way, is a notion that Karl Marx understood well. He observed that the division of labour that accompanied the Industrial Revolution divided the interest of the worker from the interest of the community, and made the worker a passive consumer. This was not, for Marx, what work should be about. At the centre of his ideas is a strong conception of meaningful work as a process of active self-realisation, rather than passive production and consumption.[39] Drawing on the labour theory of value, most notably espoused by Adam Smith and David Ricardo, Marx asserted that value is created when man exerts his labour on an object, defining work as an inherently creative process. For Marx, humans derive meaning from their observed creativity, from interacting with their surroundings in ways that produce tangible improvements and generate value.

He believed that if work is fragmented, and if the productive efforts of workers become focused on a single detail of a bigger picture, this link between production and product, between creation and the thing created, starts to fray. In the bureaucratic enterprise that has emerged since the Industrial Revolution, it is no longer possible to see work as a process of self-realisation. Most of us have become alienated from the product of our work, instead generating value that we only experience indirectly, through monetary remuneration. Increasingly, therefore, we define our own value and the value of our work, not by how much we produce, but by how much we are paid. The intimate connection between work and value that makes our productive lives meaningful is no longer apparent.

Like Marx, the philosopher Jean-Paul Sartre was also fascinated with this theme of work as a meaningful venture. His interest was in authenticity and individuality.[40] For Sartre, what is important and authentic in our working lives is the deep experience that leads to mastery. Authenticity and individuality have to be earned, not simply learnt. Sartre argued that we are defined by our interactions, and through these interactions continually choose to redefine ourselves. Since man is nothing more than the sum of his actions, a meaningful life depends on meaningful work. What is apparent in both Marx and Sartre's writing is that if we accept the workplace as distinct from the realm of enjoyment and meaning, then part of our very nature becomes diluted through this mechanical repetition, and in doing so we lose our sense of authenticity.

Broaden through sliding and morphing

The challenge with mastery is that by developing deep skills you face the danger of becoming too narrow and too inflexible. Value in the future will come through being able to combine different areas of depth to create value. This combination can happen in one of two ways.

The combination of deep skills can occur, not within your own personal skill set, but rather from the skills in your broader network. It could be that a big, diverse crowd of people can bring a variety of ideas and insights. This is an idea we will return to in the next shift when we explore the Big Idea Crowd and the crafting of a network that spans boundaries.

It's also possible to create a combination of deep skills by personally developing in more than one area. You can be sure to avoid becoming too narrow by sliding into other related areas of mastery, or morphing into something completely different. Sliding and morphing happen when you develop deep knowledge, insights and skills in one specialism and then convert this to an adjacent specialism, or rediscover a lost competence.

My friend Herminia Ibarra has studied people who make these sorts of career morphs.[41] I was reminded of her research when I joined a number of women to speak at a panel at London Business School's Women in Business Club. The panel was titled the 'road less trodden' and the panellists were women who had become serial masters. It seems to me that they were brilliant illustrations of the power of morphing to create future-proofed careers. Here are their stories.

Management consultant to documentary maker to activist

Lorella Zanardo started her working life in Italy with a degree in English Contemporary Theatre, a subject she was really passionate about. After graduation she joined one of the big consultancy firms and spent much of her career as a business consultant becoming masterful in the consultancy skills of report writing, client engagement and business analytics. In mid-career she became incensed by the way women in Italy were portrayed in the media and decided to work with a couple of friends to make a documentary about it. The documentary, *Il Corpo delle Donne*,[42] became a huge hit on YouTube with more than a million views and went on to create an enormous groundswell in Italy about the portrayal of women.

Lorella had been prepared to make a long-term investment in time, energy and education to become a management consultant. But as she became more aware of the portrayal of women in Italian TV she went back to her earlier love of theatre. She began to spend less and less time around management consultants, and more and more time around film and documentary makers. She was doing what Herminia had observed classic morphers doing – acting her way into a new way of thinking, rather than thinking their way into a new way of acting. Lorella was morphing into another area of deep knowledge by gradually exposing herself to this new world, new relationships and new roles. Over time she began to envisage and test possible futures. For her the basis of the morphing was doing rather than thinking.

Senior executive to writer to coach

Mireille Guiliano spent much of her working life in French businesses, ending up as a senior executive in LVMH. As she went around the world she noticed that women outside France often lacked self-confidence and felt uncomfortable in their skin. She decided to write a book about how Parisian women create a sense of *savoir-faire*. The book sold millions of copies around the world and she is now on her fourth book.

Like many of the morphers Herminia had observed, Mireille's morphing required her to explore what this new world could be, and then in a sense linger between identities, as she tested out what it would be to be a writer rather than an executive. As many morphers do, she often found it a strain to be trying to live in two different worlds – oscillating between her old, outdated roles and the distant possible self she could make out on the horizon. Over time she began to make an increasing investment of her time and energy in her new self. Like Lorella, one of the sources of energy for her as she made this morph was the feeling that it was enabling her to establish a greater coherence between what she did and who she was becoming.

Stockbroker to recruitment CEO to comic

Heather McGregor, after an MBA at London Business School, joined a banking group as a stockbroker, becoming one of the highest-rated brokers in the business. Having achieved mastery in that sphere she went on to run her own business. At the same time she began to hone her skills as a writer, penning the infamous 'Mrs Moneypenny' column in Saturday's *Financial Times*. In 2010 she began another switch as she prepared for a comedy run to be presented at the summer Edinburgh Festival.

These are serial masters. They have a core of highly valuable skills that they love (analytics or writing or creativity or business acumen) and around these core skills have rediscovered lost passions (Lorella's passion for creating), let initial ideas re-form into new mastery (Mireille's observation about Parisian women) or spun off into new paths (Heather's discovery of her talent for comedy). Reinvention has rippled through the layers of their lives. Although these may look from the outside like radical change (consultant to documentary writer, stockbroker to comic), in fact they often reflect a deeper continuity and change.

The rules of morphing

It seems to me that morphing will become more and more important to the future of work. Herminia Ibarra has studied these morphers and tells us that there are certain actions we can take to ensure that we balance the need to be deep with the need to morph as circumstances change.

First, rather than make big leaps into the unknown, be prepared to craft experiments that allow you to understand more deeply the opportunities you face. For Mireille this meant writing a couple of pieces for a local newspaper and then seeing the reaction others had to it. Some experiments will be unintentional, while others will be more intentional and conducted by design. Some experiments will be opportunities for you to explore possibilities, others will simply serve to confirm your hunches. These experiments are often playful – recall how Heather began to write a play for the Edinburgh Festival about her life as a columnist.

Next, in order for you to understand the possibilities for morphing, you have to create eclectic networks of people different from yourself – the Big Ideas Crowd. This eclectic network will not only bring you ideas and insights, they will also serve as a vital point of comparison. Lorella, for example, had kept up with her classmates from English Contemporary Theatre. She had gone into management consultancy, while some of them had built a life around the theatre and films. This allowed her to make more discriminating judgements about whether their lives would work for her – it was through them that she could compare and contrast. When you morph, you not only experiment and begin to build a whole new set of skills, you also begin to shift your connections. You cannot expect to morph in isolation; instead it's important to seek out people who can help you see the possibilities. This enables you to begin to grow your new self by watching and emulating the people you admire. This is important because these new peer groups will have some of the values, norms, attitudes and expectations that will be part of your new identity. Over time this new peer group becomes an important 'community of practice'.

Finally, most morphers engage in side projects as they are doing their main job. These enabled them to begin to develop new areas of expertise on the side while still working full-time in their current jobs. Others take temporary assignments, outside contracts, advisory work and moonlighting to get the experience to build up their skills in a new area. It is about being prepared to go 'back to school' – to pick up the training and credentials in the new area. This is a form of experimentation while also developing skills. Recall how John began to develop his skills as an advisor to the villages of Bangladesh at the same time as working in the retail company.

You are going to have to give yourself time if you want to morph into another area of interest. Herminia uses the French phrase *reculer pour mieux sauter* which literally means 'stepping back to better leap forward'. What seems to be important if you want to morph is that you give yourself time to reflect on the choices you have made. Even short periods of time out will be crucial in enabling you to break the frame of the past and to reframe a possible future.

Self-marketing: creating and crafting credentials

What is it going to take to help you stand out from a crowd that's becoming more global and knowledgeable by the minute? I began to understand this some years back when my friend Sumantra Ghoshal and I took a close look at companies that were successful. We discovered that much of what they did was shared across the whole sector; they were simply imitating best practice from others. However, beyond this best practice there was always something that was unusual and unique – we called these 'signature processes', and it was these that separated them from the crowd. It could be the way their executives worked together in meetings, the way they selected people for the company, or even the structure and the decision-making process. What was important was that this 'signature' was unique to them and also brought them value.[43]

The same is true of consumer brands – the most successful also go about building their own distinct signature that separates them from other brands. Marketing professor Youngme Moon[44] calls these 'hostile brands' in the sense that they separate themselves from the homogeneity around them by playing hard to get – and they don't suffer fools. She describes how the Mini Cooper, one of the tiniest cars in the US market, introduced itself to the American driving public in 2002 with the billboard that simply read 'XXL XL L M S MINI'. It then ran an advertisement in which they showed a Mini mounted on the top of a sports-utility vehicle. This was a brand that was prepared to shatter prevailing notions.

In a crowded market it is important to be clear what is different, unique and what is your signature – and that counts for corporations, commercial brands, or indeed individual skills and competencies. Over the next two decades we can anticipate the market for talent will become ever more crowded as people from across the world have opportunities to develop their capabilities. Increasingly you will be called upon to create and craft your own credentials.

How you are going to do this is an important question. As we have seen, we can assume that the proportion of people in traditional full-time work with one company will decrease as proportionally fewer people work full time, in a pre-defined job, in a large, reputable company. It is clear that these free-agent, knowledge-rich, dynamic, project-based jobs of the future are capable of being really fulfilling. However, because they are fragmented, with many different stakeholders, in a rapidly changing skill area, they are also capable of making you nearly invisible. Take Amon, for example, as he works from his home in Cairo on projects with people he has never met and in companies he has never set foot in. Amon is almost invisible. Even Jill – who has a contract for three days a week for one company – is only somewhat more visible. Certainly the company she is contracted to knows who she is and what she does. But do they really know what her potential is? Do they really understand the skills and knowledge she has developed in other spheres? Do they really know what she can bring to the table?

The problem of being invisible

We don't have to rewind corporate history to the 1990s to see how the problem of invisibility will become increasingly pervasive. Just step back to 2009 to begin to see how invisibility can actually occur.

Imagine for a moment that in 2009 you are a middle manager who has joined a big company – for example, the Mars company in their US headquarters in Hackettstown, New Jersey. Perhaps one of the reasons that clinched the deal for you was the newly renovated Mars Chocolate North America headquarters. It could be that you were blown away by the solar garden or the open-plan office and conference rooms. You were also attracted by the package and the content of the job. However, although perhaps you did not realise it at the time, what you also got with the job, beyond the solar panels and the attractive conference facilities, was visibility.

In fact, perhaps the most precious asset of this job is that you are not invisible. In fact, you are highly visible. All around you, as you take your job in the corporate HQ, there are subtle clues that give away just who you are. Your widely communicated job grade and title signal your credentials and experience. The size of your office and the brand of company car show anyone who glances into the corporate car park where you stand in the pecking order. This combination of job grade, title, office size and car brand all subtly communicate how much power you have, and they also influence whom you will get to know over the coming months. And it is not just what happens in the office. Your attendance at the corporate training programmes of prestigious business schools around the world signals your fast-track status to those in other companies. Your widely observed corporate credentials also create the initial bond that will help you establish a link with other participants who could perhaps help some time in the future.

What's more, it is not just that your credentials are clearly communicated in your job title, office size, car brand and executive training. Lest you or anyone else forget, they are also stored in the Mars sophisticated human resource system. Here in digital form are your credentials – your selection interview data, your performance appraisal scores, the ratings your co-workers gave you, your position on the succession lists, your current and likely performance and potential ratings. What this means is that at any moment in time, at any place in the world, any executive can find out who you are with ease. In Mars, as indeed in any other company of any size, you are never invisible. The company has taken the time and effort to collect your credentials for you, to take a note of what you have achieved over the years, and to even predict where they think you will need developing in the future. You had to do very little in the process of creating credentials – they did it for you.

But here is the rub. Over the coming decades it is going to be less and less likely that a corporation will make you visible and create your credentials for you. In part this is because in the future your working life will be spent more loosely connected to companies. You could, like Amon, be working on multiple projects, which have been subcontracted to you from a variety of suppliers. Or you could be like Jill, working only a couple of days a week. Or like Xui Li you could be a micro-entrepreneur somewhere in the galaxies of the ecosystem that surround a company. Even for those working full time for a company, it's still unlikely to be like Mars in 2009. For a start, the organisational structure will be flatter and less hierarchical – so there will be fewer fancy job titles to signal status. Then, concerns about carbon footprints mean that you will be working from home rather than in an office, and taking the train to work rather than the flashy car. Even when you are at work, the majority of your time will be spent on projects where the boss changes frequently, and where you are as likely to work with someone from outside the company as you are with a company employee. As a consequence, the long associations that make you visible may well be broken.

What this means is that as you work for more companies, in looser and ever more flexible ways, you will have to find other ways of getting yourself noticed – to become visible in a world of invisible people. You have three key ways of doing this. You can ensure that you create a mark or signature of recognition and actively manage your reputation. Then you can follow the lead of professional groups like lawyers and physicians and establish a professional body or what I have called a 'virtual guild'. Finally, you can make sure you stay energised and involved by creating a 'carillon' career curve and building a number of elements to create a rich working life mosaic.

Creating marks and signatures

In my study is a beautiful bookcase in which are kept my favourite books. The bookcase is rather small and is made from seasoned oak that has been hand-carved. The casual observer of this little bookcase could easily miss a rather interesting feature. On the left-hand side, just above one of the shelves, has been carved a tiny mouse. I have a friend who has a set of six dining chairs – also carved out of seasoned oak – just as beautiful as my own bookcase. If you take a look at the left-hand leg of each chair you will find the same carving of the little mouse. For any lover of carved oak, this little mouse means only one thing – that the refectory table or chair, bookcase or cupboard was created by a master carver in the workshop of Robert Thompson.[45] Since 1919 generations of craftsmen have been fashioning these beautiful objects from seasoned wood and carving the mouse, each of which can be identified with one of the craftsmen.

Master craftsmen, programmers, physicists and film-makers

It is not just master carvers who put their mark on their produce. One of the marvels of the first flowering of the internet was the creation of Linux, an extraordinary example of open source software, created by volunteer programmers who build and distribute the free software. In fact, by 2001 the 30 million source lines of the Linux code would have taken 8,000 years of development time.[46] These thousands of volunteer programmers collaborate together in what Eric Raymond has called a Bazaar[47] in which code is developed over the internet in view of everyone. First dreamed up by Linus Torvalds, leader of the Linux project, the development contrasts with the Cathedral model in which the code development is restricted to an exclusive group of software developers. The benefit of the Bazaar way of working, by the way, as Eric Raymond has argued, is that 'given enough eyeballs, all bugs are shallow'. When the source code is open, then it is available for public testing, scrutiny and experimentation, so all forms of bugs will rapidly be discovered. The challenge with this open source programming is that the contributions of individuals could be lost in the crowd, never marked or acknowledged ... they could become invisible. So what the Linux programmers do is to respect what others have built and also to note the creator of a particularly impressive piece of software.

Or take a look at any of the scientific articles that are coming out of the CERN community of physicists. Located just outside Geneva, this is one of the world's largest centres for scientific research and every year hosts thousands of scientists from 580 institutions to debate and analyse the data coming from the Large Hadron Collider (LHC). This research in particle physics throws up a torrent of experimental data within a short space of time. This data is then parcelled up to be analysed in a global computing infrastructure where thousands of computers around the world are accessed via the internet to harness their processing power. By 2010 that meant the computing resources of more than 100,000 processors from over 130 sites in 34 countries, providing more than 8,000 physicists around the world with near-real-time access to LHC data, and the power to process it. This is a collective effort of global proportions – in fact, half of the world's high-energy-physics scientists are working on CERN projects.

What is fascinating about this worldwide community is how each member signals their contribution. This could be tricky as, like the Linux programmers, they are working together in vast virtual teams, often of more than 100 people, on a single part of the data set. Yet they are able to work together by preparing their own insights, sharing them with others and then posting the first draft of their ideas on the web for other peers to comment on. What's interesting here is that every single contributor, even if it is more than 100 people, gets their name on the paper, in alphabetical order. Each one is recognised for their unique contribution. Like the craftsmen of North Yorkshire, this community wants to both work as a team and to acknowledge individual contributions.

Incidentally, the way these physicists collaborate across the world has had a profound impact on our working lives in other ways. It was at CERN, in 1989, that scientist Tim Berners-Lee wrote a proposal to develop a distributed information system. His aim was to develop a better way of sharing information between scientists across the world. By 1990 he had defined the Web's basic concepts, the URL, http and html, and had written the first browser and server software. In 1991 an early Web system was released to the particle physics community and began to spread through the academic world. By 1994 a wider range of universities and research laboratories began to use it and the steady trickle of new websites soon became a flood. The rest, as they say, is history.

Or take the film *Avatar*. I remember watching it when it first came out, and then sitting at the end to see the credits. The credits rolled, and then they rolled – and then they rolled some more. In total more than 1,000 names are credited on the *Avatar* film, from the director right down to the caterers and drivers. Everyone who worked on this gigantic $250 million project had an opportunity to be publicly recognised for their contribution (oh, and by the way, the platform that hosted the incredible 3D developments was a Linux platform).

What these master craftsmen, software programmers, physicists and film-makers are all doing is putting their mark on their work. This enables others to gauge their contributions and enables them to actively manage their reputations.

I don't want to confuse narcissism with this reputational building. It's not narcissistic to want to build a trusted personal brand – it's vital. However, building a brand in 2025 will not be simply about trumpeting to the world how marvellous you are. Remember that 'brand builders' will be a growing occupation, so there will be millions of people doing the same – and some of what they say will be overstated, unrealistic or just false.

What will be crucial is the steady crafting of a trusted personal brand – which takes you away from the band of invisibility, but does so in a way that is authentic and realistic.

What will be increasingly important is that your reputation is both enhanced and protected, in the case of the craftsman, the computer programmer or the physicist, this means doing a good job in the first place, and then telling the world how good you are.[48] Over the coming years we can expect more and more complex means by which reputation is communicated. It could be, as in eBay and Elance for example, that clients evaluate the work and then make summaries of these reputations ratings available to other potential clients.

Verified credentials

This reputation sharing will itself become an important means by which your work is both described and communicated. But of course it is difficult to make ratings of work without some form of comparison, and also without independence. That's why we can expect independent rating services to become ever more important in describing what can be done, and communicating how well it has been done in the past.

There are already several analogies for these kinds of ratings – for example, the way consumer products like cars or washing machines are evaluated by consumer associations. We can expect that people with similar skills and competencies will increasingly create some form of infrastructure in which members are elected and also rated by others. This begins to get close to the medieval guilds we considered earlier. These guilds will become increasingly important as working independently becomes the norm.

Recall that when you buy a product from eBay you know that the product will be what it says it is, and will arrive at your door. If you are a seller, then you know that you will be paid. These are crucial aspects in the management of online retail. What's important is that eBay has created a complex process of verification which ensures that both buyers and sellers are rated with regard to the extent to which they are trustworthy. We can expect that there will be more and more intermediaries working between the sellers and buyers of skills to verify and credentialise.

The company ODesk is an early example of this. The company manages a platform that enables buyers of skills to manage the hiring, firing and payment of employees. Potential hires are listed in a Web-based directory and the assignments are widely distributed in size, ranging from a few hours to many months. Once employees are hired, ODesk's software monitors them throughout the workday. It can log the frequency of their keystrokes and mouse clicks and even takes pictures at random intervals using a webcam. Workers post their performance ratings, so potential buyers of their work can assess their competence. To support this quality of service guarantee, buyers and sellers receive feedback after transactions on a scale of 1–5 stars, with 5 being the highest. Freelancers are rated based on the following: skills, quality, availability, deadlines and cooperation. Their total number of hours worked and hourly rate are also shown. Employers are also rated, based on feedback from freelancers, the total amount they've paid, number of postings, number of hires and length of membership. In addition to their overall score, both parties' profiles also come with an indication of the number of feedbacks received. Like eBay, the higher the score and the more feedbacks, the better the provider. It takes about 12 months for high-performing ODeskers to become trusted and build up a reputation, after which they become very much in demand.

Even looking at ODesk right now, it is clear that the most successful e-freelancers have taken time to develop their personal brand, have delivered quality solutions for their customers and done so in a timely way. As a result, many of these workers, especially those involved in software programming assignments, find their initial assignments extended from mere days to months or years in length. A thought here about the first trend – the move from generic to specialist. Even in 2010 on ODesk the best long-term freelancers are those who have developed a unique set of skills or capabilities that are hard to replicate or are in scarce demand. Even in 2010 generic IT skills are being bought and sold on a global basis for a global market rate. Those that command higher prices are differentiating themselves based on being either the lowest-cost resource, the most customer-attentive resource or the most knowledgeable resource.

In the future, corporate credentialising and sharing reputation can no longer be taken for granted. In its place comes an awareness of how important it is to be able to validate your contribution – whether that be through the carving of a mouse, a software sign, the name on a journal article, the listings on a credit roll or a rating on ODesk.

Joining guilds and communities

Increasingly this reputation process will come through communities of people with similar skills and competencies making use of connectivity technology to find clients, to link to others to work with in large projects, to share knowledge, and to share and protect their reputations. This is far from the centralised, hierarchical control systems of many traditional corporations.

An interesting analogy is the way in which some of the older professions such as physicians and lawyers have managed their reputations and credentials, and also how they are evolving to be a whole lot more virtual. These professional associations were created initially to calibrate and label the credentials of their members, in much the same way that the medieval guilds had. They developed often very complex systems of examinations, references and mentoring to ensure that every member of the profession had a set of validated credentials, which they would carry with them and which demonstrated their value and specialisation at any point in time.

While guilds are a medieval concept, we can expect that in the future many such guilds will flourish as professionals and workers with similar skills create virtual communities. There will be occupation-based workers' associations (such as those that already exist for physicians and lawyers); workforce brokers that match employers and workers (such as ODesk and Elance); and regionally based organisations with an interest in forwarding the interests of workers and firms in a particular geographic area.

Looking back to the story of the Mars executive, these guilds will replace the role of the traditional human resources department at Mars, in the sense that they will create the tools that let people build careers as they move from project to project across firms. So we can expect to see these guilds becoming skilled in accreditation standards, industry-wide job descriptions and salary guidelines. Some professions such as accountants and lawyers have developed these generalised systems of accreditation over decades. For other groups, such as software developers and project managers, cross-firm accreditation schemes are emerging.

Many of the old professional guilds are embracing these new technologies. These virtual communities are becoming increasingly crucial as their members hunt for jobs, discover new information or business connections, market their business to a wider and more relevant audience, or validate business decisions. For example, Sermo for US physicians, LawLink for US attorneys, NewDoc for dentists and H-Net for social science academics have all become virtual communities for their members.

Sermo is one of the largest online physician communities in the US.[49] It's where practising US physicians, spanning 68 specialties and all 50 states, collaborate on difficult cases and exchange observations about drugs, devices and clinical issues. It creates potentially life-saving insights that have yet to be announced by conventional media sources. It does this by providing a real-time meeting place where physicians get help with everything from patient care to practice management.

With regard to reputation, the physicians on Sermo rank their colleagues for the value of their postings and the quality of their answers to posted questions. Highly ranked community members are turned to for respected answers and advice. The philosophy is that no one physician is as knowledgeable as physicians working together. So Sermo operates as a research medium, harnessing the collective power of physicians' observations. It allows physicians to improve patient care through the rapid exchange of observations. In turn, Sermo clients benefit from instant insight into clinical events and medical trends.

Members join through a rapid process that verifies their status as licensed, practising physicians. Once registered they receive a pseudonym of their choice. This pseudonym and the doctor's speciality are the only pieces of information that other doctors are able to see automatically, making Sermo a credentialled but anonymous community. It uses a proprietary technology to verify physicians' credentials in real time. In doing so it has created an environment of trust and collaboration that leverages aspects of social network theory, game theory, prediction markets and information arbitrage.

Sermo is primarily an information- and knowledge-based network where problems are discussed. The focus on Lawlink, with 6,000 members, is slightly different. It allows lawyers to network and to personalise their public profile.[50] Lawyers can communicate with each other – through both Twitter Law Forums and Law Groups. They are able to rank the top law news and to moderate forums on a topic of their choosing. They can also share law documents and ask questions of others. Members are able to post and review classified ads, and over 100 new attorney job listings are posted every week.

As corporations increasingly employ people in shorter-term project work, and draw more and more of their value from partners and ecosystems, so we can anticipate the means of reputational creation and enhancement becoming more and more crucial. So for workers like Amon and Jill, who work in fluid networks of organisational tasks, joining a virtual guild will create stable communities to which they belong even as they move from project to project.[51]

Carillon career curves and mosaics

Increasingly your career trajectory will not be defined by a traditional curve, or indeed the bell-shaped curve if you decide to be a downshifter; rather it will be defined as a series of ascending bell-shaped curves – or what's termed carillon curves, in which energy and the accumulation of resources grow and then plateau, only to grow again.

This is a direct response to the demographic and longevity forces that will increasingly define your working life. Over half the children born after 2000 will live for more than a century.[52] So that's the good news. The bad news is that few of us will be able to rely on a pension that will take us beyond a normal working age of 65 with anything like the standard of living we would like. The maths is simple to work out. When pensions were first created in the developed world in the 1880s, life expectancy was below 50 years. Now let's imagine that those born in 2000 continue to work until they are 65, but more than half of them live until they are over 100. That's 35 years of retirement and a 30% ratio of working life to retirement. That's clearly economically unsustainable.

And it's not just the maths that doesn't add up. In reality many of us cannot bear the thought of 30 or 40 years of retirement. We want to continue to work and to make some productive contribution to the societies we are members of into our 70s. Work used to be a fast-paced dash, now it's a marathon – so how are you going to prepare for this?

Working full time in the 1980s and 1990s went something like this. Join a company when you are in your 20s and be prepared to work really hard to get to a middle-management role some time in your early 30s. Then, if you do well, your income and power will increase until, by your 50s, you are at the peak of your earning power and energy. Then in your early 60s it all comes to an end and you retire. That is a 'traditional' career curve – in which working resources and energy are built steadily from the 20s onwards and completely stop in your 60s, when you plummet from the peak of power and prestige. This traditional curve is not an option for the future. But what takes its place? A second curve could be a 'downshifting' career shape; this is more like a bell-shaped curve, in which career resources, energy and value are built from between 20 to 50, and then begin a process of deceleration until the point at which your contribution comes to an end – in the 70s or 80s. A third option is what Tammy Erickson calls the 'carillon' curves.[53]

Let's imagine how this carillon curve could play out. You could spend your early 20s in college and then join a large company for a period of time, let's say until you are 30 in order to really build depth and understanding and achieve mastery in a field. Then at 30 you take a year off to travel or work on a volunteer project. Then at 31 you work in a project for a number of different companies – to broaden your experience. When you return, you want a change of pace so spend the next three years in a job-share. Then perhaps in your 40s you go back to full-time education for a year to build on your mastery skills, and then morph into a second area of mastery. So in your 40s and early 50s you accelerate your energy in this second area of mastery, and then in your mid-50s take another 'gap' year to travel or volunteer, returning in your late 50s and 60s to become a micro-entrepreneur, building from the two areas of mastery, and you continue to work on this into your 70s and 80s.

That's a carillon curve involving a mosaic of building energy in new areas, making time for reflection and time for working in volunteer passions. It's a working life that is way more flexible than the traditional curve, and more encompassing of your enhanced productive lifespan than the downshifting curve. It's a working style that encompasses more flexible working options, greater possibilities for the ebb and flow of energy and excitement. Thinking about future work as a carillon curve enables you to consider how you use time, what rhythm works best for you at different stages, how the economic reality will play out with regard to periods of resource accumulation, and how to best create challenge at different career stages, and to flex the degree of responsibility you prefer at any point in time.

What is clear is that developing mastery and interesting work means that education does not stop after school or college. Increasingly, creating a valuable and interesting work life will mean a lifelong commitment to renewing and re-invigorating through learning and development. That means taking sabbaticals to realign skills, going back to the classroom to learn new skills, or being prepared to apprentice to a master.

Creating a career mosaic

The carillon curve has embedded within it many possibilities. It's about creating a mosaic from various elements that could include periods of work, learning, refreshment and development, and then work again. Each of us will create our own personal work-life mosaics – but we can expect them to be made up of a number of elements, including: periods of time for what we might call 'gap years' when you spend a significant period of time contributing to another community; time when it's really important to relearn and brush up on skills and knowledge; and times when it will be appropriate to go back to full-time education.

Recall the pleasure John had in working with his village in Bangladesh. Over the years he had chosen to spend a couple of weeks, and then later months, supporting the village. John is not alone; across the world people like John are choosing to live some of their working lives in other communities. In Voluntary Service Overseas, for example, the average age of the 1,500 volunteers is 41, and they worked in over 34 countries in tasks ranging from management consultancy to marine biology.[54] Projects Abroad has people aged 16 to 75 operating in 25 countries and working in fields ranging from teaching to human rights and journalism.[55] What is fascinating about their experience is how many, like John, find these deeply inspiring and rejuvenating experiences. Over time we can expect more companies to reduce their fixed staff costs by encouraging people to shorten their working week or take three-month sabbaticals. At the same time, voluntary sector organisations will create ever more opportunities for people to use this time resourcefully.

All over the world people are making significant investments in their skills and developments and we can expect this to increase over the coming decades. As the technology force has shown, technological developments will increasingly take learning outside the classroom to be embedded in our everyday activities and entertainments.[56] The internet has the potential to transform the way we learn as more and more of the world's books, lectures and documents will be made available – many at no or very low cost. We can also expect significant developments in e-learning. Even in 2008 the corporate e-learning market reached $17.2 billion worldwide, up from $6.6 billion in 2002, and this investment will increase over the coming decades.[57]

When you work in an online environment and face to face, you tend to learn more quickly and to retain more than if you are simply taught face to face in a classroom. It's this 'blended learning' which is the most successful way of acquiring competencies and in which we can expect to see significant developments.[58] We can also assume that video games and simulations will increasingly become places to learn. They will do this by creating highly motivating environments through challenge, fantasy and curiosity. Right now the World of Warcraft is the most advanced of these games and incentivises players to confront challenges of growing complexity. Increasingly these simulated game technologies will be used to support the continual learning that will be so crucial to careers in the future.

As you think about the future of work for yourself and those you care about, what is clear is that the traditional assumptions about careers will no longer be appropriate. Faced with the forces that will shape the context of work over the coming decades, you will need to shift – shift your assumptions, shift your competencies and shift your habits. In this first shift we looked at the way that technology and globalisation will significantly increase competition, as billions of people around the world are able to join the global talent pool, and as computers replace much of the work that was previously performed by skilled workers. You will need to stand out from the crowd, and this will require you to make significant investments in your own mastery, while also being able to identify and develop your unique 'signature'.

Yet while mastery and signatures will be increasingly crucial, it would be wrong to view them from a static perspective. The forces of longevity have brought for many the real possibility of living way into our 90s and beyond. As we saw from the maths, unless we are saving a very considerable proportion of our earnings, most of us can expect to be engaged in productive work for at least 50 years. In the past, these years were described by a traditional curve that falls at the point of retirement. Over the next couple of decades we can anticipate that this will be replaced by a series of ascending bell-shaped curves, carillon curves, which mark the ebb and flow of serial investments in both skill development and emotional replenishment.

We have the gift of three sources of capital in the five decades we may be working, and in this first shift we have taken a close look at what it will take to ensure that our intellectual capital is sufficiently deep and unique to stay the course. Let us now turn to the second shift and consider what it will take to create social capital that becomes a source of value and regeneration.

9

THE SECOND SHIFT: FROM ISOLATED COMPETITOR TO INNOVATIVE CONNECTOR

One of the marvellous opportunities of the coming decades of work will be to build your social capital in a way that was never possible in the past. With 5 billion people connected to each other in an increasingly participative way, the possibilities are endless. The challenge will be to resist the temptation to become swamped and fragmented, while avoiding the isolation that could come with a more and more virtual world. Ensuring you get the most out of a hyper-connected world will require a fundamental shift in your thinking about cooperation, connectivity and innovation.

As we have seen in the last shift, one of the great paradoxes of the future of work will be to simultaneously be a unique specialist and master, capable of standing out from the crowd, while at the same time being intimately connected to the crowd. The traditional view of work is that you became successful through personal drive, ambition and competition. This is shifting to success coming increasingly from a subtle but high-value combination of mastery and connectivity – the combination of intellectual and social capital.[1]

The reason for this and/and rather than either/or approach is simple. While your specialised competencies, know-how and networks will create value, your value on its own will not be enough. In a joined-up, global world it's clear that innovation and creativity will be one of the most important aspirations to be developed in preparation for the decades to come. This creativity and innovation will be achieved primarily by your connecting to the know-how, competencies and networks of others. It is in this synthesis or combination that real innovative possibilities lie.

This reflects the extraordinarily powerful intersection of the forces of globalisation and technology and the multiple communities that this connectivity will create. Imagine the exciting possibilities that will occur when you are connected with more than 5 billion people. You will share what they have seen and heard, you will talk about your problems and support each other, and you will form into massive communities of shared interest. You will also increasingly use your participative 'cognitive surplus' to replace much of the passive TV watching that many of us have indulged in.[2] What is also really clear about this connectivity is that it will span the globe. Not just Americans connecting with Americans – or Chinese with Chinese – but rather worldwide communities connecting on issues that interest and excite them. It's these 5 billion people who have the potential to become one of the key networks for the future, the Big Ideas Crowd.

However, as we saw in the first shift to serial mastery, it is not simply breadth that's going to be the driver of value in the coming decades, it's also the deep-dive knowledge that comes from knowing something profoundly. The basis of your mastery is personal skill and knowledge development. This is rarely developed in isolation. Instead, mastery comes from assembling a relatively small group of people who can be a sounding board and supporters along the path to mastery. This is the posse, and finding and keeping them will be a crucial aspect of combining mastery with connectivity.

While the upside of superconnectivity is clear, there are also downsides. You can feel isolation, loneliness and fragmentation as you are cut off from real people, instead living your life increasingly in virtual worlds that provide little by way of real nurturing and emotional support. As we saw in the society force, increasingly families will be dislocated, living across regions and countries, with members often working through much of their lives. For each one of us, finding a community of support and nurturing, what I call a regenerative community, will become ever more crucial.

The posse

I first learnt this term when we studied members of Generation Y. In conversation with 23-year-old Inez, a rooky management consultant, I asked her how she got her job done. To my surprise she pointed to her computer, on which was arrayed along the bottom of the screen a row of names and faces. 'These are my posse – they ride with me and we help each other out.' Her words took me back in a flash to the cowboy films I remember watching as a child, where in a small town in the Midwest of America the sheriff (played inevitably by Henry Fonda or Charlton Heston) needs a bunch of men to support him. In a matter of minutes he has rounded up the men he can trust, and it only takes a few more minutes for them to be saddled up and riding out of town. As the camera pans to the dust eddy created by the hooves of the departing horses, we, the audience, can rest assured that this posse will be able to meet any challenge in its path. In fact, so popular is the idea of the posse that a recently released and very popular video game called 'Red Dead Redemption', set in the American Old West of 1911, encourages players to form posses online and travel around the open-world environment confronting other posses, hunting and taking on challenges.

Your posse is a small group of people – my guess is rarely more than 15 – whom you know that when the going gets tough you can call on and trust to help you. Your friendship with the others can go back years; some will work in the same place as you, others will not; some you will see frequently, while others could be in a different country.

My experience with Inez and her posse reminded me of the story of Frank and Fred which I told in *Glow*,[3] a book I wrote about how to create energy and innovation at work. The story goes something like this.

Both Fred and Frank were given a really tough project to complete at breakneck speed. Fred knew immediately what to do. First he rang his wife to say he would be late home for the next couple of weeks – he knew this was a job that would totally consume him for that time. Then he closed his office door and told his PA not to disturb him, for he knew he needed time to really work through this challenge. Then he began to fathom out what he needed to do, and began to draw up the project plans. Fred's view of his work was that this was a big task that only he could solve. Of course, he acknowledged that he would have to bring in other skills at times to work on the detail, but it was he who was the master planner. Only he could really tackle the challenge, and with this in mind he wanted to remain undisturbed in order to truly focus. Fred's first reaction was to close down and concentrate.

Frank took the opposite approach. When given the challenge, the first thing he did was to remember the people he knew could help him. Within minutes he had phoned a couple of them to ask their opinion. One was a dear friend with whom he had worked over 10 years ago, and whom he knew had faced a similar challenge. His friend was able in the space of five minutes to provide Frank with some really important advice about the conditions to look out for that could derail the project. Next, Frank made another phone call, this time to someone he had met more recently and whom he had supported only last week. This person had in-depth knowledge of a couple of aspects of the project, and could give Frank his view about how to structure the approach. So in the time Fred had closed his door and spoken to his PA, Frank had already begun to assemble his posse. Here is what a great posse is and what it can do:

* It's a relatively small group of people you can assemble quickly who have some of the same expertise in common – with sufficient overlap to really understand each other and add value quickly.

* The posse members trust you – they have ridden out with you before. These are folks you have known for some time and who like and support you.

* To really attract a posse to you will take honing of some important cooperative skills like becoming skilled at mentoring, learning how to make the best of diversity, and communicating well with people, even if they are virtual.

The posse come to your rescue quickly precisely because they can understand what you are up against, and can help without distracting. Imagine if Henry Fonda or Charlton Heston assembled a posse with some people who could not ride fast, or others whose horse was lame. The whole point about a posse is that they can be assembled in a moment, and can ride with the same speed and dexterity. Their similarity and shared capabilities are a great source of advantage to the posse since it is this that brings speed and depth. This community will be increasingly important in the future, but do also realise that they have within them potential disadvantages. They can certainly come to your rescue with speed, and can help you sort out challenges with confidence. But the potential problem is that they tend to tackle everything in the same way. They can only go in one direction. That is because they are so similar to you, and so trusted by you, that they rarely move from their preferred way of thinking or acting. So if you have a challenge that is big, complex and needs innovation to solve it, then the posse is not going to do it for you. What you need for the next big idea is a much more diverse and large community – you need the big ideas crowd.

The big ideas crowd

You know how it is – someone introduces you to someone else and suddenly you find yourself enthralled by what they are saying. You can see all sorts of possibilities in their ideas and how they could influence what you do. I recall such an occasion taking place a couple of years ago in the little town I live in on the edge of the Mediterranean in northern Spain. I was sipping my morning coffee in a small café on the seafront with a friend of a friend. We have a common love of opera and I recall that's what the conversation was about. As we sipped our coffee, my new friend called out to someone walking by and introduced him to me. This stranger turned out to be one of Spain's most cele-brated makers of chocolates; in fact, he made the chocolates for the legendary El Bulli restaurant.

As he sat down to join us for a coffee I began to tell him about the book I was researching at the time. As we talked, I told him about my ideas for a concept called *hot spots* – places and times when ideas suddenly become energised.[4] In the next five minutes our voices became increasingly animated as we began to cook up an idea of his creating a box of chocolates flavoured to represent the three core elements of a hot spot. The idea was that when the book was published later that year the chocolates could accompany it. We would make a chocolate that tasted of cooperation (we chose the sweetness of caramel), a chocolate that represented networks and boundary spanning (the surprise of salt); we used wasabi mustard to flavour the chocolate representing the energy of ignition; and finally, an explosive candy to signify the hot spot.

Within a couple of weeks of meeting we had the chocolate box designed and the chocolates made. So at the launch of the book I was able to give out the boxes while I spoke about the concept of hot spots. It was a great idea – OK, perhaps not a Big Idea, but nevertheless one that amused me and possibly some others as well for the next couple of years. And let's face it, how many other books do you know that have chocolates made for them?

The chocolate maker was not a member of my posse. I had only just met him, and we inhabited completely different worlds. But it's when these different worlds collide that sometimes the sparks of innovation ignite. There are some situations when the posse will help you solve problems with ease. But you cannot expect them to be a source of real innovation; they are simply too similar to you for that. Remember how Miguel reached out across his network to the young Indian entrepreneur when he wanted to solve the problem of traffic in Lucknow. Like me in Spain, he was connecting to a big ideas crowd – people who are very different from him, and who see the world through their unique eyes. In the future we will all need a big ideas crowd because it's through this combination of ideas and insights that innovation comes. Here are some of the marks of a great big ideas crowd:

* They are people in the outer reaches of your network, often a friend of a friend. Completely different from you, yet prepared to make a connection.
* There are lots of them – your posse could be as few as three people, your big ideas network could be hundreds.

Many of those in your big ideas crowd will be virtual – you link in on Facebook or follow them on Twitter or read their blogs. So where does that leave the physical world?

The regenerative community

The challenge with our emerging global and technical world is that before you know where you are all your communities are online as the virtual world becomes more and more seductive and emotionally easy. That's going to leave you potentially isolated and lonely, with very little of the stuff we humans have always needed – kind words, warm hugs, good spirits. In the past our close communities and families were our regenerative community. They may still be in the future, but you cannot take this for granted. The forces of globalisation and the break-up of traditional families mean that we will have to be a whole lot more purposeful about creating and maintaining these warm human bonds.

That's where the regenerative community fits it. Unlike your big ideas crowd, this is not located in cyberspace; and unlike your posse, these are not people who have the same skill sets as you. Your regenerative community is real people whom you meet frequently, with whom you laugh, share a meal, tell stories and relax. They are going to be crucial to your quality of life and emotional well-being.

As I imagine the regenerative communities of the future, it seems to me that they could take a number of different forms. For some it will be the decision to live communally, sharing life with those whom you want to stay close to. For others, it will be about purposefully moving to communities where it is easier to bump into others and have easygoing daily conversation. That's why, by the way, I have a home in a small Spanish town, where the pace is more conducive to regeneration and easy friendship. For others it will be the return of the extended family, with people from all the generations choosing to stay close to each other. The emphasis is on choice. What used to be assumed now has to be purposefully crafted.

In many ways this is potentially the most perplexing and interesting aspect of networks and communities in the future, because, while the virtual will naturally evolve faster than a wink of the eye, the physical will also have to evolve – and this time we cannot expect technology to take the lead.

Assembling a posse

You have a tough call to make, a really challenging problem to be solved, or a complex task to get under way. Who do you call on? You may decide, like Fred, to do it yourself; perhaps you think you have the answers, or perhaps you want to keep all the glory to yourself. But while Fred's route may have worked when tasks were simple and easy to solve, increasingly operating as a sole worker will lead to overwork, narrowing ideas and uninspiring recommendations.

Increasingly your tough decisions will need a posse. You have always known that. How many times have you picked up the phone to a friend to help you solve a tough question – to ask their advice, find out what they have done before, try out the solutions you have come up with? We have always assembled posses, but in the coming years these are going to become ever more important.

Reflect for a moment on the people in your posse, the people whom you can turn to when, like Frank and Fred, you have a tough problem to solve. My guess is that you can probably count them on the fingers of two hands – maybe even one hand. You will notice that when you get talking to them you very quickly get into jargon, begin to get deep into the subject. If a stranger listened to your conversation, my guess is that as it progressed they would understand less and less.

Deep mutual understanding

One of the friends in my own posse is Tammy Erickson; you may have noticed her name crop up earlier. She and I have known each other now for more than ten years. Over that time we have written two articles for the *Harvard Business Review*, have worked on a research project on cooperation, and have failed a couple of times to write a book together. I don't actually see Tammy very often – she lives outside of Boston and I spend much of my time in London. But we make time to see each other. I make a point of staying on her farm outside Boston for at least a week every year, and she stays with me when she is working in London. When Tammy and I talk, it gets down to areas of mutual interest pretty quickly. We talk about some of the paradoxes in creating cooperative cultures, a topic we are both passionate about, or we talk about how to construct the outline for a book, since we are both energetic writers.

Tammy is in my posse – I know that if I contact her right now she will come to my side. She has been willing to do this in the past – to help me think through a model of cooperation when I was wrestling with it, to encourage me when my energy for a particular book was beginning to wane, to give me advice on a particularly tricky challenge I had with one of my sons. I am in Tammy's posse – she knows that if she contacts me right now I will come to her side, just as I have done in the past.

Posses are huge sources of support and value to us and will become increasingly so in the future. However, while some aspects of the posse, such as trust, have always and will always be crucial, other aspects are changing. Notice, for example, that Tammy and I do not live in the same country, and that we maintain a virtual relationship for the majority of the time. We can predict that global mastery becomes more and more important so it's less likely that the people who could potentially join your posse are going to be sitting in the same corridor, or even in the same time zone. When I looked at the posse Inez had assembled, I was struck by how many lived in other countries. Like my relationship with Tammy, she had spent time with them over the years, but they are now scattered across the world.

Posses are based on trust. Remember Charlton Heston playing the sheriff? When he assembled his posse he did not choose them necessarily because they were his best friends (although they may well have been) or the people he most liked (although he may well have liked them very much) – he chose them because he could trust them, and because he knew they would be up for the ride. They may, of course, be people he liked very much, but that was not the main criterion for his choice. To be chosen to ride out with the posse you had to be trusted to keep up with them.

I'm aware that this is stretching the analogy to its very limits, but I hope you get the point. Assembling a posse is not about bringing all your closest friends along; it's about having a network of people whom you trust and who you are also prepared to come along with you. So there are two conditions that make for a great posse: the potential network has to have people who are capable of adding value to each other, in the sense that they have sufficient overlapping fields of knowledge and competencies; and you need people who trust each other and are willing to support each other and give each other time.

Overlapping fields of interest

In the days of the Wild West shown in films, the value of the posse was the horsepower of the group as they tracked the escaping bank robbers or raced to the next town. Now, and even more in the future, the value of the posse will be measured not by its horsepower but by the depth and speed of knowledge individuals bring to solving a problem.

When Frank picked up the phone to talk with a colleague with whom he had worked on a previous job, he rapidly got deep into the topic since both were deeply knowledgeable about the topic and could quickly tease out some of the finer details. Frank and his colleague were exchanging what has been called 'tacit' knowledge, and it is this type of knowledge that is crucial to the value that a posse brings. It's the type of knowledge that Frank and his colleague have accumulated over years of experience. It's knowledge about the short cuts that make the job easier, or the special way to think about a problem that makes it quicker to solve. These deep insights are rarely written down – that's why, by the way, Wikipedia cannot replace the posse.

The challenge is that this type of tacit knowledge – in contrast to the explicit knowledge that can be written down and broadcast to the world – does not flow very easily. Thinking back to my relationship with Tammy, we talk openly and in depth precisely because we trust each other, and this long-term trust is based on a strong relationship and a deep understanding of the context in which both of us live and work.

Creating a network of supporters, and assembling a posse that can both support you and combine their expertise with yours, goes way beyond simple networking. Simple networking is about building the database and then reaching out to many people – this, as we will see, works very well in the creation of the big ideas crowd, but it does not work for the posse. These are relationships built on a deep and mutual understanding of ideas and knowledge. These come not from simply reaching out, but rather from being prepared to listen and to learn, and having the capacity to attract like-minded people to support you.

The challenge is that often classical networking can become something of a game, with the purpose of presenting yourself in the most favourable light. Too often this perfect presentation of the self becomes little more than a manipulative exchange. Rather than real conversation and exchange, there are simply the carefully staged presentations of an artificial self. These staged interactions are rarely the basis for creating a posse network, nor do they build trust.

Trust and reciprocity

Posses are assembled quickly. When Frank picked up the phone to a colleague to ask for advice, he needed it there and then. When I call Tammy I know that she can give me her thoughts on the subject in a couple of minutes. In both cases the basis of these relationships is deep trust born out of a real understanding of each other. Tammy and I know each other very well. We have invested time with each other over the years. We understand where each other is coming from, we know the biggest issues we are wrestling with, and we have an idea of the knowledge areas we are building. Most often the creation of this deep trust and knowledge comes from an intense curiosity combined with deep listening and empathy.

The posse is assembled from people with whom you have invested time in exploring and learning about their experiences. They are also assembled by learning from each other the common ground you share, and identifying the common issues you both face. It's only through this sharing of context and common ground that it is possible to work collaboratively to address particular challenges or opportunities. By doing so, you are not only drawing out your mutual experiences and knowledge, but also creating new knowledge and ideas by tapping into the flows of existing tacit knowledge.

As you both begin to see common issues and gain experience in coming together to address them, trust and the foundations for a longer-term relationship are built. One of the main means by which trust is deepened is by introducing those in the posse to each other. In the case of Tammy and me, Tammy introduced me to MIT professor Tom Mallone, whose ideas on the virtual guilds are laid out in the first shift. I introduced Tammy to my dear friend Gary Hamel, and they subsequently teamed up on a couple of projects.

Reciprocity, the easy give and take of ideas and contacts, becomes a powerful foundation for trust. Take a moment to reflect again on those people in your posse. Let me ask you a question about how you found each other. Did you find them, or did they find you? My guess is that it's a combination of both. I know that I found Tammy (well, actually we were introduced by a mutual friend) but in the case of another posse member, Julia Goga-Cooke (who now works with me on the Future of Work research), she found me. I remember sitting in my room one day and in walked Julia, saying how much she liked my book *Hot Spots*. Building a posse is not just about assembling; it's also about attracting.

The attractor

Classical networking is all about you pushing – identifying people who could possibly be helpful to you, and then finding ways to introduce yourself to these people. It's a push in the sense that it's your energy that is pushing the creation of the contact. This does not work for assembling the posse. In fact, posses are often assembled because they are attracted to each other. So the most powerful way you have of identifying promising posse members is to find ways to attract them to you. You do this through shared knowledge and a common ground of interest in addressing similar issues. It's about attracting, not pushing.

So one of the questions you face in assembling the potential posse members is, how do you create a space where people know what you are doing? In my case the space was the books I write, which make very public the issues I am grappling with. However, you don't have to write a book to create the point of attraction. What you do have to do, though, is to make a priority to discuss publicly the issues you are wrestling with, so that others can see the overlap with their own interests. That could mean making presentations, talking about your idea on your blog, joining communities of people with similar interests. To attract others to you, you have to initially go into broadcast mode, not simply to tell others of your accomplishments, but also to give a sense of the challenges you are grappling with. It is through talking about the issues you are passionate about and challenges that you face that it begins to be clear how others can ride with you.

The posse that our Wild West heroes assembled was likely to be similar people drawn from the local town. Now, and increasingly in the future, the posse will have similar interests, but look at these with different eyes; some may also be virtual. This makes it a whole lot more complex, but also potentially a whole lot more interesting and dynamic. To pull a posse together requires a range of cooperative skills probably more sophisticated than those many people have right now. The skills, for example, of interacting in a virtual environment.

Virtual support

As technology connects people in increasingly sophisticated ways, so too can we expect virtual support to become more and more the norm. What's fascinating is that by 2010 we had already begun to see the emergence of virtual communities of people prepared to mentor and support each other – in a sense to create virtual posses. In Semco, the physicians' virtual community, members post challenges they face and others reply with advice and coaching about how best they can approach these challenges. Thinking back to Rohan, the doctor in India, we can imagine that the virtual community of which he is a member will do much to support him. The virtual law firm Lawlink does something similar. In a sense these virtual communities are taking off from the normal professional ideals of supporting colleagues; or take a community like HorsesMouth, where people can post the sort of advice and mentoring they need, and then review people who are prepared – in a sense – to join their posse.[5]

As the posse, and indeed work in general, becomes more and more virtual, so too will the skill of building cooperation and enthusiasm across countries become ever more important. These virtual community skills are in their infancy in 2010, but we can expect the sophistication of understanding and competency to increase over the coming decades. For some of the people in our research consortium from technologically savvy companies such as Nokia and Thomson Reuters, working virtually has become the norm. Take David Dalpe, a member from Reuters, for example. Here are his tips for building a virtual posse.

First, the people you will want in your posse will increasingly be working in another time zone. That means you need to be super-considerate of what times they are in and practise what David calls 'sharing the pain' – so it's not always the people in

Hong Kong, for example, who have to take phone calls at midnight.

Next, it's great using collaborative tools like Yammer to keep talking – but you also have to build in-person meetings, even if it is just videoconferencing over Skype. When your posse is virtual, over-communicate rather than expecting every email to be read. It is also important in a virtual community to be honest and open about any cultural issues as they arise. Once they get swept under the carpet they don't disappear – they just fester.

Thirdly, when attracting your posse, it's not just about finding people with the right technical skills, it's also about finding the sort of people who want to cooperate and learn from others.

Finally, your posse is built on goodwill, shared learning and the expectation of support. You are there to support each other when you need it. But that does not mean that it will simply emerge without any kinds of structure. You need what David calls 'operating principles'. These could be as simple as knowing how people like to communicate and when they are prepared to help. It could be as sophisticated as regularly updating your posse on what you are doing and how your ideas are developing.

Building a big ideas crowd

Let me ask you a couple of questions. Do you think that most people find new work through recommendations from people they know well, or from people whom they hardly know? Next question. Do you think that in trying to predict the amount of computer sales over the coming six months, the more accurate forecast will be made by the head of sales of the company, or by a crowd of people most of whom are not employed by the company?

If in both cases your answer to these questions is the second alternative, then you are already familiar with the power of big, loose networks. The forces of globalisation and technology will only serve to increase these natural phenomena.

It was the sociologist Mark Granovetter who asked the first question about where people found jobs.[6] The assumption was that it is personal connections with friends, family or close work associates, what Mark has called 'strong ties', that are the source of jobs. However, what Mark found was that it was not these strong ties that are the primary source of job leads. Instead these leads don't come directly from a close friend, but rather from a friend of a friend, or indeed someone who was simply an acquaintance, and often a distant acquaintance. These were what are called 'weak ties', and the article that Mark wrote called 'The strength of weak ties' really changed the way we think about knowledge flows and networks. What makes a contact useful for finding a job is neither the closeness of their relationship nor indeed the power or position they are in. What is important is whether the person knows different people, and therefore bumps into different information. If you spend all your time with acquaintances, neighbours and co-workers who operate in the same sphere as you, they rarely tell you something you don't already know.

What Mark discovered was that having a big loose network of acquaintances has the benefit of potentially tapping into a much wider source of information, and the more diverse these acquaintances, the greater the sources of information that can be tapped into. Mark wrote his article in 1972, and since that time the concept around the big ideas crowd has become ever stronger as social media have created opportunities to tap into so many weak ties with very little effort.

So let's move into the second question, about predicting sales forecasts. The power of these big crowds was put to the test by professor of complex systems Scott Page.[7] He was interested in the extent to which accurate prediction could be made by a crowd rather than an individual. In his study he looked at the accuracy of forecasts about sales. What he discovered was that big crowds tend to outperform single predictions, even if the single individual was a highly knowledgeable person. He also discovered that the more diverse the crowd, the more accurate the forecasts, particularly if what they were attempting to forecast was a complex phenomenon.

By 2010, examples of the big ideas crowd, or crowd-sourcing, were beginning to arise in many different areas of activity – for example, 'Yahoo answers', where people come with specific knowledge areas to answer questions to which people have failed to find answers online. Or 'Mechanical Turk', which is a place where you can upload human intelligence tasks for others to address. Other crowd-sourcing activities include: Distributed Proofreaders, which allows people to proofread e-text drafts for errors; Foldit, which invites the general public to play protein folding games to discover folding strategies; GeniusRocket, which outsources advertising jobs, including copywriting, graphic design, web design and video; and IdeaBounty, an ad agency that outsources creativity.[8] And, of course, in 2009 the *Daily Telegraph* newspaper in the UK uncovered the scandal of the expenses of Members of Parliament by uploading 700,000 expenses claim documents and allowing more than 20,000 people to search through them for erroneous claims.

If this big ideas crowd is so important to the future, how do you go about developing them? Clearly, these big ideas crowds emerge, they cannot be commanded – yet it is possible to influence their speed, trajectory and shape.

There are three ways in which big, broad and diverse networks are shaped. First, people who develop big ideas crowds are well practised at taking the less trodden path. What I mean by this is that they prefer to wander outside of their normal experiences and by doing so widen their circle of acquaintances to include people who are very different from them. Next, developing a big ideas crowd is a lot about being a social chameleon. If you are going to wander into networks of people who are very different from you, then you had better be prepared to adapt some aspects of your style to fit in with them. Finally, building a big ideas crowd isn't just about 'pushing' – making sure you make contacts, networking, remembering people's names. It's also about 'pulling', attracting a diverse network of people to you because they are interested in you.

Taking the path less trodden

You create big networks of diverse people when you are prepared to devote time and resources to activities outside the norm. It could be joining a social club for an activity you would not normally do, hearing a lecture on a topic in which you are novice, or stopping by at a team meeting in another department or another company. Whatever the activity, the goal is to go to new places and see new faces. It could be about switching into a completely different community of practice than the crowd you normally learn from. It could be as simple as taking a different path to work or through the office. One study of how networks formed, for example, found that often it could be mere 'accidents' such as where a path went, or whose doorway a staircase passed, that creates new connections.[9]

Becoming a chameleon

Reflect for a moment on the various groups you are a member of, or have some knowledge of. Now for each group ask yourself these three simple questions: How do the members normally dress? What is there attitude to time-keeping? What are the most frequent words they use?

My guess is that for each of these groups you can paint a unique picture. Perhaps one group tends to dress conservatively, be sticklers for punctuality and like to use a lot of analytical words and data to pepper their speech. Perhaps another group of people you know view themselves as more creative, their dress tends to the bright and flamboyant, they have a relaxed view of time and use a language form which is more emotionally laden. Another still may have members who perceive themselves as geeky; they wear undistinguishable clothes, are more likely to want to communicate on the internet than face-to-face and talk a complex, dense technical language full of abbreviations. These are not superficial differences, but rather the manifestations of what could be deeply held group norms. They play a crucial role in how a group creates a shared identity; they underpin notions of who they are, and perhaps most importantly they also signal who should be excluded.

The challenge for the person determined to build a big ideas crowd is that the networks they want to build potentially cut across the membership of groups as diverse as these three. It's not that you have to know every member of each group, but if you want to create a big, diverse network, then bridging into one or two members of these groups will be crucial. Bridging into groups means that you have to get past the barriers they have erected that keep out 'people who are not like us'. So, the first, more traditional group will feel uncomfortable with someone who is very artsy and who they believe has less of a grip on reality than they have. The creative, artistic groups will want to be clear about your creative ideas before they will be willing to open up to you, and will be wary of anyone they see as a 'suit'; while the geek group will be fearful of over-emotionality and suspicious of authority. Of course these are wildly exaggerated stereotypes. However, this illustrates that the reason we don't tend to build big ideas crowds is that we don't have what it takes to understand the norms of the group and by doing so to gain access to their networks.

Being able to develop networks that bridge groups with very different norms is what academic Martin Kilduff has studied. He is particularly interested in the type of people who are most able to bridge across these divides. What he observed is that those who were most capable of doing so tend to have chameleon-like characteristics.[10] They seemed to be very capable of adapting their attitudes and behaviours to the demands of the group. Just like a chameleon capable of camouflaging itself to merge with its background, so too the human chameleon changes according to the context they are in. For the reptile chameleon, this is changing the colour of their body so they almost become invisible in the place in which they are resting. For the human chameleon, it's changing their speech patterns, the words they use, the beliefs they bring to the forefront, even down to the clothes they wear. This is the capacity to be supremely adaptive to the context by being highly tuned to the behaviour cues, and continuously scanning to pick up norms. By the way, these people are not simply without any internal core of beliefs, and they don't change everything about themselves. But what they seem to be good at is knowing how much of themselves to adapt and how much to keep as core.

Martin Kilduff found that part of what makes great human chameleons is a personality trait he terms 'self-monitoring'. The best chameleons are high self-monitors – adept at observing cues in a situation, and good at rapidly adapting to them. The low self-monitors struggle to be chameleons as they are less able to pick up subtle cues and then act upon them. However, the simple truth is this: whatever your personality disposition around self-monitoring, if you want to bridge your network into groups of people who are very different from you, then you'd better be prepared to observe, distinguish and then imitate some of their norms. Without this adaptation you will always be seen as an outsider to the very groups that could be crucial to your big ideas crowd.

Being an attractor

Of course you can wander around, adapting to the groups you find yourself in and making sure you tread the path less trodden. That's one of the big energy sources for the building of this big ideas crowd. But at the same time as this 'push' strategy, you will also want to create a 'pull' strategy, attracting people to you, so that different people want to adapt themselves to your group norms and wander across your path. This is important to attracting the posse, and it also plays a central role in creating a broad network of diverse groups and people. Attractors pull others towards them because they are seen as open, so others feel less anxious about approaching them, and they are seen as good at reciprocating, so their friends are keen to introduce their friends to them. But perhaps the most important pull of attraction is that they are seen as interesting and exciting, and create clear pathways along which others feel that they can approach them. It could be through their Twitter conversations, or the blogs they write that invite comments, or the articles they write for others, or the short videos they have created about their ideas. In this age of participation it's not going to be enough to simply take the path less trodden, it will also be crucial to attract others by the way you lay out your intellectual store and mastery.

Finding a regenerative community

Fragmentation and isolation could be the key emotions of your working future. Isolated in your apartment in mega-cities, working virtually across the globe, disconnected from your family, the future of work can take on a bleak and dark hue. It is what economist Robert Lane calls the 'malnutrition' model. As he says, 'My hypothesis is that there is a kind of famine of warm interpersonal relationships, of easy-to-reach neighbors, of encircling, inclusive memberships, and of solitary family life.'[11]

In the past we did not really have to think or indeed work on a regenerative community – the family and the community simply provided that for us. In the future we cannot assume this provision. What was once assumed has now to be found and crafted. The posse and the big ideas crowd can be virtual some of the time. What differentiates a regenerative community is that they are not virtual – they are physical. So one of the central aspects of crafting a regenerative community is focusing on location.

Finding places that regenerate

In a world of ever-wider aperture of choices, we have to be very thoughtful about the choices we make about the physical communities we choose to live in. As we saw in the globalisation force, more people will choose to live in the cities of the world, and to cluster around others who have the same skills and interests as they do.

It seems to me that one of the paradoxes of the future is that while the world of work becomes increasingly virtual, so too the importance of the physical increases. You cannot assume that we will find ourselves in communities which are regenerative. In the past, where we worked was pretty much dictated by where we lived, and vice versa. Take Briana's father, for example: as an assembly worker in the Detroit motor industry, he had little choice but to live within a reasonable commuting time of his factory.

But this will change, partly as work – both knowledge-based and care-based – becomes more global, and in the case of the knowledge base more virtual. We can expect therefore that the choice of where to live will be forged more by individual preferences. At the same time, we can expect these preferences to be dictated in part by a growing concern for carbon footprints. For many people it will be both economically and ethically unviable to sustain long commutes into work. We will want to live near where we work, and we will want to live in communities that nurture us.

Regenerative communities, it seems to me, are those that enable people to meet easily and converse, that are based on walking rather than the isolation of the car, and that are places where friends can live near each other, or even share a home.

Every year, newspapers and magazines such as *Wallpaper* and *Monocle* rank the best places around the world to live, whilst academics such as Richard Florida study those places that are regenerative and support a high quality of life.[12] What Richard

Florida showed in his study of the USA is that it is possible to map the happiness of citizens against the map of the country. What he discovered was that some regions and cities are able to attract, retain and then encourage happiness and rejuvenation in their citizens. Here are some of the factors he found important.

First, the place you choose to live is rejuvenating when it is a source of excitement and creative stimulation: parks, open spaces and cultural events create regenerative cycles that unleash creative energy. Aesthetics also play a key role in regeneration, and in particular the physical beauty of the place. Economists call this the 'beauty premium', and these communities tend to attract other people who are creative and open to new experiences.

Next, a place is regenerative when it allows you to be yourself, to express yourself openly and to cultivate your individuality. This sense of identity is more and more important in a world where so many people will leave their birthplace and its norms and customs. The expression of self is a great deal more likely in places that are open and tolerant of differences.

Then a regenerative community is one that allows and enables you to meet people and make friends. So communities where people walk rather than drive cars, create opportunities for bumping into other folk, or communities where there are open-air cafés do the same by encouraging people to meet and greet others.

Finally, regenerative communities are those that provide a sense of pride; it could be supporting the local team, being with great neighbours or experiencing wonderful scenery.

Where are these regenerative communities? Richard Florida studied cities and regions in the USA, and concludes that it depends in part on your life stage. For what he terms 'the young and restless', the best communities are large regions such as San Francisco and small regions such as Boulder, Santa Barbara and Ann Arbor. For those married with children, the regenerative communities are in family-friendly neighborhoods such as those in Boston, San Diego or New York. For the empty nesters, the choice is San Francisco and Seattle. Outside of the USA, the *Monocle* ranking put many of the top communities in Europe – Copenhagen, Munich, Zurich, Helsinki, Vienna and Stockholm; in Canada it's Montreal and Vancouver; in Australia it's Melbourne and Sydney, and in Asia it's Fukuoka and Kyoto. We can expect more places to join this list over the coming decades.

Having found a regenerative community in which to live, what then will be the style of living? As we have seen, family structures are moving rapidly from the traditional to the rearranged. We can also predict a greater tolerance of variety when it comes to living arrangements. My guess is that, as in many aspects of the future, the aperture of choice will increase and we will choose with more precision to build regenerative communities, perhaps by deciding to live communally, or in extended family groups, or on our own but closely linked to friends. What is clear in all these life choices is the impact that close, positive friendship will have.

Cultivating friendships that regenerate

In a future world of ever-growing distances, ever-advancing technology and ever-decreasing institutional trust, when it comes to friendship what could have been assumed now has to be consciously cultivated. We humans are highly sociable, and probably also naturally cooperative and empathic. It is in our nature to strive to create reciprocal friendships, and to surround ourselves with people who are bound to each other through the support, affection and love they have given each other in the past, and will continue to do in the future.

These strong bonds of friendship and trust have their natural home in the family. It's this unit of shared past and projected future that has historically been the place where natural support could mostly be counted on. But, as we have seen, family units are reshaping and becoming ever more separated by distance and time zones. That's not to say, by the way, that in doing so they will be less able to provide support. It could well be that social media create channels of communication through videoconferencing and virtual presence which are as frequent and as supportive as anything created in the physical world.

However, that's not the point. Family ties will always be in place, but increasingly they will be virtual rather than physical as family members locate to wherever the work is, and to wherever the clusters of regenerative communities are to be found. So where does that leave those close, loving, easy-going relationships that can be relied upon with people who understand you? These could be relationships with partners, but they need to be more than this. In a world of increasing fragmentation, increasing noise and distraction, and ever-greater distances, the creation of strong, loving friendships that go beyond the posse becomes increasingly important. It's not necessarily, by the way, the role of work to create a context or crucible for these deep, caring, regenerative relationships to be built. However, it is the role of work to create sufficient space and time for the crafting of these regenerative friendships to occur.

This is crucial, since it is time that is the resource which is most precious to the creation and sustenance of regenerative friendships. If your world becomes fragmented into slithers of time, and if it is overwhelmed by the priorities of others, then what suffers is your energy and will to invest in these deep friendships. The splintering of time and place which is so much a mark of the future means that deep friendships will not simply emerge – they have to be invested in, nurtured and cared for. What that means in reality is that a process which in the past may have happened naturally, will in the future increasingly need to be actively crafted.

In the past it would have been appropriate to create a clear divide between what we do at work – the organisation of information and the completion of tasks – and what we do out of work – the support of family and friends. But as the divide between work and non-work erodes, so too friendship becomes part of work. As my own research on the boundaries between the two showed, the cycle between work and home can bring the joys of happy friendships and partnerships into energising work. It can also work in a negative manner, bringing the loneliness of a distracted life into work. The strength and depth of our friendships both create the well-being of our life, and act as a remarkable source of energy and resilience and buffer in our work. How will these relationships emerge and be maintained in an increasingly fast-paced and disconnected world?

Sometimes in order to look forward you have to look back. I'm going to look back as far as 100 BC to the life of Roman statesman Cicero, who laid out his own thoughts about living a good life. In a series of letters he described how he saw the creation of friendship at the very heart of the good life.[13] What strikes me about Cicero's letters – and is the reason I reach back over 2,000 years to provide a signpost for friendships of the future – is the extent to which he sees friendship as a long-term investment. Not, by the way, the investment based on tit-for-tat, you do something and I will reciprocate, but rather a more cooperative, communal way of thinking about friendships.

In Cicero's letters I see many aspects of what the regenerative friendships of the future will be based on: the idea that friendship cannot simply be assumed, it has to be thought about and invested in, and that these deep, regenerative friendships have at their heart shared interests and values. That is not to say, by the way, that our friends cannot be very different from us in many ways, but it does suggest that for friendship to flourish there have to be mutual interests and shared experiences. Friendship is then strengthened on the basis of mutual goodwill and affection, and on ever-deeper conversations.

As Cicero comments: 'It is the most satisfying experience in the world to have someone you can speak to as freely as your own self about any and every subject upon the Earth' (p. 188). These relationships become regenerative precisely because they serve a whole host of purposes beyond a single purpose, and through the 'bright rays of hope it projects into the future' (p. 189). The goodwill of friendship is established by love, quite independently of any calculation of profit. The word for friendship that Cicero uses, *amicitia*, is derived from the Latin word for love, *amor*. It is this deep affection that is built from shared interests and acts of kindness and generosity. Even 2,000 years ago Cicero observed that these deep, affectionate and regenerative friendships often cease because of greed for money and ambition.

Any visitor to Rome can view, even through the ruins of that ancient city, the means by which Cicero and his colleagues conversed, shared mutual interests and became friends. The city is crossed with wide walking paths, the many temples and forums are places for rest and conversation, and Cicero, like any wealthy statesman, would also have had a private garden in which to receive guests. Ancient Rome was built for conviviality, conversation and the cultivation of friendship in a way few contemporary cities are. That's why, as we saw earlier, finding a place that creates this space for conviviality is so important to the future of work.

So how might we cultivate those regenerative relationships within the context of a working future more and more marked by loosening relationship ties and fragmentation? It seems to me that the choices we make about how we work will play important potential roles as enablers to cultivate friendship, or alternatively through fragmentation and isolation, as destroyers of friendship.

The type of work that cultivates deep regenerative friendships does so by enabling you to live in regenerative communities that encourage, as Ancient Rome did for Cicero, the natural formation of friendships. It is work that encourages the cultivation of friendships, by not overwhelming every moment of your life, but rather providing space and tranquillity for the conversations that foster regenerative friendships. And finally, it is work that supports the cultivation of friendships by creating a balance of motivation and aspiration that does not place money and power at the centre. Let me finish with a quote from Cicero that I feel could be even more important for the future than it was in the past. Here he is reflecting on a conversation with a friend, Scipio:

> But let me get back to Scipio, since he had a lot to say on the subject [of friendship]. He used to complain, for example, that people are prepared to take more trouble about everything else in the world than about friendship. Everyone has an idea how many goats and sheep he owns, but nobody can say how many friends he possesses. And an immense amount of care is devoted to acquiring the cattle, but none to choosing friends. (p. 208)

What is striking about these reflections is that what was true in Ancient Rome will be ever more true in the future – that the joys of friendship can only be achieved with time and care. This has real implications for the future or work as it puts into ever starker relief the importance of crafting a working life that creates a balance, that has the time and space to actively cultivate friendships, and that does not, as Scipio warns, place greater emphasis on material goods.

It is a paradoxical future we are entering; a world that is becoming increasingly connected and global and yet simultaneously becoming more and more fragmented and isolated. Finding a way around this paradox will be crucial to creating a working life of meaning and value. In the past it was sufficient for our relationships and networks to evolve. But, like many aspects of the future, this natural process of evolution will not be enough. What will be required will be the habits and attitudes to invest in those that will bring ideas and insight, to be prepared to reach out to others who are different, and like Cicero to put in the time and effort to find and keep regenerative friendships.

Creating time and space to cultivate friendships will be an enormous source of energy for the future. However, to do so we would be wise to heed Scipio's warning – to put development, meaning and friendship before the acquisition of material goods. This is the final shift, to which we now turn.

·

10

THE THIRD SHIFT: FROM VORACIOUS CONSUMER TO IMPASSIONED PRODUCER

This is the toughest shift of assumptions, competencies and habits. It's about shifting towards a working life that has meaning, passion and positive, productive experiences; and shifting from a working life that has the traditional deal of money and consumption as its central driver. This is a tough shift to make, and will require a deep understanding of choices, an intelligent view of consequences and a courageous approach to taking action. However, without this third shift it's hard to imagine how you can craft the future working life you want and deserve.

The shift is crucial because we are at an inflexion point in the history of the industrialisation of work. We have witnessed the steady dismantling of what might be called the 'traditional' careers, and 'traditional' work. In its place is a way of working and a new deal that could potentially create much greater freedom and opportunities. In the future you have the opportunity to work on tasks that you are passionate about and to find colleagues from whom you can learn and grow. You have the opportunity to balance your time spent working with your time meeting your obligations to family, friends and yourself. These opportunities for personal choice at work will become ever more possible as traditional careers dismantle. However, these are by no means foregone conclusions. In order to reap these opportunities, you will be called upon to make some pretty tough choices about who you are, what you believe in, and the consequence and trade-offs you are prepared to accept.

As you look into the future, what comes in the place of traditional work will, to a certain extent, depend on your focus, determination and energy. As we saw in the first shift, crafting interesting, meaningful work over the coming decades will only happen if you are prepared to devote time and concentration to building mastery, and are prepared to continue to do so throughout your working life. Similarly, it will take energy and tranquillity, vigour and enthusiasm to craft the close regenerative communities and the big ideas crowd that are so central to the second shift. Yet, as we saw in the Default Future, unless work becomes a more balanced part of our lives, and unless we make the time for these crucial activities, these shifts will not materialise.

This third shift underpins much of what I believe the future of work could and should be about. It is the shift from work that is all-consuming to a more balanced and meaningful way of working. Yet at the heart of this shift there is something much more profound. A balanced working life has been on the agenda for decades. The stresses that an unbalanced life creates are well documented, as indeed is the impact on young mothers and fathers. It's nothing new, and appears to many commentators to be unsolvable.

I believe not only that is it solvable, but that the five forces that will shape our future create an opportunity to bring force and focus to the solution. These are tough questions and issues. This is how one of the members of the Future of Work Research Consortium – let's call him Tom – describes the dilemma he faces:

> Is it possible to enjoy a high quality of life defined as a perfect work-life balance if that means an average career velocity? Given the way the media hypes heroes with headlines like 'youngest ever millionaire', etc., we are constantly fed cues that set us in fierce competition. And it is going to take a huge

amount of effort to change that. Is the media ever going to celebrate a man that was a great father, a truly development-oriented line manager who never rose beyond middle management and didn't make millions in stock options?

My guess is that these are questions that have been resonating with you, whether you are a Baby Boomer, a Gen X or a Gen Y embarking on your career. In our research consortium we also heard the voices of members who had made some important choices around why and how they worked. Here is a manager from the not-for-profit organisation Save the Children:

> Obviously I'm biased (a little) but I think that the idea of experience resonates with those of us who have already chosen to work in the not-for-profit sector. We accept that the pay we receive will be lower than we might be paid for a comparable role with a corporate and therefore that we'll have a lower 'quantity of consumption' in exchange for the quality of experience. It also ties in to the concept of pay and reward. In organisations where you can't afford to recognize achievement with pay, what reward do you give instead? For me, the important experiences are those of leadership, responsibility and decision-making which contribute to my sense of well-being at work, and, if I think back, I would have been willing to sacrifice 'stuff' in order to be able to be exposed to those opportunities earlier.

The third shift is about clarity, choices, consequences and trade-offs. We can see in these words the trade-offs she was prepared to make. It seems that the dilemmas and choices that participants of the research consortium face are shared by millions around the world. These are not new dilemmas; it is simply that the forces acting upon our future make them ever more important to face up to.

I recall seeing these dilemmas being played out some years ago as I attended a conference for the senior partners of a large professional firm. There had been concern by members of the Human Resources department of the firm about the work rate of many of these senior partners. Some appeared to be teetering on the point of work addiction, and many suffered from stress-related illnesses. So over a period of a couple of months the HR team had engaged a film crew to go round the world interviewing the young children of the senior partners. The crew asked the children to talk about what Daddy was like (for the majority of the senior partners were indeed men).

It was these child interviews that were then projected into the conference room filled with more than 100 partners. The film lasted no more than five minutes, perhaps even less. But during that time the atmosphere was charged with emotion. You can imagine what these children said about their fathers. In a poignant, caring way they described their invisible fathers. In a space of five minutes this group of 100 were confronted head on with the consequences of the choices they made. The choice to work over the weekend, the choice to come home late, the choice to leave on Sunday night. I don't imagine anyone of them was untouched by the experience – and I know for myself the emotions of that day are still seared into my memory almost 15 years later.

Of course, it is not just working fathers who are faced with tough choices and unpredictable consequences. A couple of years ago my research team and I surveyed senior executives across Europe about their work and their lives. We found that while almost 100% of the men were fathers, less than 60% of the women had become mothers, and of these the majority had only one child. When we interviewed these women – most of whom were in their mid-40s and beyond, many of them spoke of the surprise they felt at not having had children, and some spoke of their sadness.[1]

As we spoke more to them, it was clear that in fact very few had made a conscious decision not to have children. Looking back, they realised they had not always understood the real choices they faced, or indeed accurately calculated the consequences and trade-offs of these choices.

This is typical of many of the choices we make about the role work plays in our wider life. Often the consequences of our choices are slow to emerge, or do so in an unpredictable manner. Looking back on their life without children, for many of these executive women, this was the consequence of an unpredictable and slow emergence of consequences, which included, for example, their unplanned inability to conceive, their unanticipated difficulties in finding a partner or the sheer pressures of their working life.

The traditional deal at work

Why has it been so hard for us to make choices about the way we work, and what is the basis for the shift we now have to make? This third shift requires us to move from the old deal at work to a more 'future-proofed' deal. For many people the old traditional deal looks something like this:

I work ... to be paid ... Which I use ... to consume stuff ... Which makes me happy

At the heart of the traditional deal is the pursuit of high pay, and of consumption. Moreover, the simple fact is that many people in the developed economies have been spending and consuming at a more and more voracious pace over the last two decades.

Looking back to the prior decades, the extent to which this deal has been created looks ever more clear. My guess is that if my grandmothers were to be transported as children to 2010 what would most surprise them – beyond the amazement with the technology, or that in my own family of four siblings only one is still married – is the sheer amount of stuff most people in the developed world have. My family is no exception to this. We have a computer for every person, plus one 'for the house'; both my sons have a TV in their bedrooms, and we have a dishwasher, washing machine, dryer and endless household gadgets.

Consumption has been one of the headline stories of societies in the developed world over the last five decades – a story of ever-expanding consumption – of cars, houses, food and gadgets. Our patterns of consumption have always changed in part as a response to the way we live and the technologies afforded by our society. In 1874, for example, the average American family spent 56% of its budget on food; by 1901 this had fallen to 47%, which began to open up the possibility of other forms of consumption.[2] The gap left from spending on food was filled for many families with spending on cars. In the USA, for example, the number of cars went from around 20 million in the 1930s to 60 million by 1960, and more than 100 million by the early 1970s.[3] This rising urbanisation and car use began to hit China in the 1990s – which by 2009 had 26 million cars on the road.[4] In the USA, consumption also switched from food to homes – many of which were purchased with low-cost loans in the newly built suburbs that began to ring the major cities of the Western world. Home ownership was made increasingly possible by innovations in finance such as adjustable-rate mortgages and securitised sub-prime loans.

The impact of the five forces – and why the traditional deal is breaking

The old traditional deal that we worked to be paid, which we then used to consume, and this was the basis of our happiness, is certainly no longer working – if it ever worked. Here is how the five forces that are shaping your world of work are making the traditional deal look more and more fragile, and the shift to a future-proofed deal ever more crucial.

Demographic forces are calling into question the traditional deal. What is interesting about the experiences of many Gen Ys is that they saw the traditional deal being played out in hyper colour in their parents' lives. Just like the children on the video at the conference of senior partners, they have been on the receiving end of this working style for decades. They know intimately what it is like to come home late every evening, to check the mobile phone every couple of waking minutes, and to sacrifice weekends to corporate travel. They know it well, because many grew up with parents who worked like this. So for Gen Y, and indeed the generations that come after them, the consequences of choice are understood very clearly. That's not to say, of course, that they will necessarily make different choices than their parents. It could well be that a proportion will choose to work just as hard as their parents. However, what it does mean is that in making these choices their eyes are wide open with regard to the consequences. They may be prepared to work as hard as their parents, but they will want the pay and recognition that go with this. The days of 'deferred gratification' are long gone.

Global and economic forces are also putting strain on the traditional deal. Periods of austerity in the developed countries, and a realisation that the boom and bust years are set to continue, together create a view that work cannot simply be about making money and consuming – there has to be more. Plus, of course, there is an understanding that the need to reduce carbon emissions will put increasing pressure on consumption.

The forces of technology are also putting pressure on the traditional deal. Traditionally, the deal was that choices about work were made for you – in this parent–child relationship it was assumed that everyone wanted to work in the same way, and that the consequences of the deal were positive. Technology has and will continue to make it obvious that in fact people don't want the same deal, and are a great deal more aware of the consequences of the old, traditional deal. The deal has moved from parent–child to adult–adult. Not only are the consequences of choice more visible, the aperture of choice is also widening. Technological innovations are creating more and more choices for how and where we work, and we can only expect these choices to continue to widen. It's now technically possible for many workers to choose to work at home or in an office; to communicate with team members virtually or in person; and to work asynchronously rather than in the moment. The storylines for 2025 showed just how choices within this ever-widening aperture will be played out.

Technology creates greater choice; it also make the consequences of choice much more obvious. Take a look at social media, blogs and websites and see how people across the world are communicating their decisions about work, and trying to understand their consequences. Take working mothers, for example. When in 1990 I gave birth to my son I was the first professor at London Business School to become pregnant. I had absolutely no idea what to do, or the consequences of my action. I had made a choice, but frankly I had no idea how it would play out. Much has changed. Just now I googled 'working mothers'. There are 9,290,000 entries, images of working mothers, blog postings of working mothers, webzines dedicated to mothers who work, tips on how to do it, forums to talk with other working mothers … the list is endless. It's not just working mothers; dads can also play the consequences game with 14,305,000 entries to help them navigate their choices.

Social media have created a joined-up world, which brings the possibility of anyone faced with a dilemma to find out from millions of other people around the world how they made the choice and the consequences they encountered.

At the same time, societal forces are heralding an ever-growing acceptance of variety in lifestyle, and an ever-growing disaffection with large corporate life. All across the world the traditional two-parent, two-child family is being replaced by an extraordinary assortment of family structures: divorced parents remarrying and nurturing the children from both families; lesbian and gay couples bringing up children; older mothers having surrogate children. The variety seems endless. What is interesting here is that as people decide to exercise choice in their domestic lives, so too do they develop the reflexivity and intellectual muscle to exercise choices in their working lives. As lives become more diverse, there is an increasing desire to exchange traditional corporate life for something altogether more flexible.

What's more, the debate about carbon footprint puts into ever-higher relief the consequences of many traditional working practices. Is it realistic, for example, to stop people working from home, when the commute into the office uses a huge slice of their carbon footprint? Is it realistic to ask people to fly to see their colleagues in another region when videoconferencing can bring them into their office with a press of a button? The dilemmas about reducing carbon footprints highlight the consequences of more traditional working practices, and in doing so demonstrate clearly some of the benefits of more flexible patterns of work.

The configuration of these future forces creates an extraordinary opportunity over the coming decades to reshape a way of working that enables us to reconnect with what makes us happy, and to create high-quality working experiences. The breakdown of automated work, the rise of home-based working, the ever-increasing possibilities of choice and the acceptance of variety together provide the foundation for a shift in the focus of work.

The winds of change are blowing – so the question is, what will be the outcome? Can work become more balanced, more accepting of the variety of human needs and more flexible about the conditions of employment? I believe that it can; the five forces are indeed creating an enormous momentum for change, and this shift represents the foundation for what work could become over the next two decades.

However, embedded within this shift are deeper and more emotional issues. These are issues about power, status, needs and wants and the roles that money and consumption play in work. There are also issues about the way experiences are appreciated and understood. There are two sides of this issue – the fact that work, money, consumption and status are so wrapped up together that prising them apart might prove difficult. The other side of the issue is that while the power of money and consumption is often overestimated, the power of productive experiences is often underestimated.

The central role that money and status played in the traditional deal

At the heart of the old, traditional deal was the idea that we work to earn money. But as we look forward to the future of work we have to ask whether work really is just about earning money.

There is no doubt of course that money plays a key role in work. If we are paid less than we need, then all of the other experiences that work can be about really have no meaning. The workers in the low-cost factories across Asia do not, I imagine, care much these days about the wider meaning of work. As Maslow so astutely observed in 1954, there is a hierarchy of needs, and the fulfilment of security is at the very base.[5] However, what Maslow would say about these low-paid workers is that it will not be long before their needs move up the hierarchy.[6] Once security has been met, then their sense of belonging will assume greater importance (I work because I enjoy being with friends), followed by their needs for self-esteem (I work because I can develop my skills), and finally to self-actualisation (I work because it provides an opportunity for me to achieve my true potential).

And yet, even though money is at the base of the Maslow's Hierarchy of Needs, nevertheless it is often placed at the heart of the traditional deal. Why is that the case? There are a number of reasons why money has been put at the centre of the working deal – but, interestingly, these assumptions are all looking more and more like fallacies rather than realities.

We may assume that money will make us happy. Remember the traditional deal – 'I work … to be paid … which I use … to consume stuff ... that makes me happy.' Yet as many people across the world meet their basic needs, we know that this is a fallacy – more money does not bring greater happiness. We know that from lottery winners who, while initially elated by their wins, rapidly find that these feelings of elation dissipate. You don't have to be a lottery winner to be fooled by the impact of money on satisfaction. You may believe, for example, that a short-term pay rise of 25% will make you more satisfied with your working life and therefore you choose all manner of ways to earn more. However, in reality those people who are actually paid 25% more are no more likely to be happy or satisfied with their lives.[7] It seems that we can be too easily deceived by what we think makes us happy.

Why is this the case? In part it's because the more we earn, the more we change our lifestyle to accommodate our new-found wealth, and in doing so recalibrate what makes us happy. Lottery winners become progressively less interested and excited by the experiences they previously enjoyed, like reading or sitting down to a good meal. They are on what has been called the 'hedonic treadmill'.[8] Simply put, it's the human disposition to feel entitled today to what we felt thankful for yesterday, and once we have received a treat too often we become less appreciative of it over time.[9]

What these lottery winners are experiencing is declining marginal utility; the more they have, the less they appreciate it. What is crucial to recognise is that while declining marginal utility is a factor in the experience of money and consumption, it's not a factor in other forms of experience. For example, the deeper the skills and mastery you develop, or the wider the friendships you invest in, then the more you experience rising rather than declining marginal utility. The more you earn, the less you appreciate it; yet the more skilled you become in areas such as friendship and mastery, the more you enjoy it.[10]

What is true for individuals is also true for nations. The citizens of richer nations are no happier than those with less. Clearly, when communities, regions and nations have very little they are less satisfied and less happy than those that have more. People are unhappy if their children are dying of preventable diseases, if the water they are drinking is contaminated, or if they have no means to keep themselves warm in the winter or cool in the summer. However, once these basic needs are met it appears that money does not enhance either satisfaction or happiness.[11]

It is becoming increasingly clear that the money part of the traditional deal of work does not make us particularly happy or satisfied, and it also has some rather unpleasant consequences. Our appetite for money and material goods is more insatiable than our desire for other kinds of experiences. You know yourself how quickly the pleasures of a new acquisition are quickly forgotten and replaced with the desire for more. Moreover, wanting more and becoming increasingly materialistic are often associated with setting goals that are wrong for development, either because they are too easy or because they are too unattainable. Those who become increasingly materialistic are also more likely to engage in passive activities. For example, people with strong materialistic needs are likely to spend more time watching television; those who are less materialistic tend to spend more time socialising with others or planning their futures.[12]

The traditional deal has the impact of persuading us to overestimate money and status. It also persuades us to underestimate the happiness that can come from productive experiences. While the traditional deal may have money at the centre, in reality many, if not most, of the pleasures of work and personal life are not priced.[13] The aspects of your working life that bring you most pleasure are not for sale, and they are rarely available in the marketplace to be purchased. Reflect for a moment on your own emotional state over the last month, and recall those points in time when you felt happy, satisfied and joyful. Of course, some of these positive emotions will come from experiences that are bought; however, many positive emotions will come from experiences that are free: the delight of friendships, the challenge of a job well done, the fun of spending time with children, the pleasure of walking in nature, being around to see the sun rise in the morning or set in the evening.

How we learnt to love money and consumption

If we want to understand how to make the shift for ourselves, or others, we need to understand how it was that millions of people around the developed – and increasingly now, the developing – economies of the world learnt to love money and consumption. The story of consumption begins in childhood. Not surprisingly, those parents who emphasise material wealth and place this above nurturing or warmth are more likely to raise children who crave consumption. It's also not surprising that watching long hours of television can play a role in reinforcing the merits of money and what it can buy. As the psychologist Tim Kasser and his colleagues so poignantly put it: 'Those surrogate parents television sets portray the goods that money buys as the epitome of life itself; protecting children from pornography, we carelessly expose them to the vivid lessons of materialistic appeals.'[14]

Once we are out of childhood, this modelling of consumption continues. Over and over again, we learn through the traditional deal at work that to receive material rewards is good, and this connection becomes continuously rewarded and reinforced. At work this well-publicised relationship between work and pay reinforces the idea that working is about earning money. Eventually we discover, 'I must like money, because I have been working so hard for it.'[15] Over time the monetary value inherent in the work we do becomes self-reinforcing. We learn to believe work experiences are good if they enable us to earn money, and bad if they don't. As a consequence, the earning of money increasingly becomes the goal of work, ever more reinforcing our materialistic goals.

Money and work become self-reinforcing goals. But there is another reason why we have clung to the traditional working deal that has pay and consumption at its heart. In many societies money does not simply serve to create the means of consumption, it is also a social marker, which signifies status and as such has become an intimate part of identity. The acquisition of goods and services validates us as a person.[16] There are, of course, many other ways of validating identity. We can validate ourselves by our powerful friends, by the honours we acquire, through the demonstration of our athletic prowess, our kindness to children or even the making of beautiful quilts. However, in many societies around the world it is money that is the dominant validator of status, and therefore has become one of the central personal strivings. Yet when validating ourselves against others the stakes get continuously higher. Reference points change and escalate, so that 'keeping up with the Joneses' becomes an important potential driver in the link between money and work.[17]

In overvaluing money we tend to undervalue other parts of our working lives. Recall how Tom, a member of the Future of Work Consortium, described this dilemma:

> Is the media ever going to celebrate a man that was a great father, a truly development-oriented line manager who never rose beyond middle management and didn't make millions in stock options?

What Tom has noticed is that his society does not value the experiences he would like to cherish – productive experiences like being a great father or a development-orientated manager. The same, by the way, is true of other experiences such as companionship and friendship within and outside of work. Even though we may know that the working quality of life depends a great deal on companionship,[18] many companies appear to be indifferent to people and relationships. Tom may value productive relationships at work, but the context in which we work rarely does. It seems that the very process of business has created hierarchies and roles that in a sense neutralise personality and create indifference to the possibility of experiences and friendships. As the economist Robert Lane[19] observes, 'friendship is not a market commodity'.

Money has been at the centre of the traditional deal – not simply because of what it can buy, but also through what it conveys about status.

Of course, there are jobs in which money is not the goal. Take another look at the earlier quote from the manager at Save the Children:

> In organisations where you can't afford to recognize achievement with pay, what reward do you give instead? For me, the important experiences are those of leadership, responsibility and decision making which contribute to my sense of well-being at work, and if I think back I would have been willing to sacrifice 'stuff' in order to be able to be exposed to those opportunities earlier.

What she is reflecting on is that if you are in a company where the goals are not materialistic, then this reinforces your non-materialistic aspirations. What she values most is the quality of leadership, the opportunities to take responsibility and make decisions. These are the goals of her work that make a difference to her.[20]

So as the nature of work begins to be reshaped, driven in part by the velocity of the five forces, what then can work become? In this, the third shift, what work can become is a place of productive experiences, rather than simply a place designed for the fulfilment of voracious consumption.

Making the shift: putting productive experiences at the centre of the deal

What will it take to make the third shift – to think of work as a place of productive experiences, rather than simply an activity that has pay as its key driver of motivation?

We already know that work can create a wide variety of productive experiences. In the last couple of years I have asked people to reflect on the question: 'Why do I work, and how did I choose what type of work to do?' Here are some typical responses:

* I work because I enjoy the opportunity to spend time with others whose company I enjoy and from whom I can learn – I really value these relationships.
* What I love about work is being really stretched in the tasks I do – I relish the challenge to do something that is hard, that I feel I have to really work at to achieve, and that gets my adrenalin going.
* I love the opportunity the flexibility of this job gives me – I'm able to spend time with my children when they are on holiday – and that means a lot to me.
* I work to learn – I want to develop all my ideas, and for me work is a great place to learn.
* I like to work in a place in which I am able to manage others – I find leadership very, very stimulating and exciting.
* Every year I am able to take a month off to work with a charity that I support – that's really valuable to me.
* It really excites me to be in a situation where I feel I am getting better and progressing – it's great to develop my skills and feel that I am really pushing myself.

These are all productive experiences – the experience of friendship and mentoring, the experience of being stretched and developed, the experiences of leading and power, the experience of spending time with children, or with a charity. In the past the traditional view of work was that it was about earning money; in the future it could increasingly be about a complex, experience-based notion of our needs and aspirations.

The stage is set for the third shift. For much of the history of industrial work, the traditional deal for work put money and consumption at its heart. It is now possible to recast it in the future as a deal that looks more like this:

> I work ... to gain productive experiences ... that are the basis ... of my happiness

This deal does not, of course, negate the role of pay in work, for pay is important to meeting basic needs. However, in many of the developed countries of the world extra income will not be the driver of work satisfaction or happiness. Increasingly the driver will be productive experiences. The mosaic of future working lives – and the carillon curves that accompany it – requires a new deal between the individual and work that no longer puts pay at the centre, but rather places it in balance with many other sources of experiences.

This is a fundamental shift – both in the way we think about work, and in the deal that is struck between the company and the worker. What will stop this from happening over the coming decades, and what can those who want happy, fulfilled and future-proofed working lives need to make the shift? Making this fundamental shift will require you to be a great deal clearer about the choices you face, the consequences you can anticipate from these choices, and the trade-offs you may be required to make.

Choices, consequences and trade-offs

Making the shift is about being prepared to take action. It is about, for example, choosing to trade off pay for a gap year; or about choosing to become a micro-entrepreneur with all the risk that this entails; or about choosing flexible working or a job share in order to spend time with family and friends. What is clear is that in the future there will be a great deal more choice than in the past. Traditionally, it is corporations that have made choices for employees about the deal. Increasingly the deal will be fashioned by autonomous, self-directed workers. Yet this will require an altogether more reflective attitude to making choices and to facing up to the consequences.

It is not tough to make choices; we make choices all the time, in every waking minute of our lives. Yet many of us are unschooled in facing up to these choices, and understanding the nature of their consequences. To understand more deeply the nature of choices and their consequences, I have turned to the philosopher Peter Koestenbaum, who together with his colleague and friend Peter Block has thought a great deal about the nature of the choices we make.[21]

Their view is this. As we confront how we want to live our working lives in the future, and indeed to shape the institutions for those who come after us, we are faced with making decisions about our lives and being accountable for our decisions. Inevitably some of these choices will bring anxiety, and guilt from saying no either to ourselves or to others. However, what is important is that we become more aware that we are indeed making a choice, and that by doing so we are prepared to enter into debate, and through these conversations to reflect on the paradoxes that choice brings. Their message is that rather than denying choice and anxiety it is the very experience of these emotions that brings meaning, character and texture to our working lives. Failing to face up to our choices, repressing our anxiety and guilt and failing to talk about the paradoxes, we lose much of the richness of our working life. The old traditional deal was about having these choices made for us. The deal for the future is being prepared to make these choices for ourselves.

We were confronted within the Future of Work Consortium with many paradoxes and dilemmas as we talked about the future. Here is how one member described the dilemma that she faced:

> I think that sometimes the reasons that Maslow's lower levels dominate is because organisations haven't found other ways to reward/recognise staff. So, say I'm not particularly motivated by the money I'm paid (and therefore the house I own or the car I drive), but my organisation has chosen to recognise my performance using pay. I might much rather have something else, but there is nothing else and if everyone around me is being recognised through pay, then whether it motivates me or not, I still want the same level of recognition, and the organisation will do that through pay. I would be demotivated if my performance wasn't being recognised and so I will accept pay as a proxy for that recognition. So, unless I can find a way to persuade my organisation to recognise my performance in another way I'm stuck with a performance recognition system that doesn't meet my personal needs.

The dilemma that confronts her is between her own nascent needs and a corporation that recognises her primarily through her pay. In shifting to the new deal of productive experiences rather than the traditional deal of pay as the centre of the work, many such dilemmas will arise. The challenge is to understand the nature of the choices available, and to be prepared to accept the anxiety and guilt that these choices entail.

I can imagine, for example, that many of the fathers at the senior partner conference felt this dilemma. To spend time with their children would make them feel anxious about their career progression and pay, while spending time with their clients and work colleagues would make them feel anxious about their children. These are not win–win situations, and I don't believe that in the future they will be any more so. Moreover, as the trajectory of the five forces shows, the aperture of choice will only increase, and with this will come ever greater opportunities for anxiety and guilt.

What we face in this shift is the very last hurdle of the conversation that began with the storylines of the Default Future and the forces that shape these stories. It is a conversation about how the very fabric of the conditions of work will shift. While we are indeed constrained in our choices – by the company we work with, the society that frames our everyday living, the communities we care about – nevertheless we have free choice that goes beyond the family, culture and organisational context. It is indeed possible to blame the choices we make on the context in which we live, but, as Erich Fromm has argued, this could simply be 'the escape from freedom', conforming to corporate and societal norms and disregarding and disrespecting individual uniqueness.[22]

As the aperture of choice opens ever wider, and the consequences of choices are made increasingly public, so being able to make wise choices will become more and more important. It is true, of course, that the making of choices is to a large extent determined by how work is organised and rewarded in the company and country in which we live.[23]

However, beyond this context, there are times when we are confronted by the consequences of our own choices in a very explicit and profound way, like the senior executives listening to their children speak about them as fathers, or the women looking back on their lives, or even my own guilt as I see the impact my punishing work routine has had on my own parenting skills. We have all seen others painfully confront the consequences of their choices about travelling frequently and working long hours when their marriage broke down. These painful discoveries most often come when something in our lives explodes. It could be our marriage, or our health, or our children who are in trouble. It is at these points that the link between choices and consequences becomes painfully obvious. But as Robert Reich remarks, 'Is there a more reliable way to become aware of the implicit choices we're making? Do we have to await a painful discovery?'

As we become increasingly aware of the choices we are making, so we become engaged in three separate conversations.[24] The first is the debate we have been having about the shape of what lies ahead – of technology, connectivity, speed and globalisation and the impact this will have on our work. The second conversation is about what could be, and particularly about the Default Future. In this conversation we are confronting our concerns about the way our working lives could develop in a world that is potentially isolating, fragmented and has a huge underclass of the new poor. The third is the private conversation we have with those whom we are closest to about the difficulties and dilemmas we face in making choices about work.

These three types of conversations are different responses to the same set of forces. There will be occasions when we engage in all three conversations without seeing the connections between them. We see the incredible way that globalisation will develop and the opportunities it will bring over the coming decades, without realising the impact it will have on the way we and those who come after us will work. But if we are to deal effectively with the larger trade-offs before us, we must understand the connections between these three conversations. In Robert Reich's words:

It is time for a larger discussion about what combination of economic dynamism and social tranquility we want for ourselves, our families, and our society; and about the public choices we need to make in order to achieve this balance. (p. 249)

This is important since at every step of our working lives we choose – and it is in making these choices that we construct our lives. These are spontaneous choices, in the sense that they occur on a moment-by-moment basis, yet over time they create the flavour of our lives, the tone of our existence and the structure of our work.

Yet even as these choices are spontaneous, they are self-determined in the sense that we often perform them as an automatic act, without thinking. No one forces me to work every weekend, or to spend limited time with my children, just as no one forced others to buy big cars or houses. If we are to exercise our own free will, then we are required to make choices. There are always alternatives open to us, so as we consider the structure of our future working life we are called upon to engage in a deliberate choice, rather than acting automatically. To dilute responsibility 'leads to cowardice where courage is essential, or to foolhardiness when restraint is in order' (p. 47). As Koestenbaum reflects:

> By saying 'I have no choice' (and meaning it), we have chosen to betray our human nature. We have, in that sentence, freely chosen to resign from the human race and join the animal kingdom or the technocracy of machines or electronics. (p. 51)

The challenge is, of course, that in exercising our choices the alternatives themselves are fixed. Briana, for example, has different alternatives available to her than Rohan, born in rural India, or a child born in 2020 in a wealthy suburb of Boston. As each begins to craft their working lives over time, they are faced with the same challenge – to distinguish between free will (things they have power over) and objective reality (things that are not in their power) and then to accept the responsibility of free will and the inevitability of what they cannot change.

Inventing our future

As we think about the third shift, how can we go about inventing our future? In the past, of course, many of these choices about work and the future were made by the corporations in which we worked. But as hierarchical command structures, top-down decision-making and inflexible people practices are being stripped out, the aperture of choice widens. In making choices and inventing our future, we are faced with dilemmas, anxieties and guilt. Yet not making a choice is not an option. Given the ever-widening aperture of choice, what will be the wise choices for the future? I am going to make two predictions about this third shift: that the invention of a future will increasingly be framed by our individual and unique aspirations, needs and capabilities rather than by the corporations in which we work; and that in framing the motivation for our future work, the deal will move from pay and consumption towards a deal that puts experiences at the centre.

Crafting a future around what we care about

What is important to me may not be what is important to you. The sort of working future I may want may not be the future you want. We each have to craft our unique working future. This was an idea I explored in a book I wrote in 2004 called *The Democratic Enterprise*.[25] In it I argued that people would increasingly shape their work through the choices they made. I used the idea of citizenship as the framing idea, and was particularly influenced by the thinking of the philosopher David Held on the nature of democracy.[26]

The timing of the argument was not perfect. Back in 2004 many CEOs and executive board members felt very bullish about how they ran their companies, very much in control of the traditional deal, and very confident that they knew best what was right for employees. Also, at that time the available technology made the execution of many choices, such as virtual working, micro-entrepreneurship and home-working difficult. Back in 2004 the idea of individual choice did not resonate with the zeitgeist. The Western world was experiencing an economic boom, fuelled in part by the cost advantages of India becoming the back office and China the factory of companies across the USA and Europe. The world had indeed begun to globalise, but the advantage still rested firmly with the West. The five forces that are now so clearly reshaping the world had in 2004 gained much less traction. No surprise that an argument for a need to bring more choice and meaning to those that worked, to encourage companies to treat people as individuals and to encourage people to take responsibility for their actions fell on deaf ears. These were bumper years, and introspection was not on the agenda.

Since that time much has changed. The five forces, at that time nascent, are now very much to the fore. Technology has created greater opportunities for people to communicate with each other across the horizontal axis of companies, rather than to be beholden to vertical communication. It has also brought a level of transparency that makes it a great deal more obvious what choices are available, and a deeper appreciation of the consequences of those choices.

In 2004 we had discovered that people had very different needs; it was just that no one wanted to know. At that time the retail multinational Tesco had used technology stolen from marketing to profile and segment their employees in much the same way as they had profiled their consumers. Once they had collected the data about individual employees, they began to combine people with similar aspirations into segments. What they found was fascinating. Rather than all employees wanting the same ways of working, employees' aspirations for work were highly individual in reality. Of course some wanted to ascend the corporate hierarchy and to bask in the status of money. However, others wanted more than anything else to have flexible working arrangements that allowed them to occasionally spend time with their children or ageing parents during the day. Some came to work to play and have as much fun as possible, while others didn't much care what they did as long as they got paid fairly.

What was also interesting was that the people within these segments were not all the same in other aspects of their life. It was not simply that the old wanted to work hard and the young wanted to play. Some over-50s wanted to play, some under-20s wanted to work hard. It was not about gender, with all the women wanting to spend time with their kids and the men to work hard. Some women wanted to ascend the corporate ladder while some men wanted to stay at home with their children. What the executives at Tesco had discovered was that their employees were highly individualistic. These choices are indeed bound in part by the employee's personal circumstances, for example whether they had young children at home; and indeed they were shaped by their personality and aspirations. But it was impossible to make an algorithm to predict these profiles. What is clear is that as the aperture of choice widens, so to does the variety with which people decide to exercise choice.

So as we think about this third shift, what is crucial is that we both acknowledge and celebrate the variety of human needs and aspirations – for ourselves and for others. Simply put, the experiences that are important to me, and for which I am prepared to make choices, may not be the experiences that are important to you. By understanding this, we can begin to shift our view of working lives towards something that is more accepting of unique needs, and towards the idea that work can be crafted to acknowledge and meet these needs.

Consuming less and sharing

The future of work will increasingly be about our reflecting on the choices we make, with a keen eye to their consequences. While for some people the traditional deal will be the one they choose, I predict that for more and more this traditional deal will not be the one they go for. As we can already see in Gen Y, an increasing proportion of people will want a deal that has more than money and consumption as the primary drivers. Instead, as the aperture of choice widens and the consequences become clearer, so many will choose to create a fulfilling working life that enables them to create a balance. Of course this shift is not going to be easy and we can anticipate that as it emerges it will create friction with the dominant cultures in many corporations that favour the traditional deal.[27] However, although some aspects of companies and societies will discourage their employees from peeking over the maze, I believe that more and more people will want to take a peek over the wall and see what could be possible beyond the traditional deal.[28]

In making trade-offs around the future of work, what could be sacrificed are some of the big-ticket items, like homes and cars, which have been at the centre of the traditional deal.[29] Both have historically played a role in defining our sense of identity; they have become in a sense our 'social marker'. We become the woman who owns six Prada bags, the guy who drives a BMW, the child who uses an iPod. In the traditional deal it is these purchases that have defined who we are in the society in which we live. But as the future-proofed deal emerges, it is possible that our work will be defined less by what we consume, and more by the experiences we produce. What then happens to what we consume?

Perhaps we can learn to consume less? For some commentators, this change is crucial, and points to the way in which home ownership has trapped many economically and location-wise in a world that increasingly demands mobility and flexibility.[30] There is also a view that the ownership of large, gas-guzzling cars, particularly in America, has destroyed a community way of life and created dead city centres and moribund suburbs.

If our work is going to change from being less about the consumption of stuff, then we have to find different ways of living a high-quality life. Perhaps one aspect of this shift is that we will learn to share or co-own resources. Take the Cloud, for example, where complex IT programs and systems can already be shared and downloaded at the point of need. The same could be true of cars. It is now possible in many European cities to share cars. Right now, outside my home in Primrose Hill in London there is a communal car that I can use whenever I choose, and a communal bike for when the rain stops. Perhaps, as some have suggested, we will also learn to build regenerative communities by learning to share our homes.

Making the shift

Let us imagine for a moment that in the future we decide that the abundance of consumption has lost its status as our reigning aspiration. In its place could come a host of other sources of aspiration and status – the quality of our family and the depth of love with our friends, perhaps, or the creation of meaningful and exciting work, or a renewed focus on creativity and the arts.

What will create the tipping point for this shift to occur? In part it will be about the changing context of institutions and governments – but fundamentally I believe it will occur because we decide to think deeply about work. I don't expect this, however, to remain an individual thought process, but rather see the real possibility for people to converse around these issues and to be connected into ever more global movements. There have always been those who have decided to pursue another path. They joined monasteries, founded communities in remote areas or formed communes to shape their living arrangements. Now there is a possibility with globalisation and connectivity that these 'grassroots' movements could become more of a force for change. I am reminded of the Shell scenario for 2050, which describes the major difference between resource scenarios resting on governmental legislation and those relying on the power and dynamism of community groups who use technology to join up and through whom globalisation becomes a force worthy of attention.[31]

As we have seen, the shift towards experiences and away from consumption could be one of the most central hallmarks of the future of work. Restraint could be the new desire ...

Work as we know it began in earnest after the Industrial Revolution, which saw machines transform the way people worked, where they worked, how they thought about time and why they worked. As workers became treated more as machines, so the mechanisation of work placed machine-like demands. The downside of all of this was that, just like machines, we are not accountable for our actions.

The choices you are faced with are on a grand scale, as you understand more fully the shifts that will shape the context of your future. If, like many of the people I have spoken to in the course of this research, a balanced life is important to you, meaningful work is important to you, progressively developing skills is important to you, then this will require you to make the shifts that will enable these to arise, and to be held accountable for the future working life you construct.

That means changing your mind about anxiety, and rather than denying the dilemmas you face you become tough, embracing the anxiety they contain. To feel anxiety about the choices you make in the future is healthy, it's the natural state of a person who is reflecting on themselves and disclosing their feelings. You should not feel obliged to escape or deny them, but to realise that in your dilemmas there is an opportunity for illumination. As the five forces rock the foundations of what we know of work, you have an opportunity to take charge of your life – both now and in the future. You are not simply an artefact of organisational life, or a cog within the machine of your company – you are capable of making choices and of making yourself accountable for the impact of those choices. This requires you to be honest about your feelings and shortcomings, to be able to take risks beyond the point of comfort, and to be courageous in your actions.

How might you face this anxiety about how you will construct a meaningful, high-quality working life? Here we return to the second shift – for your capacity to craft a working future for yourself and those you care about will depend in part on the quality of your encounters, on your regenerative community, those few close, trusted and positive friends with whom you can spend real time in a compassionate, patient way. It's in these deep conversations that you can reveal your true feelings and share your thoughts and experiences. It is in these conversations that you can become aware of all your alternatives, consider how you have engaged with these challenges in the past and reflect on what has stopped you from taking risks.

For each one of us, the challenge is to lead a more purposeful working life, where we can create a stronger sense of who we are and what we care about, and the choices we face and their possible consequences. What this will mean in reality is to have the courage to say no; it means that you will have to actively search for a place to work that allows you to lead the purposeful working life that is important to you. That means that you will see yourself less as 'normal' and more as yourself, as an individual – making a commitment to your own lifestyle and self-definition.

It's interesting that in considering this third shift it is to philosophy that we are drawn for insights. As you look into the future you have both the freedom and the potential to pursue the values and self-concepts that are important to you. That means understanding the limits that society and organisations impose on you, and understanding that you are free to respond to those limits, but there are inevitable consequences to your actions. Your work and the organisations you work in are the playing fields where meaning is likely to be found. For each one of us the key will be our courage and our sense of the future.

PART V

NOTES ON
THE FUTURE

Beyond the complexity of the five forces that will shape our working future are a number of big truths that we should all bear in mind as we make choices and decide on acceptable trade-offs. There are clear messages in this analysis about what we tell our children – and it is to this group that the first set of notes is addressed.

Our future working life is crafted by the resources we develop and the choices we make. But it is also profoundly influenced by the context in which we live and work. This context is shaped by the organisations in which we work, be they small entrepreneurial outfits or the global multinationals that will increasingly straddle the world. These organisations are important since they shape the jobs we do, they determine the broad practices by which we are selected, promoted, rewarded and developed, and their culture has the possibility of supporting or indeed disrupting some of the aspects of the changes that will be the basis of our capacity to make choices and to craft meaningful and productive work. With this in mind, it is to the leaders of organisations that the second set of notes is addressed.

The broadest context in which we work and in which we craft our future working lives is created by the country and the government in which we live. Like CEOs, incumbent politicians will have reins of power measured by years, while our own working lives will be measured in multiple decades. Therefore it will always be the case that CEOs and politicians will take a shorter time-frame when thinking about the future than we are able to do. Moreover, it is not in the interests of politicians, keen to be re-elected, to put into too stark contrast some of the more unpalatable truths about the future – particularly, for example, working life spans and pensions. It is to politicians and governments that the final set of notes is addressed. The object here, as in all the notes, is simply to put on the table the hard facts and the implications these have in a manner that is as accurate and unbiased as possible.

If you would like copies of these three sets of notes, go to the shift website – www.theshiftbylyndagratton.com – where you can download them together with other supporting resources.

11

NOTES TO CHILDREN, CEOs AND GOVERNMENTS

Notes to children about the future of work

You have an extraordinary life in front of you. Many of you will live for over 100 years – something that was unimaginable even two decades ago. Not only will you have long lives, but also for much of that time you will be able to be working productively as medical advances push back ageing.

What will you do with your long, productive life? Finding work that excites and inspires you will be one of the keys to a good life. In the past many people joined large corporations, but I think that in your working life there will be more opportunities to create your own business, working perhaps with people from across the world. In order to do this you will have to find a skill and competence that you can master and develop deeply. Remember that achieving mastery will take time, concentration and dedication – perhaps up to 10,000 hours if you really want to develop deep skills. You will also have to become familiar and indeed skilled at working with people of different nationalities than your own, and indeed may well live far from the place you were born. This diversity will play a key role in your life because increasingly your success will depend on how creative and innovative you are – and it is in these diverse relationships that innovation often develops.

Your father and grandfather – and your mother and grandmother, if they worked – tended to spend their working life in one type of work. Over the 60 years that you may work, you have the opportunity to create much more variety in what you do. You could take one career path and then switch after 20 years, or even after 40 years. Your life will not simply have education at the beginning, work in the middle and retirement at the end. Instead you can expect to experience a mosaic that has education and development woven at different times right through it.

The potential length of your life is one of the defining opportunities and challenges of your generation – and so too will be the extent to which you will be connected to many billions of people across the world. Increasingly your actions, ideas and creativity will be transparent to others. No generation before you had the technology to do this. I believe that there is enormous potential for you to use this connectivity with billions of others to solve tough challenges and to really understand and empathise with others. Much of your time will be spent working with people virtually, and so one of the challenges you face is how to create deep friendships with a small group of people in a way that you can sustain for many years of your life. Remember that friendship brought great joy to your parents' lives, just as it will to yours.

The biggest challenge your generation faces will be how you decide to use and conserve the earth's dwindling resources of energy, water and land. Much of the technological privileges you have inherited depleted these resources to a dangerous level. In your lifetime hundreds of thousands of people around the world will be working to solve these resource challenges, and they will have access to unimaginable technology to do this. However, you cannot simply look to technology to solve this problem. It is for you and your generation to decide what trade-offs you are prepared to accept between your standard of living and the quality of your life. Much of the development of the world over the last 100 years has raised the standard of living – for you the challenge will be to raise the quality of life for yourself and others.

You will be faced with choices that go way beyond any faced by previous generations. You will be able to choose what you work on, how you work, where you work and with whom you work. But with crafting a working life come the responsibilities of wise decision-making. In particular, in an increasingly transparent world you will be faced with the consequences of your actions in a way previous generations rarely were. That means that in making choices you will have to consider the trade-offs you are prepared to make. What will be key to creating a working life that brings you fulfilment will be your capacity to meet three challenges.

The first is the extent to which you are able to invest in your intellectual capital over the period of your working life in order to build mastery in areas that interest you.

The second will be the extent to which you are able to invest in your social capital through your friendships and networks. The most valuable networks for you will be those that balance deep friendships with those whom you can trust and much wider networks with people who are very different to you.

The third challenge is to navigate between the old traditional work deal that had money and consumption at its heart to a working deal that has at its centre the capacity to be creative and productive and to live a life based more on experiences.

Notes to business leaders about the future of work

The next two decades will be particularly testing for corporate leaders across the world. Many of the traditional assumptions about work are coming under immense pressure, and many will be discarded in the coming years. Trust in business leaders is at an all-time low, and we expect this distrust to grow; the most talented will be joining with others to create a global talent pool that will increasingly make their needs and aspirations heard; and ever-increasing transparency of information will put those who lead under increasing public scrutiny. At the same time, Gen

Y are beginning to take team-leading roles in businesses, and they have particular needs with regard to the way they are managed and the type of work they are excited about doing. All these factors put increasing pressure on leaders. At the same time, the skills needed to lead groups and communities of people who are more diverse, virtual and global will be complex and challenging to select for and develop. The leadership role over the coming two decades will be to inspire followers, to manage a complex array of stakeholders, and bridge into action in some of the environmental and societal challenges that are already emerging. There are five broad areas that will be crucial to your capacity to create a business that is sufficiently resilient over the coming decades to gain from the shaping trends.

First, ever-increasing globalisation will add new markets, but will also intensify competition both for customers and indeed for talent. These customers and talented future employees will look for products and services that are innovative along a number of dimensions. In the past we looked to the developed nations as sources of this innovation, but increasingly this will become a global phenomenon. What is clear is the central role that innovation and experimentation will play in those companies that will thrive in the future. This will place an increasing importance on open innovation, and the means by which ideas from employees and customers play a role in product and service development.

Next, under the pressure of technology and globalisation, the traditional hierarchical arrangement of work will rapidly morph into something much more organic. We can expect that increasingly work will be performed in short- or long-term projects bringing talent from across the corporation. We will also see the growing importance of ecosystems that are collaborative relationships with the joint ventures, partnerships and micro-entrepreneurs that are arrayed around the business. Reaching out into these ecosystems in a cooperative way will be crucial to the rejuvenation and innovative capability of the business. It will be increasingly important to tap into the skills of the growing proportion of the world's most talented people who will choose to build their own business rather than work for another.

Most companies have worked implicitly on the basis of a parent–child relationship with employees – making decisions about where work takes place, when people work, and how and what they work on. Increasingly your talented employees will want an adult–adult relationship in which more of these decisions about the placing and scoping of work are made by them rather than by you. At the same time, with the expectation that many Gen Zs will live for more than 100 years, working lives over 60 years will become the norm. Your company will be called upon to change its assumptions about the productivity of the over-60s and 70s. This level of personalisation and flexibility appears potentially chaotic, but technological platforms will increasingly make this a viable option. As a result you will be called upon to ensure that human resource policies are future-proofed, particularly with regard to flexible working, individualised training and team-based work design.

You can also expect a subtle shift in the role that pay plays in the motivational make-up of employees. Early research on the work aspirations of Gen Y suggests that they will place ever-greater emphasis on meaningful and developmental work. It appears that many will also want to create a high-quality working life that enables them to make work/life choices in a more proactive way. They will also want to work their 60 years in a mosaic that has sabbaticals, learning *and* work as core components. Your capacity to deliver to this flexibility will be crucial in attracting talent.

Finally, many companies were developed on the tradition of competition as the basis of success. Increasingly, the sources of competitive advantage will come from the capacity to build cooperative partnerships across various ecosystems. That will bring to the centre stage the capacity to create cultures of cooperation, trust and inclusion. We know that a primary driver for these cooperative cultures will be the extent to which others see you and your team working collaboratively with each other and the role models you create. So, while the creation of future-proofed strategies will be crucial, in an ever more transparent world it is to your own behaviour that employees will look for inspiration.

Notes to government ministers about the future of work

Over the coming decades we can expect a significant shift in work as the forces of technology and globalisation, societal changes, demography and longevity, and energy resources impact on government around the world in a number of ways.

First, the forces of globalisation, which initially saw India emerge as the back office and China as the factory of the developed world, will continue. However, over the coming decades an increasing proportion of high-value, knowledge-intensive work will be distributed to the developing economies. This will create a surge in what has been termed frugal innovation and will see the rapid globalisation of innovation and R&D.

Moreover, in a combination of globalisation and technology, more than 5 billion people across the world will become connected to each other via the internet and potentially to the Cloud, which will hold much of the world's knowledge. This hyper-connectivity will create enormous grassroot opportunities for rapid developments in education and community building. A government's capacity to enable every citizen – particularly the young – to access a computer and the Cloud will in the longer term create a crucial boost to productivity and innovation. Those regions where children do not have access to the knowledge of the Cloud will rapidly become the backwaters of the world.

Related to these advances, we can expect rapid technological advances to occur in the way that people learn skills and acquire knowledge, and that this will become increasingly important as high-value work will require the mastery of deep skills. Expect to see computerised simulations, e-learning and blended learning rapidly replace traditional classroom teaching. As a result of these rapid grassroots developments in innovative education we can anticipate traditional positional advantage rapidly eroding as the talent markets of the world join up. Supporting every young person to gain marketable skills using the rapidly evolving learning technologies will be a key priority for governments.

As a result of these forces, those with high-value skills (in biotechnology, renewable energy or design, for example) will increasingly choose to cluster near each other. We can anticipate that these clusters of mastery and skill will become more and more crucial to the economic health of a region. While these clusters are emergent rather than designed, nevertheless a government's willingness to support high-quality educational and cultural institutions will play a key role in the process of attracting and embedding these clusters.

Next, with regard to societal forces there are a number of factors in motion that will impact on how work gets done over the coming decades. Across many countries, citizens' trust in institutions, big businesses and governments is decreasing and is unlikely to increase. We can expect that ever more prevalent transparency and sharing of information will only serve to exacerbate this. As Generation Y and Z assume the mantle of citizenship, we can expect those with a common goal to develop these agendas on the world stage. These active world communities will be increasingly technologically enabled, and over time will become joined up in a way that goes beyond country boundaries.

With regard to the forces of demography and longevity we can expect some significant impacts. A key proportion of the Gen Z cohort is expected to live beyond the age of 100. In one generation this will transform our assumptions about work, age and ageing. Many of these healthy Gen Zs will want to work productively into their 70s and 80s and it will be a priority for governments to find ways to support these aspirations. This will also require a review of the current pension arrangements and a closer look at how people save for their retirement. However, while many in the developed world will live significantly longer, we cannot anticipate that fertility rates in most regions of the world will increase. The increasing proportion of the over-60s in many developed countries will place an intolerable burden on the young. Opening borders to migration of both the skilled and those prepared to play caring roles will be crucial if this burden is to be eased.

Finally, the issues of dwindling energy resources will profoundly impact on the future of work. As the cost of energy increases and carbon tax becomes a reality, so companies will be required to transform the way that work gets done. Expect more home-based working, the rapid rise of technologically enabled virtual working and the move of some manufacturing capability back to the home market. Requiring corporations to take account of their carbon footprint will serve to accelerate this transformation.

BIBLIOGRAPHY

Akerlof, G. A. and R. J. Schiller (2009) *Animal Spirits: How Human Psychology Drives the Economy, and Why It Matters for Global Capitalism*, Princeton, New Jersey: Princeton University Press.

Anderson, P. (1972) More is different, *Science*, 177: 393–6.

Ashton, T. S. (1948) *The Industrial Revolution (1760–1830)*, Oxford: Oxford University Press.

Bem, D. J. (1972) Self perception theory. In L. Berkowitz (eds), *Advances in Experimental Social Psychology, Vol 6*, New York: Academic Press.

Bolchover, D. (2010) *Pay Check: Are Top Earners Really Worth It?* London: Coptic.

Bornstein, D. (2007) *How to Change the World: Social Entrepreneurs and the Power of New Ideas*, Oxford University Press USA (and others).

Bostrom, N. (2009) The future of humanity. In J. K. B. Olsen, E. Selinger and S. Riis (eds), *New Waves in Philosophy of Technology*, New York: Palgrave Macmillan.

Brickman, P. and D. T. Campbell (1971) *Experienced Utility and Objective Happiness*, Princeton, New Jersey: Princeton University Press.

Brickman, P. and D. T. Campbell (1971) Hedonic relativism and planning the good society. In M. H. Appley (ed.),

Adaptation-Level Theory: A Symposium, New York: Academic Press, pp. 287–302.

Brynjolfsson, E. and A. Saunders (2010) *Wired for Innovation: How Information Technology Is Re-shaping the Economy.* Cambridge, MA: MIT Press.

Campbell, A. *et al.* (1976) *The Quality of American Life*, New York: Russell Sage.

Child, J. and A. Prud'Homme (2006) *My Life in France*, New York: Knopf.

Christensen, C., M. Horn and C. Johnson (2008) *Disrupting Class: How Disruptive Innovation Will Change the Way the World Learns.* New York: McGraw Hill.

Cicero, translated by M. Grant (1971) *On the Good Life*, London: Penguin Books

Comfort, A. and S. Quilliam (2004) *The Joy of Sex*, London: Mitchell Beazley.

Concours Group (2004) *The New Employeee/Employer Equation.* Concours Group.

Crafts, N. F. R. and C. K. Harley (1992) Output growth and the British industrial revolution: a restatement of the Crafts-Harley view, *Economic History Review*, 45(4): 703–30.

Crosby, F. J. (1991) *Juggling: The Unexpected Advantages of Balancing Career and Home for Women and Their Families*, New York: The Free Press.

Csikszentmihalyi, M. (1997) *Creativity: Flow and the Psychology of Discovery and Invention*, New York: Harper Perennial.

Csikszentmihalyi, M. and J. LeFevre (1989) Optimal experience in work and leisure. *Journal of Personality and Social Psychology*, 56: 815–22.

David, E. (1970) *A Book of Mediterranean Food*, Harmondsworth: Penguin Books.

Davis, M. (2008) *The Planet of Slums*, New York: Verso.

Deci, E. L. and R. M. Ryan (1985) *Intrinsic Motivation and Self-Determination in Human Behaviour*, New York: Plenum.

Diamond, J. (2005) *Collapse: How Societies Choose to Fail or Succeed*, New York: Viking.

Dickerson, S. and M. Kemeny (2004) Acute stressors and cortical responses: a theoretical integration and synthesis of laboratory research, *Psychological Bulletin*, 130(3): 355–91.

Dossani, R. (2005) Origins and growth of the software industry in India. Working Paper, Stanford University, Shorenstein APARC. Available at http://aparc.stanford.edu/people/rafiqdossani

Drucker, P.F. (2008) *The Essential Drucker*. London: Harper Paperbacks

Elster, J. (1986), Self-realization in work and politics: the Marxist conception of the good life, *Social Philosophy and Policy*, 3, pp. 97. http://journals.cambridge.org/action/displayAbstract?fromPage=online&aid=3093292

Equality and Human Rights Commission (2008) Sex and Power Report.

Erickson, T. (2008) *Plugged In: The Generation Y Guide to Thriving at Work*, Maidenhead: McGraw-Hill.

Erickson, T. (2008) *Retire Retirement: Career Strategies for the Boomer Generation*, Boston: Harvard Business School Press.

Erickson, T. (2010) *What's Next, Gen X: Keeping Up, Moving Ahead, and Getting the Career You Want*, Boston: Harvard Business School.

Festinger, L. (1950) Informal social communication. *Psychological Review*, 57: 271–82.

Finnel, S. (2006) 'Once upon a time, we are prosperous: the role of storytelling in making Mexicans believe in their country's capacity for economic greatness'. Unpublished senior essay, Yale University.

Fischer, C. (1994) Changes in leisure activities, 1890–1950. *Journal of Social History*, 27(3): 453–75.

Florida, R. (2002) *The Rise of the Creative Class: And How It's Transforming Work, Leisure, Community and Everyday Life*, New York: Basic Books.

Florida, R. (2008) *Who's Your City: How the Creative Economy Is Making Where to Live the Most Important Decision of Your Life*, New York: Basic Books.

Florida, R. (2010) *The Great Reset: How New Ways of Living and Working Drive Post-Crash Prosperity*. New York: HarperCollins.

Fowler, J. and N. Christakis (2009) Alone in the crowd: the structure and spread of loneliness in a large social network, *Journal of Personality and Social Psychology*. 97(6), December.

Fromm, E. (1941) *The Escape from Freedom*, New York: Rinehart.

Gallup Management Journal, 26 May 1999. Item 10: I Have a Best Friend at Work: The twelve key dimensions that describe great workgroups (part 11)

Gartner (2010) http://www.gartner.com/technology/initiatives/ cloud-computing.jsp. The Cloud Security Alliance, 'Top threats to Cloud computing' (www.cloudsecurityalliance.org/ topthreats/csathreats.v1.0.pdf).

Ghoshal, S. and J. Nahapiet (1998) Social capital, intellectual capital and the organizational advantage, *Academy of Management Review*, 23(2): 242.

Gibson, W. (1999) The science in science fiction, *Talk of the Nation*, 30 November 1999 Timecode 11:55, NPR.

Giddens, A. (1991) *Modernity and Self-Identity: Self and Society in the Late Modern Age*, Stanford, CA: Stanford University Press.

Giddens, A. (1992) *The Transformation of Intimacy: Sexuality, Love and Eroticism in Modern Societies*. Stanford, CA: Stanford University Press.

Gills, B. K. and W. R. Thompson (2006), *Globalization and Global History*, London: Routledge.

Giu, M. and L. Stanca (2009) *Television Viewing, Satisfaction and Happiness: Facts and Fiction*, University of Milan-Biocca, Department of Economics Working Paper Series, 167.

Gladwell, M. (2008) *Outliers*, London: Little, Brown.

Goffman, E. (1990) *The Presentation of Self*. London: Penguin.

Goodin, R. E., J. M. Rice, A. Parpo and L. Eriksson (2008) *Discretionary Time: A New Measure of Freedom*, Cambridge: Cambridge University Press.

Granovetter, M. S. (1973) The strength of weak ties, *American Journal of Sociology*, 78(6): 1360.

Gratton, L. (2004) *The Democratic Enterprise: Liberating Your Business with Freedom, Flexibility and Commitment*, London: Financial Times Prentice Hall.

Gratton, L. (2007) *Hot Spots: Why Some Teams, Workplaces and Organisations Buzz with Energy – and Others Don't*, Financial Times Prentice Hall (UK), Berrett Koehler (US).

Gratton, L. (2009) *Glow – Creating Energy and Innovation in Your Work*. Financial Times Prentice Hall (UK), Berrett Koehler (US).

Greenhaus, J. H. and N. J. Beutell (1985). Sources of conflict between work and family roles, *Academy of Management Review*, 10: 76–88.

Haberl, H., Erb, F. Krausmann, W. Gaube, A. Bondeau, C. Plutzar, S. Gingrich, W. Lucht and M. Fischer-Kowalski (2007) Quantifying and mapping the human appropriation of net primary production in the Earth's terrestrial ecosystems, *Proceedings of the National Academy of Sciences*, USA, 104(31), p. 12942.

Hagel III, J., J. Seely Brown and L. Davison (2009) *The Big Shift Index*, Deloitte Center for the Edge.

Hagel III, J., J. Seely Brown and L. Davison (2010) *The Power of Pull: How Small Moves, Smartly Made, Can Set Big Things in Motion*, New York: Basic Books.

Heilbroner, R. L. (1994) Do machines make history? In M. R. Smith and L. Marx (eds), *Does Technology Drive History? The Dilemma of Technological Determinism*, Cambridge, MA: MIT Press.

Heilbroner, R. L. (1995) *Visions of the Future: The Distant Past, Yesterday, Today, Tomorrow*, New York: Oxford University Press.

Held, D. (1996) *Models of Democracy*, Cambridge: Polity Press.

Hobsbawm, E. J. (1962) *The Age of Revolution: Europe 1789–1848*, London: Weidenfeld & Nicolson.

Horx, M. (2006) *How We Will Live, A Synthesis of Life in the Future*. New York: Campus; London: Cyan Books.

HSBC Insurance (2005) *The Future of Retirement Study*, HSBC.

Ibarra, H. (2003) *Working Identities: Unconventional Strategies for Reinventing Your Career*. Boston, MA: Harvard Business School Press.

Kahneman, D. and J. Snell (1992) Predicting a changing taste: Do people know what they will like?, *Journal of Behavioral Decision Making*, 5(3).

Kapoor, A. (2009) Regional disparity in India: why it matters. http://blogs.hbr.org/cs/2009/06/regional_disparity_in_india_wh.html.

Kasser, T., R. Ryan, M. Zax and A. Sameroff (1995) The relations of material and social environments to late adolescents' materialistic and prosocial values, *Developmental Psychology*, 31: 907–14.

Kilduff, M. and W. Tsai (2003) *Social Networks and Organizations*. London: Sage.

King, R. (2010) *People on the Move*, London: Myriad Editions.

Klein, S. (2007) *The Secret Pulse of Time: Making Sense of Life's Scarcest Commodity*, Cambridge, MA: Marlowe & Co.

Koestenbaum, P. and P. Block (2001) *Freedom and Accountability at Work: Applying Philosophic Insight into the Real World*. San Francisco, CA: Jossey-Bass Pfeiffer.

Kubey, R. (1990) Television and the quality of life, *Communication Quarterly*, London: Routledge.

Kulananda and D. Houlder (2002) *Mindfulness and Money: The Buddhist Path to Abundance*. London: Broadway Books.

Kurweil, R. (2006) *The Singularity is Near*, London: Gerald Duckworth & Co.

Landes, D. S. (1998) *The Wealth and Poverty of Nations: Why Some Are So Rich and Some So Poor*, New York: W.W. Norton & Co.

Lane, R. E. (1991) *The Market Experience*, Cambridge: Cambridge University Press, p. 309.

Lane, R. E. (2000) *The Loss of Happiness in Market Democracies*, New Haven, CT: Yale University Press.

Leadbeater, C. (1996) *The Rise of the Social Entrepreneur*, London: Demos.

Leadbeater, C. (2008) *We-Think: Mass Innovation Not Mass Production*, London: Profile Books.

Lebergott, S. (1968) Labour force and employment trends. In E. Sheldon and W. Moore (eds), *Indicators of Social Change*. New York: Russell Sage, pp. 97–143.

Levitin, D. (2007) *This is Your Brain on Music: Understanding a Human Obsession*, London: Atlantic Books.

Li, T. and R. Florida (2006) Talent, technology innovation and economic growth in China, *The Martin Prosperity Institute*, University of Toronto. Available at creativeclass.com.

Lowe, G. S. and G. Schellenberg (2005) *What's a Good Job? The Importance of Employment Relationships*. CPRN Study No. W12005.

McGregor, D. (1960), *The Human Side of Enterprise*, London: McGraw Hill.

Maddison, A. (1998) *Chinese Economic Performance in the Long Run, Paris:* Organization for Economic Cooperation and Development.

Mainemelis, C. and S. Ronson (2006) On the nature of play: ideas are born in fields of play – towards a theory of play and creativity in an organizational setting, *Research in Organizational Behavior* 27: 81–131.

Malone, T. (2004) *The Future of Work: How the New Order of Business Will Shape Your Organization, Your Management Style, and Your Life*, Boston, MA: Harvard Business School Press.

Malone, T., R. Laubacher and M. S. S. Morton (eds) (2003) *Inventing the Organizations of the 21st Century*, Cambridge, MA: MIT Press.

Mandel, M. (2009) The failed promise of Innovation in the US, *Business Week*, 3 June.

Manning, P. (2004) *Migration in World History*, London: Routledge.

Maslow, A. (1954) *Motivation and Personality*, New York: Harper & Row.

Maslow, A. (1972) *The Farther Reaches of Human Nature*, New York: Viking.

Massimini, F. and A. Delle Fave (2000) Individual development in a bio-cultural perspective, *American Psychologist*, 55(1): 24.

Moon, Y. (2010) *Different: Escaping the Competitive Herd*, Crown Publishing Group: Random House Group.

Mortimer, J. T. and J. Lorence (1985) Work experience and occupational value socialization: a longitudinal study, *American Journal of Sociology*, 84: 1361–85.

Nordhaus, W. (1997) Traditional productivity estimates are asleep at the (technological) switch, *Economic Journal*, Royal Economic Society, vol. 107(444), September, 1548–59.

Owen, N. A., O. R. Inderwildi and D. A. King (2010) The status of conventional world oil reserves: Hype or cause for concern?, *Energy Policy*, 38: 4743.

Page, S. E. (2007) *The Difference: How the Power of Diversity Creates Better Groups, Firms, Schools and Societies*, Princeton: Princeton University Press.

Putnam, R. (2000), *Bowling Alone: The Collapse and Revival of American Community*, New York: Simon & Schuster.

Ramankutty, N., A. T. Evan, C. Monfreda and J. A. Foley (2008) Farming the planet: 1. Geographic distribution of global agricultural lands in the year 2000, *Global Biogeochemical Cycles*, 22, GB1003, p. 19.

Reich, R. (2001) *The Future of Success: Working and Living in the New Economy*, New York: Alfred A. Knopf.

Rifkin, J. (1995) *The End of Work: The Decline of the Global Labor Force and the Dawn of the Post-Market Era*, New York: Tarcher/Putnam.

Rifkin, J. (2009) *The Empathic Civilization: The Race to Global Consciousness in a World in Crisis*, Cambridge: Polity Press.

Robinson, S. L. and D. M. Rousseau (1994) Violating the psychological contract: Not the exception but the norm, *Journal of Organizational Behavior*, 15: 245.

Rosenthal, E. (2006) Empty playgrounds in an aging Italy, *International Herald Tribune*. http://www.iht.com/articles/2006/09/04/news/birth2.php

Rubin, J. (2009) *Why Your World is About to Get a Whole Lot Smaller*, New York: Random House.

Sanderson, W. and S. Scherbov (2008) *Rethinking Age and Aging*. Population Bulletin, December.

Sartre, J.-P. (1943) *Being and Nothingness: A Phenomenological Essay on Ontology*, London: Routledge.

Sawhill, I. and J. E. Morton (2007) *Economic Mobility: Is the American Dream Alive and Well?*, Washington, DC: Economic Mobility Project.

Saxenian, A. L. (1999) *Silicon Valley's Immigrant Entrepreneurs*, San Francisco, CA: Public Policy Institute of California.

Sayre, K. (2010) *Unearthed: The Economic Roots of our Environmental Crisis*, Notre Dame: University of Notre Dame Press; http://ocw.nd.edu/philosophy/environmental-philosophy/unearthed/chapter-6-the-rising-tide-of-human-energy-use.

Schumpeter, J. A. (1945) *Capitalism, Socialism and Democracy*, New York: Harper, 1975; orig. pub. 1942.

Scitovsky, T. (1977) *The Joyless Economy*, New York: Oxford University Press.

Sennett, R. (2008) *The Craftsmen*, London: Allen Lane.

Shafiee, S. and E. Topal (2009) When will fossil fuel reserves be diminished? *Energy Policy*, 37(1): 181–9.

Sheehy, G. (1976) *Passages*, New York: Dutton.

Shirky, C. (2010) *Cognitive Surplus: Creativity and Generosity in a Connected Age*, London: Allen Lane.

Shrum, L. J., R. S. Wyer Jr and T. C. O'Guinn (1998) The use of priming procedures to investigate psychological processes, *Journal of Consumer Research,* 24(4): 447.

Smil, V. (2006) *Transforming the Twentieth Century: Technical Innovations and Their Consequences*, Oxford: Oxford University Press.

Smith, M. R. and L. Marx (eds) (1994) *Does Technology Drive History? The Dilemma of Technological Determinism*, Cambridge, MA: MIT Press.

Tai, L. (2008) *Corporate E-learning: An Inside View of IBM's Solutions*, Oxford: Oxford University Press.

Tapscott, D. and A.D. Williams (2010) *MacroWikinomics: Rebooting Business and the World*, London: Atlantic Books.

Twenge, J. (2007 The age of anxiety? Birth cohort change in anxiety and neuroticism, 1952–1993, *Journal of Personality and Social Psychology*, 79(6): 1007–21.

US Department of Education, Office of Planning, Evaluation, and Policy Development, Washington, DC (2009) *Evaluation of Evidence-Based Practices in Online Learning; A Meta-Analysis and Review of Online Learning Studies*. Accessed at http://www.ed.gov/rschstat/eval/tech/evidence-based-practices/finalreport.pdf.

van Steenbergen, E. F., N. Ellemers and A. Mooijaart (2007) How work and family can facilitate each other: Distinct types of work-family facilitation and outcomes for women and men. *Journal of Occupational Health Psychology*, 12: 179–199

Wright, L. and B. L. Stewart (2009) Exploring corporate e-learning research: what are the opportunities,? *Impact: Journal of Applied Research in Workplace E-learning*, 1(1): 68–79.

Willetts, D. (2010) *The Pinch: How the Baby Boomers Stole Their Children's Future*. London: Atlantic Books.

Women in Business Institute, London Business School (2009) *The Reflexive Generation: Young Professionals' Perspectives on Work, Career and Gender*, London: London Business School.

LEARNING MORE ABOUT THE SHIFT

I am absolutely committed to supporting people and organisations to understand and plan for their working future. I hope that this book has given you a point of departure. To continue on the journey, we have developed a number of resources to support you.

Your first port of call is www.theshiftbylyndagratton.com where you can download a short *Future of Work Workbook* that I hope you will find useful. I developed it for the elective class I teach at London Business School and it's a very useful road map to some of the decisions you have to make.

I have made a number of short Shifts videos that you can take a look at and download. You will find these also on the website.

Finally, to receive tips about the future of work directly to your phone, download *The Shift* from the App Store now. This app combines text, images and video to show you what the future of work will look like, and how best to prepare yourself for it. You can also submit your own tips for others to read and share your favourite tips with friends and colleagues.

Download now from www.shiftbylyndagratton.com/app.

Why not also go to our Hot Spots Movement website – www.hotspotsmovement.com – and do sign up for our monthly *Hot Spots Newsletter* to keep updated on progress. It's a great resource and comes to your inbox free every month.

If your company needs more support, I have Future of Work team members in the USA, Europe and Asia who are actively working with companies across the world to help them become future proofed and develop their own future signature. We run *workshops*, research and write *reports* and prepare *business profiles*. If you'd like to know more about our approach and capability, just drop an email to tina@hotspotsmovement.com and she will arrange a time to talk with you.

We would love to hear your ideas and insights about your own or your company's working future. You can follow me on Twitter, join the Shifts group on Facebook and LinkedIn, or simply drop me a note – lyndagratton@theshift.com

ACKNOWLEDGEMENTS

Creating an understanding about the extent to which work will shift has been the result of a deep collaboration between researchers and executives. My Future of Work research team, headed by Dr Julia Goga-Cooke, has been inspirational. Julia's capacity to bring insight, joy and excitement to what became a very complex project was crucial, and thanks also to Tim Cooke for his eagle-eye reading of early drafts. Max Mockett brought his deep understanding of historical trends, particularly those of the Industrial Revolution, to the analysis, and he has also been the right-hand man on the long task of creating a coherent argument about the five trends. A thank you also to Rose Abdollahzadeh for her insights on the role of migration in globalization. Andreas Voigt's ideas on the nature of cooperation have been a really useful touchstone. The wonderful visualisation of Marzia Arico became the standard by which we presented ourselves to the world, and you can see her work in the App and on the website. My incredible business manager and speaking agent Tina Schneidermann helped me to create time for the ideas to be written up into a book, whilst Jayna Patel brought her organisational wizardry.

However, whilst my research team has been central to this endeavour, without the executives who joined us at the Future of Work Consortium many of the ideas would not have surfaced. I am particularly grateful to the group that met at London

Business School in October 2009 and for the insights they brought to the storylines that became such an important part of the future scenarios. With over 200 executives involved it's hard to thank any single contributor, but over the course of the study Ian Gee, Mathew Hanwell, Bill Parsons, Nigel Perks, Heather Sawyer, Bethany Davies Swanson, Ari-Pekka Skarp, Andrea Elliot, Stephen Sidebottom, Hala Collins, Balaji Ethirajan, James Chapman, Eric Brunelle, Dawn Crew, Joan Coyle, Paul Kane, Nupur Singh, Ritu Anand, Jane Hodgen, Elly Tomlins, David Dalpe, Gail Sulkes, Yves Zischek, Mandy Bromley, Karen Rivoire and Stephen Remedios did much to add their own insights and ideas.

The financial support for the Future of Work Consortium was provided in part by the companies who took part. However, as in much of my research, the financial support of the Singapore's Government's Ministry of Manpower was a real bonus. I am also grateful to the Asian insights that came out of conversations with members of the government, in particular Leo Yip, Peck Kem Low, Shirlyn Ng and Alvin Teo. The Asian membership of the FoW research was crucial to creating a global view and I am indebted to my colleague Heidi Baker Kingman in the Singapore group of the Hot Spots Movement for her support and insights.

My intellectual home over the last 20 years has been the London Business School. It's a wonderful privilege to teach at this world-class institution and to be a member of a community of outstanding scholars. In particular I would like to thank the chair of the Organisational Behaviour group, Madan Pillutali, and the Dean of the School, Sir Andrew Likierman, for creating such a stimulating intellectual and understanding home. I also want to acknowledge the support of Julian Birkenshaw for all his support through the Innovation Centre, and Michael Blowfield for his observations about carbon.

I'm blessed with some wonderful friends who listened, argued and made suggestions as I began to formulate my ideas about the future of work – a particular thanks to Peter Detre, Tammy

Erickson, Gita Piramal, Peter Moran, Gary Hamel, Dominic Houlder and Dave Ulrich.

As always my family are a source of inspiration and support – my sons Christian and Dominic Seiersen, my mother Barbara Gratton, and my brothers and sister, Jack, Richard and Heather. Our collective children, Barbara's grandchildren – the 'Regenerative Generation' – gave me an idea of what it means to be facing the future of work, and it is to them that this book is dedicated.

Finally, thanks to my wonderful agent Caroline Michel and to my editor at HarperCollins Helena Nicholls, who made the whole process go smoothly and with such elegance.

NOTES

Introduction: Predicting the future of work

1. T. S. Ashton (1948) *The Industrial Revolution (1760–1830)*, Oxford: Oxford University Press; E. J. Hobsbawm (1962) *The Age of Revolution: Europe 1789–1848*, London: Weidenfeld & Nicolson.

2. N. F. R. Crafts and C. K. Harley (1992) Output growth and the British industrial revolution: a restatement of the Crafts-Harley view, *Economic History Review*, 45(4): 703–30.

3. D. S. Landes (1998) *The Wealth and Poverty of Nations: Why Some are So Rich and Some So Poor*, New York: W.W. Norton & Co.

4. J. A. Schumpeter (1945) *Capitalism, Socialism and Democracy*, New York: Harper, 1975; orig. pub. 1942.

5. Philosophers such as Nick Bostrom at Oxford University's Future of Humanity Institute make this point very clearly. For an overview of his thinking see N. Bostrom (2009) The future of humanity in J. K. B. Olsen, E. Selinger and S. Riis, S (eds), *New Waves in Philosophy of Technology*, New York: Palgrave Macmillan. See also Institute Faculty of Philosophy, Future of Humanity Institute, James Martin 21st Century School, Oxford University, www.nickbostrom.com.

6. William Gibson (1999) The science in science fiction, *Talk of the Nation*, 30 November 1999, Timecode 11:55, NPR.

7. R. L. Heilbroner (1995) *Visions of the Future: The Distant Past, Yesterday, Today, Tomorrow*, New York: Oxford University Press.

8. V. Smil (2006) *Transforming the Twentieth Century: Technical Innovations and Their Consequences*, Oxford: Oxford University Press.

9. These figures are drawn from the United Nations Population Division (2004).

10. Nikolai Dmitriyevich Kondratiev was a Soviet economist and it was Schumpeter who brought Kondratiev's ideas to the West. The Kondratiev theory is this: capitalism not only has short-term business cycles, but much longer ones running from 50 to 75 years. In the upswing of each

long-term cycle, periods of prosperity were longer and robust – recessions short-term and shallow. In the downswing of the long cycle, prosperities became shorter and shakier, while recessions were harsher and more stubborn and persistent. The end of each upswing was marked by an enormous build-up of assets, followed by a devastating crash of asset values. These crashes can be understood as the collapse of stock values in 1929, and the devastation of 2008. Following the collapse of assets the system would enter a period of crisis. This period is often called 'The Kondratiev Winter'. During this period the system must adapt to new ways of doing business and modes of production and the technological developments of the last period subjected to a learning curve to create a new economic paradigm.

1. The five forces

1. M. R. Smith and L. Marx (eds) (1994) *Does Technology Drive History? The Dilemma of Technological Determinism*, Cambridge, MA: MIT Press; see particularly Robert Heilbrowner's chapter, 'Do machines make history?'

2. This is a point Robert Reich makes forcibly in R. Reich (2001) *The Future of Success*, New York: Alfred A. Knopf.

3. B. K. Gills and W. R. Thompson (2006), *Globalization and Global History*, London: Routledge.

4. These institutions helped reduce natural and artificial barriers to trade in many countries. The natural barriers to globalisation generally resulted from the high cost of transporting both goods and information, whereas artificial barriers resulted from governments putting in tariffs and quotas in order to protect their nascent industries. By incentivising trade liberalisation, and investing in transportation technology such as containerisation, the emerging international institutions gradually changed the foundations of international trade.

5. WTO, International Trade Statistics, 2007.

6. T. Erickson (2010), *What's Next, Gen X: Keeping Up, Moving Ahead, and Getting the Career You Want*, Boston: Harvard Business School.

7. National Center of Health Statistics, 2000.

8. www.internetworldstats.com

9. I. Sawhill and J. E. Morton (2007) *Economic Mobility: Is the American Dream Alive and Well?*, Washington, DC: Economic Mobility Project, focuses on the income of males 30–39 in 2004 (those born in April 1964–March 1974) prepared by Pew's Economic Mobility Project and based on Census/BLS CPS March supplement data.

10. Erickson (2010) op. cit.

11. William H. Frey, an analyst for the Brookings Institution Think Tank.

12. E. Rosenthal (2006) Empty playgrounds in an aging Italy, *International Herald Tribune*. http://www.iht.com/articles/2006/09/04/news/birth2.php

13. Unknown (2000) Aging populations in Europe, Japan, Korea, require action, *India Times*. http://www.globalaging.org/health/world/overall. htm. Retrieved 2007-12-15.

14. With regard to birthrates, for example, the more educated the female population becomes in a region, then in general we can expect the birth rate to fall.

15. T. Erickson(2008) *Plugged In: The Generation Y Guide to Thriving at Work*, Maidenhead: McGraw-Hill.

16. The mental life of human beings has continuously been transformed by developments such as language, literacy, urbanisation, division of labour, industrialisation, science, communications, transport and media technology.

17. A. Maslow (1954) *Motivation and Personality*, New York: Harper & Row, p. 91.

2. Fragmentation: a three-minute world

1. As far back as 1998 psychologists were observing the extent to which managers were being interrupted by technology.

2. J. Diamond (2005) *Collapse: How Societies Choose to Fail or Succeed*, New York: Viking.

3. S. Klein (2007) *The Secret Pulse of Time: Making Sense of Life's Scarcest Commodity*, Cambridge, Mass: Marlowe & Co.

4. R. E. Goodin, J. M. Rice, A. Parpo and L. Eriksson (2008) *Discretionary Time: A New Measure of Freedom*, Cambridge: Cambridge University Press.

5. According to author, musician, neuroscientist Daniel Levitin in *This is Your Brain on Music: Understanding a Human Obsession* (2007) London: Atlantic Books, an expert or master of any craft is measured by that person practising their craft for 10,000 hours.

6. Goodin *et al.* (2008) op. cit.

7. In R. Sennett (2008) *The Craftsmen*, London: Allen Lane, the sociologist Richard Sennett paints a vivid picture of how medieval craftsmen learnt their arts and how contemporary masters use concentration and time as the building block of their competencies.

8. Elizabeth David's descriptions of how to make Mediterranean food: E. David (1970) *A Book of Mediterranean Food*, Harmondsworth: Penguin Books Ltd.

9. Julia Child and Alex Prud'Homme (2006) *My Life in France*, New York: Knopf.

10. This wonderful example comes from Sennett (2008), pp. 182–3.

11. C. Mainemelis and S. Ronson (2006) On the nature of play: ideas are born in fields of play – towards a theory of play and creativity in an organizational setting, *Research in Organizational Behavior* 27: 81–131.

12. In 1965 the co-founder of Intel, Gordon Moore, predicted that the number of transistors in integrated circuits would continue to double 'for at least ten years'.

13. Surveys in 2009 of the corporate use of technology at work showed that telepresence is not widely available, the take-up software as a service was low, and desktop virtualisation was in its infancy. With regard to Cloud computing there was almost no corporate take-up. In 2010 there was indeed considerable activity, either progress at the beta test level or evaluation – but there is still much to play for. By 2010 there is also a growing concern about the security of the Cloud. Gartner (2010) http://www.gartner.com/technology/initiatives/cloud-computing.jsp. The Cloud Security Alliance, 'Top threats to Cloud computing' (www.cloudsecurityalliance.org/topthreats/csathreats.v1.0.pdf).

14. There is a TED video by super-inventor Pranav Mistry, who is pioneering 'Sixth Sense', which promises to seamlessly connect the physical and digital world and allow us to work more intuitively. TED is a really useful resource about the future of technology. http://www.ted.com/talks/pranav_mistry_the_thrilling_potential_of_sixthsense_technology.html

15. MIT's *Technology Review*, 2009, described 'Intelligent software assistant' as one of its ten emerging technologies.

16. The number of companies from Brazil, India, China or Russia in the *Financial Times* 500 list went from 15 to 62 between 2006 and 2008.

17. There are many other examples of the growth in the multinationals from emerging economies. For example, in 1990 Lenovo did not exist, in 1995 it bought IBM's personal-computer business and became the world's fourth largest PC-maker. South African Breweries (SAB) was a local brewer in 1990, yet by 2010 it was one of the three largest beer companies in the world.

18. This rapid development of the emerging economies may have only taken off since the mid-1990s, but all the trends suggest that this rise will continue faster and further. According to Adrian Wooldridge of *The Economist*, there are four reasons for this. The companies in emerging markets have increasing access to the capital markets, enabling them to move into the mega-deals previously only in the domain of developed economy companies; they have huge and growing populations of both workers and consumers; they are skilled at volume, and will continuously seek new markets; and some of the best Western companies are already looking to emerging markets as sources of innovation and growth. For example, 20% of Cisco's most talented people are located in their innovation hub in Bangalore.

19. This data comes from the UN Population Division.

20. In fact it is predicted that the working population in the more developed countries will actually fall between 2010 and 2030 from 835 million to

795 million, while the working population of the less developed regions is expected to increase by around 1 billion people.

3. Isolation: the genesis of loneliness

1. Research has shown that we value, above all other aspects of work, our relationships with our co-workers. G. S. Lowe and G. Schellenberg (2005) *What's a Good Job? The Importance of Employment Relationships*. CPRN Study No. W|2005.

2. *Gallup Management Journal*, 26 May 1999. Item 10: I Have a Best Friend at Work: The twelve key dimensions that describe great workgroups (part 11)

3. See, for example, the study by J. Fowler and N. Christakis (2009) Alone in the crowd: the structure and spread of loneliness in a large social network, *Journal of Personality and Social Psychology*. 97(6), December.

4. M. Horx (2006) *How We Will Live, A Synthesis of Life in the Future*. New York: Campus.

5. Perhaps these 'transhumans' will view cyber relationships with as much warmth and goodwill as we currently view face-to-face relationships.

6. Work- and home-life spillover can have both positive and negative effects. See e.g. F. J. Crosby (1991) *Juggling: The Unexpected Advantages of Balancing Career and Home for Women and Their Families*, New York: The Free Press; J. H. Greenhaus and N. J. Beutell (1985) Sources of conflict between work and family roles, *Academy of Management Review*, 10: 76–88.

7. See e.g. E. F. van Steenbergen, N. Ellemers and A. Mooijaart (2007) How work and family can facilitate each other: Distinct types of work-family facilitation and outcomes for women and men. *Journal of Occupational Health Psychology*, 12: 179–300.

8. In our research, my colleagues and I have discovered that this positive cycle – particularly between home and work – can have an incredibly beneficial impact on well-being and the capacity to withstand the strains of work. If we leave home feeling fulfilled, supported and cared for, then this can provide a crucial shield to the challenges of work.

9. UNFPA State of the World Report, 2007.

10. P. Manning (2004) *Migration in World History*, London: Routledge, p. 5.

11. R. King (2010) *People on the Move*, London: Myriad Editions.

12. UNDP Human Development Report, 2009, p. 21.

13. Ibid., p. 25.

14. Philippine Overseas Employment Administration, Overseas Employment Statistics, 2009.

15. K. Sayre (2010) *Unearthed: The Economic Roots of our Environmental Crisis*, Notre Dame: University of Notre Dame Press; http://ocw.nd.edu/philosophy/environmental-philosophy/unearthed/chapter-6-the-rising-tide-of-human-energy-use.

16. During the Industrial Revolution energy consumption doubled roughly every 75 years. By the twentieth century energy consumption had increased to double every 25 years. As of 2010 nearly 7 billion people make up less than 1% of the total biomass of the Earth, yet consume nearly a quarter of global net primary production and use nearly 35% of the Earth's surface for their own productive needs. H. Haberl, K. H. Erb, F. Krausmann, W. Gaube, A. Bondeau, C. Plutzar, S. Gingrich, W. Lucht and M. Fischer-Kowalski (2007) Quantifying and mapping the human appropriation of net primary production in the Earth's terrestrial ecosystems, *Proceedings of the National Academy of Sciences*, USA, 104(31), p. 12942; N. Ramankutty, A. T. Evan, C. Monfreda and J. A. Foley (2008) Farming the planet: 1. Geographic distribution of global agricultural lands in the year 2000, *Global Biogeochemical Cycles*, 22, GB1003, p. 19.

17. http://www.grida.no/publications/rr/food-crisis/page/3571.aspx.

18. By 2005, Exxon-Mobil admitted that all the easy oil and gas reserves had been found, and that future supply would be significantly more challenging to guarantee. http://www.boston.com/news/world/articles/2005/12/11/price_rise_and_new_deep_water_technology_opened_up_offshore_drilling/.

19. S. Shafiee and E. Topal (2009) When will fossil fuel reserves be diminished? *Energy Policy*, 37(1): 181–9.

20. N. A. Owen, O. R. Inderwildi and D. A. King (2010) The status of conventional world oil reserves: Hype or cause for concern?, *Energy Policy*, 38: 4743.

21. http://www.eia.gov/oiaf/aeo/woprices.html.

22. These prices do not accurately reflect the potential and very challenging extraction conditions. For example, the majority of US fossil fuel is found beneath the Gulf of Mexico. This is a treacherous region of the world, subjected to hurricanes – Katrina and Rita ravaged 167 offshore platforms – with deep oil reserves that require highly technically challenging deep sea drilling, which can be both hazardous and costly, as the BP explosion and oil spill of 2010 demonstrated. What is clear is that the traditional forms of energy are becoming increasingly hard to access, increasingly scarce and, therefore, increasingly expensive.

23. It would appear that draconian energy restrictions are inevitable. Yet to bring in such measures would disappoint the aspirations of hundreds of millions of people who will be forced to adopt austere policies that may well hinder their economic growth. It is neither economically nor politically feasible to expect China and India to stop climbing the ladder

of prosperity. So we can expect that over the coming decades industrialisation will continue and the urgency with which industrialising countries modernise will continue. As a result of this ambition, estimates are that the presently industrialising world could be responsible for almost 90% of growth in energy demand by 2050 (http://www.iea.org/techno/etp/etp10/English.pdf). Moreover, without a structured network of incentives, energy guidelines and climate policies, this growth rate will mean that the production of easily accessible oil and gas will quickly prove insufficient to guarantee future prosperity. It is indeed true that abundant coal exists in many parts of the world; however, transportation difficulties and environmental degradation ultimately pose limits to its extraction and use. Meanwhile, while alternative energy sources such as unconventional oil and synthetic fuels may play a much more significant part in the energy mix, experts believe that there is no 'silver bullet' that could completely resolve supply–demand tensions. As a consequence, we can anticipate that over the next two decades the supply of fossil fuels will struggle to keep pace with demand.

24. http://www.statistics.gov.uk/cci/nugget.asp?id=12.
25. http://www.tuc.org.uk/work_life/tuc-17223-f0.cfm.
26. T. Erickson (2010) *What's Next, Gen X: Keeping Up, Moving Ahead, and Getting the Career You Want*, Boston: Harvard Business School.
27. National Center of Health Statistics, 2000.
28. A. Giddens (1992) *The Transformation of Intimacy: Sexuality, Love and Eroticism in Modern Societies*. Stanford: Stanford University Press, p. 96.
29. K. O'Hara (2004) *Trust: from Socrates to Spin*, Cambridge: Icon Books. These figures are presented on page 312.
30. R. Putnam (2000), *Bowling Alone: The Collapse and Revival of American Community*, New York, NY: Simon & Schuster
31. As psychologist Denise Rousseau has shown, these violations of implicit work contracts are the norm rather than the exception: S. L. Robinson and D.M. Rousseau (1994) Violating the psychological contract: Not the exception but the norm, *Journal of Organizational Behavior*, 15: 245.
32. R. E. Lane (2000) *The Loss of Happiness in Market Democracies*, New Haven: Yale University Press.
33. Philip Brickman and Donald Campbell (1971) *Experienced Utility and Objective Happiness*, Princeton, New Jersey: Princeton University Press.
34. C. Fischer (1994) Changes in leisure activities, 1890–1950. *Journal of Social History*, 27(3): 453–75.
35. Clay Shirky (2010) *Cognitive Surplus: Creativity and Generosity in a Connected Age*, London: Allen Lane.
36. Putnam (2000), op. cit.
37. M. Giu and L. Stanca (2009) *Television Viewing, Satisfaction and Happiness: Facts and Fiction*, University of Milan-Biocca, Department of Economics Working Paper Series, 167.

4. Exclusion: the new poor

1. David Bolchover (2010) *Pay Check: Are Top Earners Really Worth It?* London: Coptic.

2. This is particularly pertinent for Briana in the USA. In 2010 the richest 20% were on average nine times richer than the poorest 20%. André lives in Belgium where the gap is considerably less; in Belgium the richest 20% were four times richer than the poorest 20%.

3. J. Twenge (2007) The age of anxiety? Birth cohort change in anxiety and neuroticism, 1952–1993, *Journal of Personality and Social Psychology*, 79(6): 1007–21.

4. S. Dickerson and M. Kemeny (2004) Acute stressors and cortical responses: a theoretical integration and synthesis of laboratory research, *Psychological Bulletin*, 130(3): 355–91.

5. Anxious people are also less likely to be innovative and flexible because their anxiety tends to have a 'freezing' effect on their capacity to change and adapt. However, there are ways to reduce anxiety.

6. E. Goffman (1990) *The Presentation of Self*. London: Penguin.

7. Women in Business Institute, London Business School (2009) *The Reflexive Generation: Young Professionals' Perspectives on Work, Career and Gender*, London: London Business School.

8. G. A. Akerlof and R. J. Schiller (2009) *Animal Spirits: How Human Psychology Drives the Economy, and Why It Matters for Global Capitalism*, Princeton, New Jersey: Princeton University Press.

9. These stories or narratives can be used to great effect by leaders. For example, the waxing and waning of economic confidence in Mexico reached a peak under the presidency of José Lopez Portillo, who built a narrative of Mexico as the 'underdog' – a story of the triumph of the weak over the powerful and arrogant. At the same time, he published a book about an Aztec god who was expected to reappear at a time of great transformation. It became the base for a story of Mexico's future greatness – fortuitously supported by the discovery of major new oil reserves in Mexico. The narrative and idea of undreamt-of wealth took hold of the imagination of the people and the country began to act as if it was already rich. Real GDP rose by 55% over the six years of his presidency, but faltered when he left – with 100% inflation and growing unemployment. S. Finnel (2006) 'Once upon a time, we are prosperous: the role of storytelling in making Mexicans believe in their country's capacity for economic greatness'. Unpublished senior essay, Yale University.

10. As Akerlof and Schiller (2009, p. 55) remark, 'The stories of young people making fortunes were a contemporary re-enactment of the nineteenth-century Gold Rush.'

11. US Department of Labor's Dictionary of Occupational Titles.

12. Robert Reich (2001), *The Future of Success*, New York: Alfred A. Knopf, p. 5.

13. Adrian Wooldridge 'The world turned upside down', *The Economist* special report on innovation in the emerging markets, 17 April 2010 – see Economist.com/specialreports.

14. However, India's growing economic regions in Bangalore, Hyderabad, Mumbai and parts of New Delhi are quickly pulling away from the rest of the country. Though China is not without economic inequality, in India the problem is much more severe and certainly in 2010 appears not to have been adequately addressed. It looks as if India is failing to develop as an integrated whole, and has stopped short of using its regional competencies to construct an amalgamated platform for development. The national average per capita GDP was $978 in 2010, but in certain areas such as Bihar the figure was as low as $200 (Dr A. Kapoor (2009) Regional disparity in India: why it matters: http://blogs.hbr.org/cs/2009/06/regional_disparity_in_india_wh.html). In fact, Stanford University's Rafiq Dossani has gone as far as to argue that India's technology and business services base – these are the industries that are growing the fastest – in fact lacks the broad employment base enjoyed by Chinese manufacturers. (R. Dossani (2005) *Origins and growth of the software industry in India*, Working Paper, Stanford University, Shorenstein APARC. Available at http://aparc.stanford.edu/people/rafiqdossani). A particularly telling aspect of this is that by 2010 93% of Chinese adults could read and write, while the number in India was 66% (United Nations Development Programme Report, 2009, p. 171). Without the capacity to engage with the mass of the population, we can expect that globalisation could very well serve to simply deepen the country's internal economic, political and social divisions.

15. It's what Martin Woolf in a *Financial Times* article referred to as the 'grasshopper and the ant' paradigm (http://www.ft.com/cms/s/0/202ed 286-6832-11df-a52f-00144feab49a.html).

16. R. Florida (2008) *Who's Your City: How the Creative Economy Is Making Where to Live the Most Important Decision of Your Life*, New York: Basic Books.

17. In reality, as Richard Florida's research shows, there were in 2008 roughly two or three dozen places that dominated the global economy. The most populous was India's Delhi–Lahore region with 120 million people; there were then 8 regions with more than 50 million people; another 12 were home to 25 to 50 million; and 33 more had between 10 and 25 million people. Population density, of course, is only a rudimentary measure of economic activity. Some large regions can be primarily simple manufacturing, while other small cities like Helsinki can be immensely innovative and productive.

18. M. Mandel (2009) The failed promise of Innovation in the US, *Business Week*, 3 June.

19. R. Florida (2002) *The Rise of the Creative Class*, New York: Basic Books, p. 74.

20. http://ww2.unhabitat.org/programmes/guo/documents/Table4.pdf.

21. This represents a twofold increase from 1990, in which the total world slum population was just over 720 million.

22. M. Davis (2008) *The Planet of Slums*, New York: Verso.

23. Human Development Report, 2005, p. 60.

24. Economic inequality produces economic, political and social problems. However, many commentators are arguing that the solution to inequality is not just about income distribution – it's also about inclusion and capacity sharing. It is not enough to construct after-the-fact redistributive mechanisms to ensure the rural poor are not left behind financially. In order to guarantee growth in the long run, governments need to ensure that growth itself is inclusive. In India, the National Rural Employment Guarantee Act has entitled every rural household to spend nearly a third of each year improving their local village infrastructure. This sort of scheme goes further than handing out benefits from the city, as it encourages the development of rural capacity and ownership in a combination of indigenous knowledge and technological inputs from more advanced regions. At the moment these types of schemes are limited, but they are gaining traction as the benefits begin to become clear. The governments of Africa and Latin America, as well as those of China and India, would do well to push these innovative practices as far as they can.

25. http://www.who.int/whr/1998/media_centre/50facts/en/index.html.

26. When a US group was asked in 2004 at what age they planned to retire, 24% said before the age of 60; another 25% between 61 and 65; 16% said 66 to 75; while 34% said they planned to never retire. The Concours Group (2004) *The New Employeee/Employer Equation*.

27. HSBC Insurance (2005) The Future of Retirement Study, HSBC.

28. Stanford University economist John Shoven. By 2009, under the influence of the baby boom, pension assets in the USA had grown from less than 2% of national wealth in 1950 to almost 25% by the end of 1993. For the next 15 years, until 2008, the private pension systems continued to be a major source of savings for the US economy. However, as the Baby Boomers began to retire in large numbers, the pension funds combined for the first time to become net sellers, rather than buyers, of assets. As a consequence, the savings generated by the pension system began to fall precipitously starting about 2010, and the system became a net seller by 2024.

29. As studies by the Oxford Institute of Ageing have shown, the over-60s are more likely to be affected by long-term poverty than other age groups because they are unprepared for retirement: they lack financial literacy,

they overestimate the financial robustness of their retirement investments, and they have underestimated their own longevity (http://www.ageing. ox.ac.uk/research/themes/work/longevity).

30. David Willetts (2010) *The Pinch: How the Baby Boomers Stole Their Children's Future*. London: Atlantic Books.
31. http://www.thisismoney.co.uk/work/article.html?in_article_ id=487225&in_page_id=53928&position=moretopstories
32. J. Rifkin (1995) *The End of Work: The Decline of the Global Labor Force and the Dawn of the Post-Market Era*, New York: Tarcher/ Putnam.
33. http://www.ipcc.ch/publications_and_data/ar4/syr/en/spms2.html.
34. http://www.grida.no/publications/vg/climate2/.
35. http://www.ipcc.ch/publications_and_data/ar4/syr/en/spms2.html.
36. http://www.actoncopenhagen.decc.gov.uk/en/ambition/ evidence/4-degrees-map/.
37. http://www.guardian.co.uk/business/2007/dec/09/water.climatechange.
38. http://www.unep.org/dewa/vitalwater/index.html.
39. http://www.mckinsey.com/App_Media/Reports/Water/Charting_Our_ Water_Future_Full_Report_001.pdf.

5. Co-creation: the multiplication of impact and energy

1. C. Leadbeater (2008) *We-Think, Mass Innovation Not Mass Production*, London: Profile Books.
2. The words 'cognitive surplus' are used by C. Shirky (2010) *Cognitive Surplus: Creativity and Generosity in a Connected Age*. London: Allen Lane.
3. Douglas McGregor (1960) *The Human Side of Enterprise*, London: McGraw Hill. 1960.
4. Abraham Maslow (1972) *The Farther Reaches of Human Nature*, New York: Viking.
5. For more on the cooperative endeavour, see for example Howard Rheingold on the power of cooperation: http://www.ted.com/talks/ howard_rheingold_on_collaboration.html.
6. S. E. Page (2007) *The Difference: How the Power of Diversity Creates Better Groups, Firms, Schools and Societies*. Princeton, New Jersey: Princeton University Press.
7. Scott E. Page (2007).
8. On the international level, the World Bank has a dedicated staff of 200 people working on the issue of information and communication technologies for development. Individual countries are also making the push; e.g. the Egyptian Ministry of Communications and Information Technology was actively involved in the extension of 'e-access', with the development of ICT projects at the communal level (http://www.mcit. gov.eg/news.aspx).

9. In an attempt to foster a knowledge-based economy, the Rwandan Ministry of Education has supplied children throughout the country with over 100,000 XO computers – the most significant commitment by any African nation (http://www.globalpost.com/dispatch/education/100408/rwandas-schoolyard-tech). These differences in regional connectivity rates will have a profound impact on the development of these regional economies and the people.

10. http://globaltechforum.eiu.com/index.asp?layout=rich_story&channelid=5&categoryid=15&doc_id=10370.

11. http://www.ulib.org/ULIBAboutUs.htm.

12. http://www.e-learningforkids.org/aboutus.html.

13. http://www.facebook.com/note.php?note_id=76191543919.

14. http://www.google.com/adplanner/static/top1000/.

15. Economist Special Report, 1/30/2010, Vol. 394, Issue 8667.

16. L. J. Shrum, R. S. Wyer Jr and T. C. O'Guinn (1998) The use of priming procedures to investigate psychological processes, *Journal of Consumer Research* 24(4): 447.

17. R. Kubey (1990), Television and the quality of life, *Communication Quarterly*, London: Routledge.

18. Shirky (2010), op. cit.

19. P. Anderson (1972) More is different, *Science*, 177: 393–6.

20. D. Tapscott and A.D. Williams (2010) *MacroWikinomics: Rebooting Business and the World*, London: Atlantic Books.

21. T. Erickson (2010) *What's Next, Gen X: Keeping Up, Moving Ahead, and Getting the Career You Want*, Boston, Mass: Harvard Business School.

22. This is an argument made forcibly by J. Rubin (2009) *Why Your World is About to Get a Whole Lot Smaller*, New York: Random House.

23. World Bank – World Development Indicators via Google Public Data.

24. http://www.eia.doe.gov/oiaf/ieo/pdf/ieoreftab_1.pdf.

25. However, it is important to note that in 2010 the energy use of individuals in China and India was significantly lower than in the US or Russia. It is predicted that individual energy use will remain below that of the average consumer in the developed world for many decades to come. In 2010 the average American used more than five times the energy of the average Chinese, and nearly 15 times as much energy as the average Indian.

6. Social engagement: the rise of empathy and balance

1. J. Rifkin (2009) *The Empathic Civilization: The Race to Global Consciousness in a World in Crisis*. Cambridge: Polity Press.

2. Home schooling in the USA increased by about 75% between 1999 and 2007 (http://www.usatoday.com/news/education/2009-01-04-

homeschooling_N.htm). Although predominantly for moral or religious reasons, factors such as family time, child welfare and family finances have continued to increase as considerations for parents.

3. Women in Business Institute, London Business School (2009) *The Reflexive Generation: Young Professionals' Perspectives on Work, Career and Gender*, London: London Business School.

4. A. Giddens (1991) *Modernity and Self-Identity: Self and Society in the Late Modern Age*, Stanford, CA: Stanford University Press.

5. Gail Sheehy (1976) *Passages*, New York: Dutton.

6. A. Comfort and S. Quilliam (2004) *The Joy of Sex*, London: Mitchell Beazley.

7. In 1995 in the USA, data from Catalyst Research revealed that 0.2% of Fortune 500 companies had female CEOs; 10% of the board seats were held by women. By 2009 the percentage of female CEOs had risen to 3%; and of board seats held by women to 15%. There were 3 US Fortune 500 CEOs in 2000; by 2010 there were 15. These are US data, but are representative of many countries across the world. Globally, less than 5% of CEOs were women in 2010. Resources on women at work: Catalyst Research Catalyst, 2009; Catalyst Census: Fortune 500 Women Board Directors (2009); Catalyst Census: Fortune 500 Women Executive Officers and Top Earners (2009); Bureau of Labor Statistics, unpublished tabulations from the 2009 Current Population Survey (2010). The analysis of future trends does not demonstrate a great deal of change. For example, in 2009 the UK's Equality and Human Rights Commission calculated that at the current rate of progress it would take 70 years for women to gain equal representation on the boards of the FSTE 100 (Equality and Human Rights Commission [2008] *Sex and Power Report*, p. 4).

8. Third Bi-annual European PWN Board Women Monitor, 2008.

9. In 1992 the sociologist Anthony Giddens asked, 'What do men want?' A. Giddens (1992) *The Transformation of Intimacy: Sexuality, Love and Eroticism in Modern Societies*, Palo Alto, CA: Stanford University Press, p. 60.

10. Ibid., p. 111.

7. Micro-entrepreneurship: crafting creative lives

1. http://www.alibaba.com.

2. J. Hagel III, J. Seely Brown and L. Davison (2010) *The Power of Pull: How Small Moves, Smartly Made, Can Set Big Things in Motion*, New York: Basic Books.

3. J. Hagel III, J. Seely Brown and L. Davison (2009) *The Big Shift Index*, Deloitte Center for the Edge.

4. T. Malone (2004) *The Future of Work: How the New Order of Business Will Shape Your Organization, Your Management Style, and Your Life*, Boston: Harvard Business School Press, p. 81.

5. C. Leadbeater (2008) *We-Think: Mass Innovation Not Mass Production*, London: Profile Books, p. 219.

6. Lasse Gjertsen, a self-taught filmmaker from Larvik.

7. He is very involved with one called *Witness*, which works under the banner 'See it, film it, and change it.'

8. E. Brynjolfsson and A. Saunders (2010) *Wired for Innovation: How Information Technology Is Re-shaping the Economy*. Cambridge, MA: MIT Press.

9. W. Nordhaus (1997) Traditional productivity estimates are asleep at the (technological) switch, *Economic Journal*, Royal Economic Society, vol. 107(444), September: 1548–59.

10. This is a combination that has created the winning formulas we now see in companies such as Apple, Google, Nokia, IBM or BMW. As a consequence, as innovation productivity rises, so less and less value of a company is held in the physical assets, and more and more in intangible assets. In June 2010, for example, Apple had a market capitalisation of $234 billion, which placed it as one of the most valuable companies in the world, with huge market shares in the computing, music and mobile phone industries. Their latest product, the iPhone 4, sold 1.5 million in its first day.

11. For example, the computing power that cost $4,000 in 1987, by 2007 would cost $38.

12. A survey carried out in 2009 by Pew Global Attitudes Project asked Chinese people: 'Is the economic situation good or bad?' 84% responded 'good' (in the USA, France, Spain, Britain and Japan the percentage is less than 18%). Indians were almost as positive, with 66% responding 'good'.

13. A. Maddison (1998) *Chinese Economic Performance in the Long Run*, Paris: Organization for Economic Cooperation and Development.

14. In this focus on saving, the Chinese have been deeply influenced by Lee Kuan Yew, the long-time prime minister of Singapore. In 1955 he started the Central Provident Fund that required employees and employers each to contribute 5% of their income to the fund, rising steadily until in 1983 it was 25% each – a total of 50%. The sums collected were invested and, largely because of the CPF, the gross national savings rate in Singapore has been in the vicinity of 50% for decades. This high-saving model became a model for China, which copied Singapore's saving achievements and has achieved significant economic growth for decades as a result.

15. G. A. Akerlof and R. J. Schiller (2009) *Animal Spirits: How Human Psychology Drives the Economy, and Why It Matters for Global Capitalism*, Princeton, New Jersey: Princeton University Press.

16. It is no surprise that in the 2010 *Financial Times* listing of the world's most valuable companies, two Chinese banks (the Industrial and Commercial Bank of China and the China Construction Bank) were in the top ten.

17. This rise up the value chain was reflected across Chinese manufacturing. In 2008, for example, Huawei, a telecoms company, had applied for more patents than any other firm that year. And it is not only Chinese companies that are investing in the emerging knowledge economy of the country; in 2010 Fortune 500 companies had 98 research and development facilities in China (and 63 in India).

18. The top ten regions in China account for 16% of the nation's population, yet are home to nearly 45% of the talent-producing universities and 60% of China's technological innovations (T. Li and R. Florida [2006] Talent, technology innovation and economic growth in China, *The Martin Prosperity Institute*, University of Toronto. Available at creativeclass.com.)

19. However, this is beginning to be addressed within India and China, where there is an increasing focus on management education. The *Financial Times* three-year average ranking of business schools included three from the emerging markets among the world's top 20: Hong Kong University of Science and Technology Business School (=14), the Indian School of Business (16) and the China Europe International Business School (=14) (http://rankings.ft.com/businessschoolrankings/global-mba-rankings).

20. A McKinsey study published in 2005 calculated that only 25% of India's engineering graduates, 15% of its finance and accounting professionals and 10% of those with more general degrees were sufficiently qualified to work for a multinational company. For the moment, the quality of Indian universities is substantially lower than their Western counterparts and falls short of what is demanded by the multinationals. In 2010 a study by the Indian company Aspiring Minds revealed that only 4% of India's engineers were adequately qualified to work in a software product firm and only 18% were employable by an IT services company after six months of further training (The engineering gap, *The Economist*, 00130613, 1/30/2010, 394 (866)).

21. A. L. Saxenian (1999) *Silicon Valley's Immigrant Entrepreneurs*, San Francisco, CA: Public Policy Institute of California.

22. By 2010 the M-PESA money-transfer service was being used by more than 9.5 million Kenyans, transferring the equivalent of 11% of the country's GDP each year.

23. Increasingly Western firms are investing in emerging markets, and at the same time a growing number of multinational companies are based outside the West. Some have multiple facilities, GE's healthcare business spent $50 million and Cisco more than $1 billion on R&D facilities in Bangalore, and Microsoft's R&D centre in Beijing is its largest outside of

the USA. 'The world turned upside down: *Economist* special report on innovation in the emerging markets' April 17th 2010 – see Economist. com/specialreports

24. P. F. Drucker (2008) *The Essential Drucker*. London: Harper Paperbacks

25. W. Sanderson and S. Scherbov (2008) *Rethinking Age and Aging*. Population Bulletin, December.

26. Older people tend to have fewer disabilities than people of the same age in earlier decades, and now there is some evidence that cognitive decline is being postponed as well. University of California, Berkeley and Max Planck Institute for Demographic Research, Human Mortality Database (www.mortality.org and www.humanmortality.de, accessed 1 Feb. 2008). United Nations (UN), Department of Economic and Social Affairs, Population Division, World Population Prospects: The 2004 Revision (2005).

27. R. Kurzweil (2006) *The Singularity is Near*, London: Gerald Duckworth & Co.

28. A global survey in 2005 found some differences across countries, but generally there are five reasons why people want to work in later years: for the money, to gain continued mental stimulation, to keep physically active, to keep connected with others, and finally, to have something meaningful/valuable to do with their time. The interesting aspect is that, taking the average for across the group, all five reasons were about equally important. (HSBC Insurance (2005) The Future of Retirement Study, HSBC.)

8. The first shift: from shallow generalist to serial master

1. For example, Ford opened their first plant outside the US in 1911, while Philips opened facilities in Brazil in 1924, Australia in 1927 and India in 1930.

2. We need to be able to fit into networks of well-trained individuals that contribute different skills – much like guilds in World of Warcraft do … 'They also learn to welcome collaboration as an opportunity to learn faster by focusing on a set of individual strengths while being exposed to the diverse perspectives and experiences of those with complementary strengths. At the end of the day, this is the most powerful contribution of WoW. This disposition creates an amplifying effect throughout the game. Players seek out other players who share this point of view, and they end up performing better than players who bring more conventional ideas to the game.'

3. David Bolchover (2010) *Pay Check: Are Top Earners Really Worth It?* London: Coptic.

4. This example comes from David Bolchover (2010) *Pay Check: Are Top Earners Really Worth It?* London: Coptic.

5. Business Week – http://www.businessweek.com/technology/content/aug2010/tc2010082_406649.htm

6. Note: The UK's CBI report on skill shortages can be found at http://www.cbi.org.uk/pdf/20091123-cbi-shape-of-business.pdf.

7. http://www.deccanherald.com/content/84978/indian-bpo-facing-huge-churn.html.

8. http://english.peopledaily.com.cn/90001/90778/90860/6857605.html.

9. http://www.computerworld.com/s/article/9121385/U.S._agency_sees_robots_replacing_humans_in_service_jobs_by_2025).

10. See for example the UK Government's Department of Business, Innovation and Skills analysis of 20 future professions presented 2010 in *The Shape of Jobs to Come*.

11. Advocacy groups can arise quickly and with broad support from petition websites such as http://petition.co.uk/ as well as platforms such as Facebook.

12. D. Bornstein (2007) *How to Change the World: Social Entrepreneurs and the Power of New Ideas*, Oxford University Press USA (and others); C. Leadbeater (1996) *The Rise of the Social Entrepreneur*, London: Demos.

13. http://www.census.gov/epcd/www/smallbus.html.

14. http://stats.bis.gov.uk/ed/sme/.

15. Look at http://www.kickstarter.com/ for example.

16. http://www.gototurkey.co.uk/health-and-spas.html.

17. http://www.euromonitor.com/Industry_Trend_Hippocratic_holidays.

18. In the Bay Area of California, for example, one in six of the 1.6 million biomedical jobs in the United States were located.

19. http://www.newscientist.com/article/dn19254-green-light-for-first-embryonic-stem-cell-treatment.html.

20. http://business.timesonline.co.uk/tol/business/career_and_jobs/graduate_management/article5792471.ece.

21. http://beta.thehindu.com/opinion/lead/article4752.ece?homepage=true.

22. http://www.upiasia.com/Society_Culture/2009/07/14/chinas_college_grad_employment_statistics/3617/.

23. R. Florida (2002) *The Rise of the Creative Class: And How It's Transforming Work, Leisure, Community and Everyday Life*, New York: Basic Books.

24. German futurist Mathias Horx (2006) *How We Will Live: A Synthesis of Life in the Future*. London: Cyan Books.

25. Florida (2002), op. cit.

26. L. Gratton (2007) *Hot Spots: Why Some Teams, Workplaces and Organisations Buzz with Energy – and Others Don't*, Financial Times Prentice Hall (UK), Berrett Koehler (US).

27. This might also be a factor of the qualitative difference between skill and artistic talent. A bad doctor can be trained to be a good one through

intensive courses, as can a lawyer. But it is much more difficult for a bad designer/artist to become a good one because they depend on talents that are more inherent. It's also more down to tapping into the zietgeist or anticipating what's next, which is more difficult to teach than other disciplines.

28. R. Reich (2001) *The Future of Success: Working and Living in the New Economy*. New York: Vintage Books.

29. Horx, op. cit, p. 121.

30. Horx, op.cit.

31. http://news.bbc.co.uk/1/hi/uk_politics/5273356.stm.

32. R. Sennet (2008) *The Craftsman*, London: Allen Lane.

33. S. Ghoshal and J. Nahapiet (1998) Social capital, intellectual capital and the organizational advantage, *Academy of Management Review*, 23(2): 242.

34. Daniel Levitin (2007) makes this estimation in *This Is Your Brain On Music*, London: Atlantic Books; while Malcolm Gladwell (2008) repeats it in *Outliers*, London: Little, Brown & Co.

35. C. Mainemelis and S. Ronson (2006) On the nature of play: Ideas are born in fields of play – towards a theory of play and creativity in an organizational setting, *Research in Organizational Behavior*, 27: 81–131.

36. Abramis (1990, p. 364) refers to a study with 589 employees: 'I cannot believe that people pay me to do my hobby.' Play in Work, *American Behavioural Scientist*, 33 (3) 353-373

37. M. Csikszentmihalyi and J. LeFevre (1989) Optimal experience in work and leisure. *Journal of Personality and Social Psychology*, 56: 815–22; E. L. Deci and R. M. Ryan (1985) *Intrinsic Motivation and Self-Determination in Human Behaviour*, New York: Plenum; F. Massimini and A. Delle Fave (2000) Individual development in a bio-cultural perspective, *American Psychologist*, 55(1): 24.

38. M. Csikszentmihalyi (1997) *Creativity: Flow and the Psychology of Discovery and Invention*, New York: Harper Perennial.

39. J. Elster (1986), Self-realization in work and politics: the Marxist conception of the good life, *Social Philosophy and Policy*, 3, pp. 97. http://journals.cambridge.org/action/displayAbstract?fromPage=online& aid=3093292

40. J.-P. Sartre (1943) *Being and Nothingness: A Phenomenological Essay on Ontology*, London: Routledge, p. 246.

41. H. Ibarra (2003) *Working Identities: Unconventional Strategies for Reinventing Your Career*. Boston: Harvard Business School Press.

42. English translation: *Women's Bodies*.

43. L. Gratton and S. Ghoshal (2005) Beyond best practice. *Sloan Management Review*, 46(3): pp. 49–57.

44. Y. Moon (2010) *Different: Escaping the Competitive Herd*. Crown Publishing Group: Random House Group.

45. Robert Thompson's workshop was in the wild moorlands of Yorkshire in the north of England.

46. In fact, by 2001 (study Red Hat Linux 7.1) the 30 million source lines of the Linux code would have taken 8,000 years of development time. http://www.dwheeler.com/sloc/redhat71-v1/redhat71sloc.html.

47. Eric Raymond has called this way of working a Bazaar: http://catb.org/esr/writings/homesteading/cathedral-bazaar/.

48. T. Malone (2004) *The Future of Work: How the New Order of Business Will Shape Your Organization, Your Management Style, and Your Life*, Boston: Harvard Business School Press.

49. Sermo was the largest online physician community in the US by 2010.

50. Lawlink, one of the largest US sites for lawyers.

51. T. Malone, R. Laubacher and M. S. S. Morton (eds) (2003) *Inventing the Organizations of the 21st Century*, Cambridge, MA: MIT Press.

52. The UK government statistics on age can be found at http://www.cdc.gov/nchs/hus.htm. The article, appearing in the medical journal *The Lancet*, shows that, based on current trajectories, more than half of all babies born in industrialised nations since the year 2000 can expect to live into triple digits. The trends included in the article show that many Western nations will have the most people living past 100, with half of all babies born in 2007 in the USA likely to live to age 104. http://abcnews.go.com/Health/WellnessNews/half-todays-babies-expected-live-past-100/story?id=8724273.

53. T. Erickson (2008) *Retire Retirement: Career Strategies for the Boomer Generation*, Boston: Harvard Business School Press, p. 79.

54. http://news.bbc.co.uk/1/hi/magazine/7401326.stm.

55. The Bookend Generations, http://www.ft.com/cms/s/0/b147d61a-5b9e-11de-be3f-00144feabdc0.html cites this study: https://www.worklifepolicy.org/index.php/action/PurchasePage/item/278.

56. C. Christensen, M. Horn and C. Johnson (2008) *Disrupting Class: How Disruptive Innovation Will Change the Way the World Learns.* New York: McGraw Hill.

57. C. L. Waight and B. L. Stewart (2009) Exploring corporate e-learning research: what are the opportunities? *Impact: Journal of Applied Research in Workplace E-learning*, 1(1): 68–79; L. Tai (2008) *Corporate E-learning: An Inside View of IBM's Solutions.* Oxford: Oxford University Press.

58. US Department of Education, Office of Planning, Evaluation, and Policy Development, Washington, D.C. (2009) *Evaluation of Evidence-Based Practices in Online Learning; A Meta-Analysis and Review of Online Learning Studies.* Accessed at http://www.ed.gov/rschstat/eval/tech/evidence-based-practices/finalreport.pdf.

9. The second shift: from isolated competitor to innovative connector

1. This combination of social and intellectual capital was at the heart of a seminal article written by Sumantra Ghoshal and Janine Nahapiet. S. Ghoshal and J. Nahapiet (1998) Social capital, intellectual capital and the organizational advantage, *Academy of Management Review*, 23(2): 242.

2. On a very simple level, the strength of the big crowd is phenomenal – even in its most passive state. The small piece of software reCaptcha is meant to tell humans from computers apart by offering distorted words for users to recognise. About 200 million Captchas are solved by humans around the world every day. But rather than simply wasting the user's time, the service is being used to digitise books and newspapers that computers fail to decypher. http://www.google.com/recaptcha/learnmore.

3. L. Gratton (2009) *Glow – Creating Energy and Innovation in Your Work*. Financial Times Prentice Hall (UK), Berrett Koehler (US).

4. L. Gratton (2007) *Hot Spots: Why Some Teams, Workplaces and Organisations Buzz with Energy – and Others Don't*. Financial Times Prentice Hall (UK), Berrett Koehler (US).

5. http://www.horsesmouth.co.uk/.

6. M. S. Granovetter (1973) The strength of weak ties, *American Journal of Sociology*, 78(6): 1360.

7. S. E. Page (2007) *The Difference: How the Power of Diversity Creates Better Groups, Firms, Schools and Societies*. Princeton: Princeton University Press.

8. http://en.wikipedia.org/wiki/List_of_crowdsourcing_projects.

9. L. Festinger (1950) Informal social communication. *Psychological Review*, 57: 271–82.

10. M. Kilduff and W. Tsai (2003) *Social Networks and Organizations*. London: Sage.

11. R.E. Lane (2000) *The Loss of Happiness in Market Democracies*, New Haven: Yale University Press.

12. Richard Florida (2008) did the same for US cities in his book *Who's Your City?*, New York: Basic Books.

13. Cicero, translated by M. Grant (1971) *On the Good Life*, London: Penguin Books.

10. The third shift: from voracious consumer to impassioned producer

1. My research team and I surveyed senior executives across Europe about their work and their lives.

2. R. Florida (2010) *The Great Reset: How New Ways of Living and Working Drive Post-Crash Prosperity*. New York: HarperCollins.

3. With regard to growth, we can predict that between 2010 and 2035 world energy consumption will increase by nearly 50%, with the majority of this growth emerging from developing countries (http://www.eia.doe.gov/oiaf/ieo/highlights.html). The consequence of this vast expansion in energy consumption will be to swell carbon dioxide emissions by more than 30% (http://www.oecd.org/dataoecd/45/29/42414080.pdf), which will result in the rise of global temperature by around 0.2 °C (http://www.ipcc.ch/publications_and_data/ar4/syr/en/mains3-2.html) every decade. This will have clear and immediate effects on regional and global ecosystems and economies, as well as eventually causing greater health concerns, more food shortages, more forest fires and longer droughts (http://www.actoncopenhagen.decc.gov.uk/en/ambition/evidence/4-degrees-map/). World growth will also severely affect the accessibility of fresh water, meaning that it will equal oil in terms of demand. Competition for access to a diminishing supply of fresh water will cause increasing socio-political tensions, with two out of every three people living in water-stressed areas by 2025 (http://www.unep.org/dewa/vitalwater/index.html).

4. http://www.businessweek.com/news/2010-02-25/china-2009-private-car-ownership-jumps-34-to-26-million-units.html).

5. A. Maslow (1954) *Motivation and Personality*. New York: Harper.

6. In fact by 2010 this was already occurring as workers in a number of Chinese factories were beginning to voice their concern with their living arrangements and the little time they had with family and friends.

7. S. Lebergott (1968) Labour force and employment trends. In E. Sheldon and W. Moore (eds), *Indicators of Social Change*. New York: Russell Sage, pp. 97–143.

8. P. Brickman and D. T. Campbell (1971) Hedonic relativism and planning the good society. In M. H. Appley (ed.), *Adaptation-Level Theory: A Symposium*, New York: Academic Press, pp. 287–302.

9. Nobel prizewinner Daniel Kahneman and colleague Jackie Snell confirmed this – that once we receive a treat too often we become less appreciative of it over time. D. Kahneman and J. Snell (1992) Predicting a changing taste: Do people know what they will like?, *Journal of Behavioral Decision Making*, 5(3).

10. R. Lane (1991) *The Market Experience*, Cambridge: Cambridge University Press, p. 309.

11. Lane (1991), op. cit.

12. Ibid., p. 149.

13. T. Scitovsky (1977) *The Joyless Economy*. New York: Oxford University Press.

14. T. Kasser, R. Ryan, M. Zax and A. Sameroff (1995) The relations of material and social environments to late adolescents' materialistic and prosocial values, *Developmental Psychology*, 31: 907–14.

15. D. J. Bem (1972) Self perception theory. In L. Berkowitz (eds), *Advances in Experimental Social Psychology, Vol 6*, New York: Academic Press.
16. Lane (1991), op. cit., Ch. 6.
17. My colleague from London Business School, Dominic Houlder, writes convincingly about this in Kulananda and D. Houlder (2002) *Mindfulness and Money: The Buddhist Path to Abundance*. London: Broadway Books.
18. A. Campbell *et al.* (1976) *The Quality of American Life*, New York: Russell Sage.
19. Lane (1991), op. cit., p. 96.
20. J. T. Mortimer and J. Lorence (1985) Work experience and occupational value socialization: a longitudinal study, *American Journal of Sociology*, 84: 1361–85.
21. P. Koestenbaum and P. Block (2001) *Freedom and Accountability at Work: Applying Philosophic Insight into the Real World*. San Francisco: Jossey-Bass Pfeiffer.
22. Erich Fromm (1941) used the phrase as the title of his book, *The Escape from Freedom*, New York: Rinehart.
23. R. Reich (2001) *The Future of Success*, New York: Alfred A. Knopf.
24. Ibid.
25. L. Gratton (2004) *The Democratic Enterprise: Liberating Your Business with Freedom, Flexibility and Commitment*, London: FT Prentice Hall.
26. D. Held (1996) *Models of Democracy*, Cambridge: Polity Press.
27. However, maybe this friction will simply highlight what Robert Lane has called the 'cultural lag': 'most continue to emphasize the themes that have brought them to their current eminent positions. In these circumstances, individuals are not, in any practical sense, free to go against the culture that nurtures them. Furthermore, there are immediate rewards for working within the system – the immediate rewards (reinforcements) of more money are persuasive, even captivating, so much so that they discourage a peek over the wall of the maze to see what else is there' (Lane, 1991, p. 60).
28. Consider also the argument of the German anthropologist A. L. Kroeber who believed great civilisations go through life-cycles. Each culture develops distinctive configurations that are the basis of success. The greatness of each culture passes away when its possibilities have been exhausted. The end comes when a theme is simply repeated without innovation or experimentation. Cultures die, not in grand cataclysmic events, but as a failure to adapt, a monotonous repetition of what has been done before.
29. This is the belief of marketing professor Youngme Moon (2010) *Different: Escaping the Competitive Herd*, New York: Crown Publishing Group, Random House.
30. Richard Florida calls it *The Great Reset* (Florida, 2010).
31. Shell scenarios are available on the company's website.

INDEX